Cinema Genre

Cinema Genre

Raphaëlle Moine

Translated by Alistair Fox
and Hilary Radner

Blackwell Publishing

© 2008 by Raphaëlle Moine
Translation © 2008 by Alistair Fox and Hilary Radner
First published in French as *Les genres du cinéma* by Nathan-Université, 2002.
Second edition published by Armand Colin Publisher, 2005

BLACKWELL PUBLISHING
350 Main Street, Malden, MA 02148-5020, USA
9600 Garsington Road, Oxford OX4 2DQ, UK
550 Swanston Street, Carlton, Victoria 3053, Australia

The right of Raphaëlle Moine to be identified as the author of this work has been asserted in accordance with the UK Copyright, Designs, and Patents Act 1988.

First published 2008 by Blackwell Publishing Ltd

1   2008

Library of Congress Cataloging-in-Publication Data

ISBN-13: 9781405156509 (hardback)
ISBN-13: 9781405156516 (paperback)

A catalogue record for this title is available from the British Library.

Set in 10/12.5pt Meridian by Graphicraft Limited, Hong Kong
Printed and bound in TJ International Ltd, Padstow, Cornwall

The publisher's policy is to use permanent paper from mills that operate a sustainable forestry policy, and which has been manufactured from pulp processed using acid-free and elementary chlorine-free practices. Furthermore, the publisher ensures that the text paper and cover board used have met acceptable environmental accreditation standards.

For further information on
Blackwell Publishing, visit our website at
www.blackwellpublishing.com

Contents

Contents

Translators' Note

Unless noted otherwise, the translation given of quotations from works originally written in French is that by the translators of this book.

Foreword

Janet Staiger

What is it that draws us repeatedly back to the same questions: questions of authorship, national production, media specificity, pleasures and displeasures, and, here, genre? Why do certain questions continue to compel thought and conversation among scholars? I certainly do not know the answer to my query, but it is my delight to introduce *Cinema Genre* to a new audience. Raphaëlle Moine's book, translated by Alistair Fox and Hilary Radner, is an admirable and original contribution to a stellar array of recent scholarship on the matter by renowned authors such as Rick Altman and Steve Neale. A synthesis of Euro-US research, *Cinema Genre* offers a compact and clear review of inquiries into explaining the production, textual features, and social functions of films that industry workers, consumers, and scholars feel compelled to group together. Moreover, Moine's array of examples to explicate the positions goes beyond the standard hegemony in English-language scholarship of primarily Hollywood examples. Tackling the topic from the point of view of a French scholar results in numerous examples from European cinema that will enliven the transnational understanding of patterns of filmmaking – although obviously we all need to expand our familiarity with genres beyond these regions.

What any good synthesis of the research does, and what Moine excels with, is to point out what the research has accomplished and what yet needs to be achieved. A major matter as she suggests is to explain the social functions of films that repeat textual patterns. Moine points out that scholars have attributed both ideological and ritual explanations to genre films. As is commonly expressed in the field, ideological theories propose that viewers' pleasures in watching these films are suspect – that the movies have a repressive or manipulative function. On the contrary, ritual theories are liberal, seeing these pleasures as building communities and reinforcing cultural beliefs. Moine introduces the important objection that both approaches neglect more contemporary representations of viewers as situated individuals with some agency in interpreting and responding to the cinemas they view. Indeed, research on cult movie viewers indicates that some audience members seek out the same formulas over and over again; other viewers will even watch the same film multiple times. In a survey that Barbara Klinger reports on in her recent *Beyond the Multiplex* (2006), she found at least five reasons her college students give for repeat viewing: the pleasure of familiarity with the movie; the desire to obtain mastery over a complex film; the assurance that the mood they seek will be achieved; the enjoyment of retrieving an earlier experience; and mastery of a film for social exchange among friends.

Moine also objects to the ideological and ritual functions on the grounds that they assume a homogeneous (or undifferentiated) audience. Certainly, the wide variety of profitable genres indicates that whatever ideological or ritual functions might exist, those functions do not appeal or work for everyone. Again, one possible consequence of the renewed energy in genre studies is the potential for researching in more subtle ways the sorts of audiences who enjoy particular genres or who would never attend some types of films.

Moine chooses to argue for Altman's semantic-syntactic-pragmatic approach to analyzing the textual features of genre films. Beyond further research in social functions and audiences is the application of this approach to genres beyond the musical. Moine explains that Altman's study considers the semantic features of the musical to be the format as a story, the feature length of the film, characters paired for romance, performance suited to the rhythms of the music, and sounds of both a traditional diegetic fictional world and a musical. Syntactical features of the musical include a narrative that alternates between the paired characters, the coupling of the lovers with the success of the other actions in the story, the use of music and dance to underscore these causal events and to create continuity, and the possibility of the sound features of the film becoming more important than the narrative progression.

What makes the semantic-syntactic method a compelling textual approach is that it is easy to see how substitutions and alterations of the various features could produce changes in the genre, allowing for a descriptive history of generic change. Thus, scholars might try to map out the changing history of the Hollywood musical (Altman's example is the Hollywood musical of the 1920s–1960s) or the semantics and syntactics of musicals in various countries. They might also articulate the semantics and syntactics of other genres. Easier might be genres such as the various versions of the romance, horror, western, gangster, melodrama, or war film. More difficult might be traditionally recognized genres such as the women's film, comedy, cult, epic, science fiction, or social problem movie.

A third area for further research is asking whether any grouping of films constitutes a genre. Moine surveys the research on early cinema that discusses the variety of categories by which movies were sold to the nickelodeon and early film exhibitors. Elsewhere in thinking about meaningful categories of producing and viewing for television (for instance, news, cartoons, and reality shows), Jason Mittell in *Genre and Television* (2004) has argued for defining groups on the basis of "cultural" categories. Does any grouping constitute a genre? Is there a genre, for example, of "baseball" movies? Teen movies? Trick films? Shorts? Parodies? Would the explanations for audiences' preferences or the semantic-syntactic textual approach work for these groupings? Or are these something else, again?

Thankfully, the intelligent and exceptionally accessible *Cinema Genre* gives us a platform from which to begin to address these further questions. Moine's explanations and synthesis of scholarship on genre studies to date will reward those of us immersed in these questions, will save newcomers extensive work in sorting out what has gone before, and will hopefully encourage sustained investigation in these and new questions in the field of genre studies.

Introduction

Cinematic genre is a notion that is familiar to any viewers seeking to choose which film they wish to see, to describe a film in a few words to a friend, or to identify, characterize, and distinguish groups of films that have common traits. It is also a central concept in the film industry, as well as in film history. Nothing is more common among viewers, whether ordinary filmgoers or scholars, than the habit of classifying according to generic categories – from the western to science fiction, through melodrama and the musical – in order to situate and rank recurring narrative, ideological, and aesthetic forms and elements within cinematic production as a whole. Similarly, cinema histories draw upon generic designations to describe whole chapters in the filmic production of a period. The history of cinematographic language, forms, movements, and techniques is thus marked by numerous discussions about genres as characteristic of a cinema or era, such as the "burlesque" of silent cinema, or the Italian "spaghetti western" of the 1960s and 1970s. Finally, from an economic perspective, there is general agreement that genres (which exploit a convergence of narrative, iconographic, and stylistic conventions through a play of repetition and variation) should be seen as a rational system for producing and exploiting images, with Hollywood providing a canonical example, especially during the classical era. This common ground allows schematic contrasts to be made (especially in French film criticism) between two different types of cinema: on one hand, a "genre cinema" that is commercial and formulaic, and on the other hand, an "auteur cinema" that is liberated from the institutional, economic, and ideological constraints of other genres that it avoids, borrows from, or transgresses. The values inherent in this contrast can also be reversed – with a highly inventive, spectacular, and entertaining genre cinema (that draws upon the brand image of American cinema) being contrasted with an off-putting, self-indulgent, soporific auteur cinema.

My reason for alluding to these widespread popular assumptions in this introduction is to draw attention to the way in which genres influence our relationship with the world of cinema.

Consideration of genre, however, has not always received a lot of attention from theorists of cinema. A comparison of scholarly literature in English on cinema with that in French is revealing in this regard. Whereas numerous American and British scholars have been reflecting on the notion of cinematic genre since the beginning of the 1970s, and have produced various studies on a number of cinema genres, mostly from Hollywood, genre remains a poor relation in French criticism, which prefers either to study auteurs, or to engage in the more aesthetic activity of identifying movements, schools, styles, or tendencies in its own national cinema.

In the first American studies of cinema, the presence of genres was seen as an obstacle to artistic development at Hollywood, and before the 1970s only a few isolated works were devoted to American genres – in particular, the western and the gangster film (e.g., Warshow 1962a, 1962b). In the following decade, in response to the debate surrounding auteurship (*la politique des auteurs*) pursued first in France during the 1950s by *Cahiers du cinéma*, then picked up in the United States by Andrew Sarris under the term "auteurism," several scholars tried to demonstrate the influence of generic conventions on the production and reception of films. The crisis that the Hollywood system underwent during this period, and along with it the system of genres, possibly also contributed to make the "old" Hollywood genres a subject of study. The work of Kitses (1969) on the western and that of McArthur (1972) on the gangster film both adopt the same structure: after a general analysis of genre based on structuralist principles, they deal with prominent auteurs who have been associated with a genre, thus attempting to combine the study of genres with auteur studies. It is really during the 1970s, when departments of film studies began to appear in Great Britain and the United States, that genre studies developed. The very large number of articles devoted to American genres in the journals *Movie, Screen, Jump Cut, Journal of Popular Culture, Journal of Modern Literature, Film Culture, Film Comment,* and *Literature/Film Quarterly* bear witness to this growing interest and the variety of approaches adopted by scholars. For example, articles in *Jump Cut* tended to have an ideological bias inspired by Marxism, while pieces in *Journal of Popular Culture,* which was more strictly historical than other journals, focused on the archetypal and collective dimension of genres. Three books attest to the predominance in American thought of the idea that genres are vehicles of cultural archetypes: Stuart Kaminsky's *American Film Genres* (1974), Stanley Solomon's *Beyond Formula: American Film Genres* (1976), and John G. Cawelti's *Adventure, Mystery and Romance: Formula Stories as Art and Popular Culture* (1976). Thomas Schatz's book, *Hollywood Genres: Formulas, Filmmaking and the Studio System* (1981), confirmed the dominance of approaches that saw genres as a social consensus, and showed that the interest of scholars in American universities remained focused on the period of classical Hollywood cinema. In the course of the 1980s, and then again in the 1990s, a greater range of studies of, and reflection on, genres appeared, as the rest of this book will more amply confirm. It is sufficient to indicate here that such studies aim to integrate "ordinary films" into the corpus of genres, along with the outstanding examples, to a much greater extent. Although still centered on Hollywood cinema, these studies pay more attention both to the "prehistory" of genres from the classical period, and also, at the other end of the historical chain, to contemporary productions (Neale 2002). They also link genres more closely to issues relating to production and marketing, reception, and gender. Generally, they are more attentive to the cultural and historical mediating contexts in which genres exist, as well as to the history of genres and the process whereby they become transformed. The vitality of research on genres is evident in the very large number of publications devoted to genre(s) in the course of the 1990s. Confirmation of this fact is found in the significant additions made by Barry Keith Grant to his *Film Genre Reader* (published in 1986) when its second edition (*Film Genre Reader II*) appeared in 1995.

While generic studies have achieved real academic visibility in Anglo-American scholarship, French research, although very dynamic in other areas of cinema studies, seems to have completely neglected the study of genres. This has also had the effect, with regard to French cinema as portrayed by French scholars, of giving the impression that this cinema, which has as many "popular" and "commercial" films as it does auteur films, is nevertheless a genre-less cinema. While a number of serious books have recently appeared testifying to the existence and vitality of genre-study in French scholarship – for example, Jean-Loup Bourget (1985) on Hollywood melodrama, Jean Gili (1983) on Italian comedy, Jean-Louis Leutrat (1987) on the origins of the western, or Anne-Françoise Lesuisse (2002) on *film noir* – these are all studies devoted to a single genre. One can add to these works a number of overviews, dictionaries, and encyclopedias that survey genres and movements (Serceau 1993; Virmaux and Virmaux 1994; Pinel 2000), but the only work recently published in France that is devoted solely to the theory of genres, or of genre itself (issue number 20 of the journal *Iris*, 1995), is a collection of articles compiled as an initiative of the Association québécoise des études cinématographiques.

Several factors help to explain this reluctance of French scholarship to engage with the concept of film genre. The empirical nature of generic categories makes the issue of film genre a difficult one to theorize, so long as the attempt at theorization remains attached to an essentialist notion of genre. This is because film genres are always easier to recognize than to define, being often impure, because the mixing of genres invalidates any attempt to achieve a rigorous taxonomy. It is also because many film genres appear to perpetuate or recreate genres that already exist in another medium. While the notion of literary genres, as Jean-Marie Schaeffer has observed, derives its importance and theoretical legitimacy from the fact that it has been linked historically since Aristotle, and even more so since the end of the eighteenth century, to the definition of literature itself – for the simple reason that not all verbal practices are literary or artistic – the same is not true for cinema (Schaeffer 1989, pp. 8–10). One could even advance the opposite proposition for the seventh art: even if the concept of cinematic genres could be restricted to genre cinema, the prevalence of genres in popular and commercial cinemas, as well as their strong economic and ideological roots in mass culture, put them well outside the artistic field. The notion of cinematic genre, therefore, is one that is seldom visited, because it does not seem easy to visit. Finally, in order to avoid the *aporia* soon encountered by any theory of genres that aims to identify fixed and distinctive traits, and to move beyond the inherent limits of the study of specific cases, the issue of genre must be decentered.

There are other ways of looking at film genre apart from a dogmatic kind of categorization whereby genre is regarded as the product of similarities within a group of filmic texts, or of the canon to which these are deemed to conform. As certain Anglo-American scholars, in particular, have demonstrated during the past twenty years, genres function simultaneously as a discursive act, a communication tool, and a means of cultural, ideological, and social mediation. The process whereby genres are designated and recognized – and sometimes denied – by the different agents involved in the world of cinema (producers, directors, critics, ordinary viewers, etc.) is just as important to the study of genres as the comparative analysis of filmic texts. Cinematic genres, then, are not exclusively film genres; they are also categories of production and interpretation. From this perspective, a theory of cinematic genres must reconcile both textual and contextual approaches. In this regard, the strong division that exists between these two types of film analysis in the French context explains why French scholars have been reticent to examine the issue of genre within this new frame of reference, in which the concept of genre derives its meaning and operative value from the complex play of interactions between films and their contexts of production and reception.

The aim of this book, then, is to develop a comprehensive theoretical consideration of the notion of genre, of genres, and of the "generic gesture." To this end, I have chosen to center this study on both the *theories*, and also the *uses* and *practices*, of film genres. The goal of this book, therefore, is not to present a digest of cinematic genres, and my intention is not to answer the question "in what genre should one place this or that film?" – to echo the terms in which students often formulate a query, daunted by their encounter with the unavoidable difficulty of having to come to grips with generic categories in order to assign a genre to a film, and then expect an authoritative answer from their teacher. That is why I do not put in question the validity or pertinence of existing generic categories, whether they have been forged by the film industry, by scholarly or critical thought (theoretical or historical), or by the most ordinary social uses of the cinema. It is not, in fact, a matter of criticizing all these "generic gestures," but of grasping their meaning and function. Furthermore, I shall be dealing here with a vast collection of uses for, and thoughts about, genre, and not merely with genre cinema, which represents only one of the possible cinematic uses of genre. In the same spirit, I have not restricted the field of investigation solely to Hollywood cinema as do most American works on this topic. Hollywood genres, while they constitute a particularly rich and structured system, constitute only one use (or group of complex uses) of genre by cinema. The dominant position of American cinema, the major influence it has exerted on other cinemas (including its genres), and the large number of analyses that have been applied to it, have had the effect of rather skewing the examination of cinema genres. This volume inherits, and undoubtedly suffers from, this skewing, but one of its intentions is, modestly, at least to open or point to paths that allow one to think about different generic regimes, among which figures Hollywood classicism. The present study attempts, then, to steer a course between two reefs: the flattening of the question of genre under the Hollywood paradigm, on one hand, and the elaboration of "local" genre theories that are specific to each context, on the other. As the reader will eventually discover, this work does not pretend to be exhaustive, because its vocation is not encyclopedic, and if certain genres are only lightly touched upon, that is solely due to the material limits of the book, as well as those of its author, her culture, and her tastes. Let us signal, nonetheless, that the scant presence of the documentary, and of the genres of documentary cinema (if one views the latter as a form that contrasts with fiction), alluded to briefly in the first two chapters, is a deliberate choice. Problematical issues, such as the distribution of the documentary,[1] seem to me to be too specific to be integrated and articulated in a coherent and pertinent manner in a general work, which remains, then, devoted to fictive cinema genres.

A few words, finally, about the path that I invite the reader to follow. The first chapter, starting with the classificatory uses of genres, emphasizes the contradictions arising from the taxonomic vertigo inherent in this use of genre. The two following chapters move from the empiricism of generic labels to deal in turn with two different types of generic definition, viewing them in relation to the theories of cinema and culture that determine them: on one hand, structural definitions that seek the rules and distinctive traits of genre in film texts, and, on the other, functional definitions that contemplate the economic, ideological, cultural, and communicative utility and services of genre. In the fourth chapter, I will return at greater length to the functioning of genre as a category of interpretation, which permits the consideration of different levels of genericity and the mixing of genres – two accepted facts that static and essentialist conceptions fail to take into account. The relationship between genres and history is the subject of the fifth and sixth chapters. In the former, I examine the theoretical frame in which the history of a genre might be thought about, before raising questions about the inscription of genre in history, the determination of genre by its context, and by the historicity of generic regimes in which the corpora of genres, generic labels, and the uses of genre simultaneously take form and come into being.

Note

1 On this subject see Guy Gauthier (1995) *Le Documentaire. Un autre cinéma*, Paris, Nathan, "Nathan cinema"; and François Niney (2000) *L'Épreuve du réel à l'écran. Essai sur le principe de réalité documentaire*, Brussels, De Boeck Université.

Chapter 1
In the Genre Jungle

In our current discourse on artistic practices, we commonly use generic distinctions to characterize a particular work: for example, when we say that Leonardo da Vinci's "Mona Lisa" is a portrait, and that Vincent van Gogh's "Sunflowers" is a "still life"; when we describe the novels dealing with the investigations of Georges Simenon's Inspector Maigret, or of Agatha Christie's Hercule Poirot, as "whodunits," and the romances in the Harlequin series as "format romances"; or when we call Shakespeare's *Macbeth* a tragedy, and Molière's *The Miser* a comedy. We thus invoke the idea of genres (pictorial, literary, theatrical, etc.) to identify, classify, and differentiate particular works. The same is true with cinema. At the beginning of the twenty-first century, a film viewer will readily use the terms "musical" to describe *Singin' in the Rain* (Donen/Kelly, 1952), "comedy" to refer to *There's Something About Mary* (Farrelly Brothers, 1998), or "vampire film" to characterize *Nosferatu* (Murnau, 1922). Similarly, critics often make use of generic categories in both popular and scholarly publications – whether at the beginning of an article, or in the body of the text – to introduce a new film and situate it in the landscape of cinema. Like other cultural productions, films, both in our discourse and our consciousness, are arranged in a geography organized by genres.

Cinematic Genre: An Empirical Category

.

As a way of approaching this topic, one can begin with the common use of the concept of genre – defined as an empirical category that serves to name, differentiate, and classify works on the basis of the recurring configurations of formal and thematic elements they share. This is to say that any viewer (along with any critic, cinema historian, or theoretician) who assigns a film to a generic category will be familiar with, and recognize, the generic category concerned. To regard *Gunfight at the OK Corral* as a western is to conclude that this American film directed by John Sturges in 1957 embodies many of the elements that are associated with the "western" genre. In assigning a film to a genre, we give it an identity that is greater than the sum of its specific components. We attribute to the film a *generic identity*. In addition, if we admit that the generic category is a recognized category (at least by those who use it) and that it conveys an understanding of the world of cinema that is culturally pertinent to a given community, it is possible to assign a film to a genre without having to make reference to other films in that genre. For example, the "western" usually involves an action that takes place in the American West in the second half of the nineteenth century; emblematic locations such as the small Western town, the saloon, or the desert; stereotypical characters such as the sheriff, or the gambler; gunfights; and plots that are designed either to establish or transgress the law. The viewer who shares this common cultural knowledge probably does not need to appeal to his or her memories of other westerns to determine that *Gunfight at the OK Corral* belongs to this genre, given that it tells the story of the bloody, vengeful fight of the Marshall Wyatt Earp, his brothers, and the professional gambler, Doc Holliday, against the Clanton brothers in Tombstone, a small town in the West.

It is important to recognize that in current usage the notion of genre always designates an abstract category that serves to group films together, as well as referring to the particular body of films

2

that are grouped together in the category concerned. Cinematic genres, as is the case with literary, theatrical, pictorial, or musical genres, thus comprise both a *class of works* and a *group of works* (the contents of the class). In giving a generic identity to a film, therefore, it is not enough for us simply to place it in a category; we must also link it to a series of other films that present similar thematic, narrative, and formal traits. The nexus of common elements that constitute a genre results from the identification of these elements in many films, with the number and recurrence of the elements permitting recognition of the similarity across them. For example, the genre of the "musical" could only become established once the Hollywood studios had produced numerous films at the beginning of the 1930s in which love stories were told through a mixture of spoken dialogue, song, and dance. A significant number of films embodying analogous characteristics are thus a necessary precondition for the establishment, recognition, and consciousness of a genre, even though the number required cannot be precisely quantified.

Conversely, a generic category that has become established and recognized, once it has entered film reading-habits as part of a collective "knowledge," can short-circuit the need for comparison with other films of the same genre because of its summative descriptiveness. Spectators can thus classify a new film in a genre through two different approaches: either they can refer directly to the features that characterize a genre without reference to other films that constitute it, or they can compare this new film with other films in the genre, discuss the resemblances, and then either reinforce the generic category, perhaps adding a new element, or else question its adequacy in the light of the new case. This linked critical rereading of films and genres, as we shall see in the course of this book, is the foundation of the work of historians and theoreticians of genre, even though there is no reason to think that it is their exclusive prerogative.

The case of films recounting the story of the colonists in the Eastern parts of what was not yet the United States of America, before Independence, shows why the existence of a minimum number of films with comparable features is a necessary (if insufficient) condition for creating a generic category. Even though *Birth of a Nation* (Griffith, 1915), *Drums Along the Mohawk* (Ford, 1939), *Unconquered* (De Mille, 1947), the different versions of *The Last of the Mohicans* (Tourneur and Brown, 1920; Seitz, 1936; Sherman's 1947 film *Last of the Redmen*; Mann, 1991), or Disney's *Pocahontas* (1995) and *Pocahontas II: Journey to the New World* (1998) all manifestly deal with settlers becoming established in New England – in the context of the pioneers' clash with the Indians, and the war between the French and the English – the small number of such films has not allowed for the establishment of an "eastern" genre. Because these films do not take place either west of the Mississippi, or during the second half of the nineteenth century, they have become a controversial subject among those who specialize in the western. Those who see a similarity to the western in the plots of these movies (the settling of, and battles along, a frontier) and in their characters (Indians, guides, families of colonists) often include them in the "western" genre under the label of "Pennsylvania western." Such critics even include in this sub-genre of the western a film like *High, Wide and Handsome* (Mamoulian, 1937), which takes place in Pennsylvania, but well after Independence, in 1859.

All attempts at classification involve not only selection and grouping, but also exclusion. That is why, by assigning a film to a genre, we distinguish it from other films. The ideal aim of this classifying activity is to create a typology of films, which will itself be linked to a typology of cinematic genres. To use generic criteria to characterize a film, then, is to incorporate it into a larger category of works, in accordance with a logic of differentiation. There are, nevertheless, other ways of grouping films, and other typologies besides genre typologies for ordering the world of films that do not depend upon global similarities in structure, form, or content. Films can be grouped around a director, an actor, a country, a period, a producer, a school, and so on. Thus, *Gunfight at the OK Corral* can belong to the group of films directed by John Sturges, to the group of films featuring Burt Lancaster (or Kirk Douglas, or Lee Van Cleef, or Rhonda Fleming, etc.), to the group of American films from the 1950s, to the group of films produced by Paramount, or to the group of films that constitute the cinematic saga of the Earp brothers. It is not a question of discussing here the relevance of these classifications, but of acknowledging that genre is just one possible mode of cinematic classification. We should note, however, that categorization of films by genre always depends upon the mediating definition of an *abstract* generic label, whereas the criteria that determine other possible groupings of films are immediately apparent and readily identified because they derive from *concrete* attributes that are either intrinsic to the films themselves, or pertain to the making of the films (Aumont and Marie 1988, p. 190).[1] Only classification by schools requires an abstract construction of categories, especially if one is not going to limit the definition of "school" to those that are named after a theorist, a manifesto, or an aesthetic program, and if one is going to take into account, for example, the notion of national cinematic schools. Moreover, identification by genre is a cultural habit of long-standing, not only in the occidental tradition, but also in the Japanese tradition. Genres perpetuate in cinema the practice of genericity, which distinguishes works of art through their shared traits (incidentally, a topic in the field of literature that has been an inexhaustible subject of debate and redefinition from the time of Aristotle's *Poetics*).

Finally, although I have deliberately retained only the current meaning of genre in this initial approach to the concept, it is appropriate to recall that the construction, awareness, and manipulation of generic categories is, in the movies as in all cultural productions of an industrial nature, a phenomenon that cuts across both the production and reception of films, given that producers, distributors, and exhibitors on the one hand, and popular audiences, critics, and film theorists and historians on the other, make use of descriptors drawn from genre theory. In all probability, this last point is responsible for the power of the notion of genre in cinema, while at the same time it helps to explain the extreme variability of typologies.

Every Use Has Its Own Typology

A summary (but by no means exhaustive) examination of the different generic classifications in cinema is sufficient to indicate the diversity of generic categories, the various ways in which they are used, and their contents. We will dwell on some of these typologies not in order to mock the naïveté or impressionism of this or that taxonomy, but for the sake of examining what each one deals with, how it functions, and whether it functions.

Viewers' guides

The existence of two guides to entertainments being presented in Paris (*L'Officiel des spectacles* and *Pariscope*) provides an opportunity for comparison. The way in which these two booklets classify films by genre and attribute a genre to each film shows them making the same use of generic categories. However, while these two guides have the same function and address an identical readership, an attentive reading of them brings to light real divergences between their respective classifications.

In contrast to a guide like *Time Out*, *L'Officiel des spectacles* and *Pariscope* are published as small-format booklets designed to be held in the hand or put in a handbag, and have almost no editorial content. These two guides (that appear weekly) restrict themselves to listing pieces currently being performed in the theater, films currently being screened in cinemas, exhibitions, museums, and guided tours. Practical information is given for each show or cultural event (dates, hours, venue, price) and a very brief description that allows the Parisian reader/spectator to place them among the very large number of cultural and artistic events presented in Paris and its suburbs ("the Paris region"). The practical purpose reflected in these guides and their modest price (35 centimes for *L'Officiel des spectacles* and 40 centimes for *Pariscope*) make them an indispensable *vade mecum* for the Parisian viewer.

Because of the great number of cinema halls located in Paris and its suburbs, from multiplexes to art-house cinemas, cinema occupies an important part of these guides (around one third of their approximately 200 pages), which, moreover, are presented for sale in kiosks each Wednesday, the same day that new films are released in France. Both of the guides offer a classification of films according to genre. In *L'Officiel des spectacles*, the titles of films currently being screened are divided under two headings: *Exclusivités* (new releases) and *Reprises* (repeats). They are then presented in alphabetical order, preceded by a letter or an abbreviation that indicates the film's genre. It is the same in *Pariscope*, which until 2004 also offered a second list of films presented by genres.[2] The function of these generic ascriptions is identical in both booklets. The distinctive features of films are quickly identified by their title, their country of origin, their date, their distribution, their director, and a short description – but the mention of a genre, through relating each film to a larger category, gives it a more precise definition capable of steering the choice of viewers through the several hundred films being shown in Parisian cinemas. That is why all films, without exception, are given a generic identity, enabling the guides to divide up the larger group of films through this means. Generic designations in these guides have the function of locating and constructing a horizon of expectation for the reader and prospective viewer. For example, in seeing the ascription "Adventure" before *Journey to the Centre of the Earth* (Levin, 1959), he or she can expect to follow the breathtaking story of the exploits of a hero in an exotic, dangerous, and hostile world, and not to see a scientific documentary on geological magma. Generic determinations used in these guides are assigned by the editors, but, given that the weekly has to serve the needs of all those who go to the cinema, these attributions rely on an implicit consensus with those that are used by the "ordinary viewer."[3]

Now, despite an identical use of genre in the two guides and a comparable readership, the systems of classification are not the same. *L'Officiel des spectacles* divides films between 16 genres: Adventure; Biography; Comedy; Drama; Terror, Horror; Fantastic,

Science-Fiction; War; Historical; Cartoon, Wildlife; Karate; Musical Film; Dramatic Comedy; Police, Spy; Erotic; Western; Miscellaneous. Up until 2004, *Pariscope* proposed 22 categories: Animated Film; Adventure; Dramatic Comedy; Comedy; Short Film; Cartoon; Documentary; Psychological Drama; Drama; Erotic; Fantastic; Dance Film; Musical Film; *Film noir*; Political Film; War; Horror; Karate; Police; Science-Fiction; Thriller; Western.

I shall leave a more detailed comparison to the reader, in order simply to highlight five main points here:

1 The difference between the generic categories employed concerns their number as much as their name.

2 The genres that are common to both lists are those that serve to classify a large number of films (such as "Comedy" or "Dramatic Comedy"), but certain ones, currently not well represented, reflect a past heyday, like the label "Western," which is almost entirely reserved for repeats, or "Karate," which is really a relic of the vogue for martial arts films popularized by Bruce Lee.

3 The categories used are extremely diverse: their contours are sometimes fluid ("Dramatic Comedy," "Drama") or, to the contrary, very precise ("Karate," "Western"); they indicate as much a commonality of subjects, themes or contents, as they do production techniques ("Cartoon") and differences of format ("Short Film").

4 The films are not given the same generic identity. Thus, in 2002, *Microcosmos* (Nuridsany/Perennou, 1996), a film dealing with the life of insects and other tiny animals in an ordinary French field,[4] is assigned to the "Cartoon-Wildlife" genre in *L'Officiel des spectacles*, marked with a "J" (*jeunesse*) to indicate a film suitable for children. In *Pariscope*, however, it is identified as a "Documentary." But this divergence does not derive merely from whether or not a category exists in the two guides; *Dancer in the Dark* (von Trier, 1999) was an example of a musical film for *L'Officiel des spectacles*, and of a drama for *Pariscope*.

5   The difficulty of dividing films accurately into a comprehens-
    ive map of genres is evident even in the text of the booklets.
    The "Miscellaneous" category of *L'Officiel des spectacles* is a catch-
    all for all films that have not been able to be assigned to the
    15 other genres, attesting to the irreducible residue that
    remains after all attempts to classify objects – a phenomenon
    well known to all those who have sought, at least once, to
    organize their library or their collection of videos into a
    system. Moreover, the generic identity of films, doubtless
    because it does not completely fulfill its navigational function,
    is sometimes completed in the text accompanying the pre-
    sentation of works by a supplementary denomination – the
    equivalent of a sub-genre, without, however, being lexical-
    ized as a sub-genre (that is, defined as sub-category that can
    be reused in a systematic way) by the guide. Comedies can
    thus be listed variously as "for children," "of manners,"
    "romantic," and so on.

Reference volumes: dictionaries and encyclopedias

Dictionaries and encyclopedias about cinema, cinematic genres,
and filmmaking movements that are designed to compile an inven-
tory of works in particular cinematic genres also propose their
own categories. Generally, for each entry about a genre they give
a name, a list of characteristics, a historical overview, and a list
of the main films in the genre. Having done this, they tend to
reduce the number of films in a particular genre – probably for
practical, editorial, and pedagogical reasons – to a handful of titles,
mostly of films that have received acclaim. Inevitably, as the alert
reader might anticipate, there is no perfect agreement in this type
of work concerning the name, the number, the size, and the definition of the genre![5] Moreover, as is the custom with all dictionaries, cinema dictionaries make frequent use of cross-references
between genres. Thus, Vincent Pinel in his *Écoles, genres et mouvements au cinéma* explicitly invites his readers to refer to four other
genres in the definition that he gives for the historical film:

As time recedes, all films become "historical" – that is, historical objects. However, these are not historical films in the sense that I am proposing here: fictive films in which the action takes place in a reconstructed past. The historical film, thus defined, does not constitute a genre in the narrow sense of the term but a vast domain that encompasses, entirely or partially, most of the great screen genres, particularly the "western" and the war film.

In addition, the historical film does not include only fiction (see Documentary, and Montage). (Pinel 2000, p. 120)

Even if the implicit reference to *all* other genres raises a doubt about the soundness of the "historical film" as a category, this system of cross-referencing has the virtue of underlining an important fact that previous classifications have not taken into account – the mixing of cinematic genres.

There are also many more genres catalogued in these reference books than the standard ones. Indeed, they itemize all the cinematic genres to which reference has been made at one time or another throughout the history of cinema, as well as the history of scholarship on cinema. Furthermore, they do not restrict themselves to describing the state of contemporary film production, the nomenclature in use today, or even the categories that have been established by critics.

Lack of agreement over cinematic categories

The classifications that we have just seen propound generic categories that differ in number, name, and content, as well as in their definitions (even if we have until now provisionally overlooked that last point in order to grasp the rationale of the various types of divisions). An examination of the film lists and names used by the film industry confirms the variability of the categories that are used. It is the same with the names of genres produced, used, or studied by film critics and historians, for whom constituting, organizing, and discussing the classifications and groupings of films in an informed and rigorous manner is a major preoccupation. Thus Steve Neale, in order to propose a panorama of Hollywood genres, retains 16 principal genres from among the various possibilities, chosen because they fit the two following criteria: they have been the subject of a detailed examination by film scholars, and their theoretical definitions coincide with the designations of the film industry (2000, p. 51). However, these genres, which he accepts as uncontested, are far from being incontestable. In fact, Neale admits in the introduction to his study that scholars are in general agreement about a dozen genres, while he himself begins with ten genres that are identified by Richard Maltby: four undisputed categories (the western, the comedy, the musical, the war film) and four supplementary categories (the thriller, the gangster film, the horror film, and the science-fiction film), and two categories that stand apart from the others because they have been the subject of numerous and significant studies and discussions (*film noir*, and melodrama) (Maltby 1995, p. 116). To this list of categories, which clearly do not all have the same status, Neale adds six other genres: the detective film, the epic, the social problem film, the teenpic (in which the principal characters are generally adolescents, and which is aimed at a teenage audience), the biopic, and the action-adventure film. In addition, these 16 genres are constantly subject to reworking by producers, as well as being the subject of debates and redefinitions, as Neale proceeds to demonstrate in his detailed examination of the scholarly literature dedicated to each genre. Even if the field is restricted to Hollywood cinema – that is, to a cinema which is often considered to be constructed and organized around genre – this variation in naming is inescapable.

Generic categories are not the same for everyone, everywhere, in all periods, because they depend upon different contextual relations with cinema. This means that they cannot have the same meaning or the same function in all these different contexts. Classifying films by genre is to practice a kind of labeling game, comparable to that which Jean-Pierre Esquenazi (inspired by Wittgenstein's account of "language-games") has detected in

11

the use of genres in television programming (1997, p. 105).[6] Practiced by a community (of spectators, producers, critics, etc.), this labeling game presupposes shared systems of reference that are often implicit, and is, above all else, the result of habits of production and reception. Even though these labels are used almost automatically by those who share the same understanding of the world of cinema, they nevertheless produce useful generic distinctions.

In fact, several possible labeling games exist in parallel. Each devolves from a vision and a practice of the cinema that is specific, but shared. All impart meaning and have classificatory value because they depend upon a prior agreement between those who employ them. Adopting the metaphor of a card game, one might say that the different communities who concur with a classificatory system agree about the cards (the corpus of films considered) and the rules of the game (the criteria that serve to determine the distinguishing similarities and differences between films). The recurrence of certain generic labels in the different typologies that I noted previously (such as the western, the comedy, the war film, the musical, or the science-fiction film) do not derive solely from the purity of the filmic forms that they designate; they also illustrate a broader cultural consensus (one that is perhaps less rigorous on account of its inclusiveness) that transcends and traverses the specific communities of producers, directors, critics, and viewers.

An Impossible Typology?

There is no known universal typology of genres capable of dividing up the cinematic landscape definitively into groups of films, given that such a typology would need to be built on distinctions accepted by all, and to be organized in terms of stable categories. It is necessary, therefore, to examine catalogues of film genres to ascertain the principles according to which the various conventional genres are organized.

Different levels of characterization

A comedy, by its very nature, provokes laughter or smiles (assuming that it is successful). A western deals with life on a frontier – that of the American West at the time of its conquest (1840–90). As brief as these definitions might be, they suffice to demonstrate that the criteria enabling these two genres to be defined cannot be put on the same level. Comedy is recognized by the response it attempts to arouse in its viewers, the western through its thematic content. Beyond these two examples, we can observe that the properties that serve to characterize and identify genres are not always of the same nature. With cinema, the justifications for different generic categories are as varied as those used to distinguish literary genres. Jean-Marie Schaeffer remarks:

> When we run through the list of names of common genres, it very quickly becomes apparent that the heterogeneity of the phenomena they identify derives very simply from the fact that these names do not all operate at the same discursive level, but refer sometimes to one, sometimes to another and the most often, the several of them at the same time. (1989, p. 81)

This literary theorist identifies five distinct levels of differentiation that can all be used to construct generic categories, even though they do not pertain to the same phenomena. Three of these levels (the level of *enunciation*, the level of *destination*, and the level of *function*) derive from the fact that a work is not only a text, but also performs an act of communication: "a message transmitted with a specific aim by a given individual in particular circumstances, received by another individual in particular circumstances, with a purpose that is no less specific" (Schaeffer 1989, p. 80). Thus, the level of enunciation corresponds to the question "Who speaks?," that of destination to the question "To whom?," and that of function to the question "With what effect?" The other two levels (the *semantic* level and the *syntactic* level) are about the materialized message – that is, the text, or,

13

for our purposes, the film. The semantic level corresponds to the question "What is said?" and the syntactic level to the question "How is it said?" These five levels of differentiation that have been established in the discourse about genres will be very useful to an understanding of where and how the distinctions between film genres are played out, in terms of one or more of the five different levels (Schaeffer 1989, pp. 82–115).

The level of function

This level may be used, for example, to distinguish documentary genres (assuming, hypothetically, that we accept the documentary as a genre, and not merely a form). The enunciation of a documentary occurs through an informative mode that "established its scientific method on the strict recitation of facts in the order of their occurrence, in the conviction that truth would emerge from this 'faithful' representation of phenomenal reality," while other genres present themselves generally as fictive representations, being the outcome of an invented enunciation (Guynn 1990, p. 13).

The level of destination

Some of the film genres that we have already met, such as the children's film, are defined through specific destinations – that is, the audience(s) to which they are directed – while other generic categories do not assume *a priori* the existence of a particular spectator. In the same way, a home movie in Super 8 or on video by the member of a family for the most part addresses the family that made it, and which forms its subject. Not surprisingly, such films are rarely exhibited at public screenings! The impact that intended destinations can have is illustrated by the suppression and subsequent release of Raymond Depardon's film *1974, une partie de campagne* (*A Summer Outing*), which is a documentary tracing the election campaign of Giscard d'Estaing, a candidate for the presidency of France who was elected and served as president from 1974 to 1981. Given that the former president, the central character in the documentary, had largely financed Depardon's film, he was able to exercise a control and censorship over its distribution. In fact, apart from several special showings in which Depardon personally presented his work as a documentary filmmaker, *1974, une partie de campagne* was not shown in the commercial cinema before 2002. Valéry Giscard d'Estaing explains that up until this date the film, in his eyes, had been equivalent to a set of holiday snapshots, having been made for sentimental reasons without any commercial motive, as a personal memento of his campaign.[7] In 2002, to lend support to a new presidential campaign in which he was not personally involved, he reversed his decision because, according to him, the destination of the film appeared to have changed. A private film – a sort of home movie (albeit made by a professional filmmaker, in a format that was not customary for the genre!) – had become with time an object of general interest for public consumption, a documentary with historical value attesting to a dimension of political life (an election campaign).

The level of function
The names of genres can be defined by the function that they seek to perform, by their "project," as it were. Certain genres have an *illocutionary* function – that is, they express the communicative aim that the films and their creators wish to achieve. Thus, a documentary is often employed to inform viewers of how things are. Other genres have a *perlocutionary* function – that is, they aim to change the behavior of viewers, to induce a particular response in them.[8] Thus, a comedy solicits laughter, an erotic or pornographic movie solicits sexual excitement, and a horror film the emotion of fear or dread.

The semantic level
Many genres are distinguished by semantic elements: their themes, their motifs, or their topic. The western is characterized by spaces (mountains ranges, deserts, canyons, etc.), locations (saloons, banks), characters (cowboy, horse, communities of farmers, saloon singer, sheriff, etc.), objects (wagons, coaches, colts and shotguns), situations (confrontation between hero and villain, river crossings, Indian attacks on the wagons, gunfights, etc.),

all of which belong to the American West at the end of the nineteenth century.[9] Similarly, other genres are defined by their distinctive semantic elements; for example, the martial arts film is characterized by samurais, monks and their students, aerial combat, unarmed combat, and sword fights that resolve conflicts between good and evil, and an ethos of detachment and bodily and spiritual self-mastery. Fantasy and horror films contain supernatural beings or inhuman creatures (devils, spirits, living-dead, giant monkeys, hybrid creatures of all sorts) that behave in an unnatural manner (sorcerers, mad scientists), and populate disturbing spaces (crypts, cemeteries, castles in ruin, haunted homes, isolated houses, ancient buildings, etc.). Contemporary wars are the topic of the war film, which recreates military events (battles, ambushes, front lines, etc.), magnifies heroic actions, or raises doubts and questions about the usefulness of armed combat, retracing the story of simple soldiers or officers, who are variously admirable, or dangerous.

The syntactic level
Jean-Marie Schaeffer aggregates formal elements at this level. In this regard, because "film" as a form is not the same as "text" as a form, and because the term "syntactic" may have different meanings, what should be grouped together at this level may be subject to debate. The technical aspects of filmmaking provide criteria that operate at this level, giving rise, for example, to the cartoon (which we have already encountered) as a generic category. One can also view the alternation between realistic scenes with dialogue and scenes with singing and dance numbers as being a formal element that distinguishes the musical. One might, if need be, enlarge the syntactic level to include narratological features that partially characterize certain genres, such as the flashback – a favored narrative technique in *film noir* – or the use of focalization from the perspective of the viewer, which often generates the effects in comedies, or in suspense genres such as the thriller.

One must acknowledge the plurality and composite nature of generic references. Commentators do not always invoke the same level when making distinctions between genres. It is obvious, for example, that even though most genres are largely based on a convergence of semantic and thematic features, this level is completely absent from what we refer to as the "documentary," the name of which does not imply any particular subject. It is hypothetically possible to describe a generic category by mechanically referring to the five levels. For example, one might say that melodrama uses a fictive mode of expression (enunciation); that it addresses, particularly in the United States, women spectators (destination); that it makes audiences cry (function); that it emphasizes conflicts between generations, between the sexes, or between desire and the law (semantic); and that it is often told through a flashback, or through a story told by the voice of a narrator who is also one of the characters in the story (syntactic). To do this, however, would be to address historically determined categories through a scheme that takes no account of context – such as the sexual branding of the genre, or the use of the flashback, which is not a universal feature of melodrama.

Different frames of reference

The degree of precision with which common generic categories are conceptualized is extremely variable, as can be seen both in the understanding of a genre (its defining criteria) and in its application (the number of films that are deemed to be included in it). The more general the definition of a genre, the more indistinct its boundaries become, meaning that more and more films are able to be included in the category – as with comedy or drama, for example. Moreover, each of these genres is named after a dramatic type. Cinema thus inherits a long theatrical tradition in which certain genres were defined, developed, and transformed. Indeed, the term "drama," which originated in the eighteenth century as an intermediate genre between comedy and tragedy, after two centuries of changes and reformulations ended up by referring loosely to all plays in the theater at the end of the nineteenth century having a serious tone, and in which the action

17

consisted of violent and pathetic confrontations between characters placed in a specific historical or social framework. The term then migrated to the cinema, where it was used in the early years of filmmaking to classify films that were neither documentaries nor comedies. Subsequently, it was extended to cover a field so vast that it became necessary to specify the nature of the drama (romantic, historic, psychological, social).

In contrast to these broad, inclusive frames of reference – which are often transnational, trans-artistic, and transhistorical, and so large that they tend to lose their operational value – we find very precise categories, such as the "gore" or "splatter" film, born in 1963 with *Blood Feast* (Lewis), in which horror combines with repulsion, with the specific aim of explicitly showing violence, rather than merely suggesting it: mutilated and cut up corpses, horribly wounded and lacerated bodies, blood spattered in streams. Similarly, certain Asian cinematic genres, particularly those found in Hong Kong cinema, may appear singularly idiosyncratic, especially to a Western spectator. One thinks, for example, of *Wu xia pian* with its sword fights, as illustrated in the 1960s Hong Kong movies by King Hu (*Come Drink with Me*, 1965; *A Touch of Zen*, 1972), and Chang Cheh (*Tiger Boy*, 1960), or *kung fu* films and aerial battles, as in *Fist of Fury* (Luo Wei, 1972) in which the Chinese Chen-Chen, played by Bruce Lee, a student of the school of *kung fu*, confronts the Japanese directors of a karate school in Shanghai during the 1940s who had killed his master. Even without entering into the Chinese distinction between the two genres of *Wu xia pian* and *kung fu* (based on the type of martial art used), the larger genre that unites the martial arts film still often strikes the French viewer, from an occidental perspective, as a very narrow category.

These differences between broad general categories and narrow precise categories do indeed result from different conceptual framings, insofar as they derive in part from the broader global artistic and cultural system in which the genres are conceived and received. Cinematic genres embody traces of other literary or visual genres, and share any degree of indeterminacy or precision that may inhere in them. In addition, the perception of this degree is inevitably influenced by the culture of the specta-tor. Hong Kong spectators do not consider the notion of martial arts film too narrow and limited, and the aficionados of the horror film would find the simple distinction between horror movies and gore films inadequate, preferring to subdivide the horror film into thriller, gore, psycho-killer, slasher, splatter,[10] stalker,[11] and so on. The traces that remain from this earlier fram-ing also explain the recurrent uncertainty about the boundaries between genres and sub-genres from which certain differences between common and scholarly typologies derive. Some make gangster films, *film noir*, detective films, and the thriller into auto-nomous genres, while others incorporate them into one large, complex genre – the crime film.

The mixing of genres

One of the perverse effects of a typology designed to divide and construct categories is to give the illusion that genres are pure and impermeable. In actuality, we know that genres are often hybrid, as is evident in the alliance of the silent western first with the burlesque comedy, and later with melodrama in the 1920s. Furthermore, certain of the distinctions between genres appear to be purely conventional. The western, in its classical form, could be included in the genre of the historical film because it recounts episodes, inspired by real or fictitious events, that take place in a reconstructed past located in the far West. This would not be the case, however, for a large number of westerns made during the 1920s that did not delve back very far in history – one needs to acknowledge that in the 1920s the settlement of the West was still a relatively recent event – and could even be set in a time that was contemporaneous with their filming. The formation and permanence of the western as a genre distinct from the historical film, therefore, derive from the desire to adopt a narrower frame of reference to define films about the American West that is designed to encompass them all. Apart from being based on a large number of films on this topic, this frame of reference also derives from ideological motivations, making the formation of the American nation a separate category in the cinematic production dominated by Hollywood from 1910 onwards.

The number of films that draw upon several genres are legion. Abel Gance's *Napoleon* (1927) is both a historical film and a biopic; *Seven Brides for Seven Brothers* (Donen, 1954) relies on the musical and the western; *Some Like It Hot* (Wilder, 1959) is a comedy, but also borrows from the gangster film; *Dance of the Vampires* (Polanski, 1967) is both a fantasy film and a comedy; and so on. Undoubtedly, the lack of awareness of genre-mixing displayed in typologies is attributable to the fact that, in an effort to be rationally ordered, they tend to compile their classification according to a scientific biological model. However, as Jean-Marie Schaeffer has observed, "Biological classification relies upon a set of inclusive relationships, in which the indivisible unit resides in its organic constitution, belonging to a specific class" (1989, p. 71). The same does not apply in the classification of objects made by human art or craft, such as films, which do not inherently belong to a genre, but can be conveniently grouped in a genre owing to the common traits they present. Thus, the film *Napoleon* can be viewed as a biopic because, in common with other films, it recounts the life of a man; it can also be considered a historical film because its actions, relying on the reconstruction of a historical period, ally it with other films that depict the past, without necessarily choosing the biographical route. By way of contrast, Napoleon as a person, considered from a biological point of view, belongs entirely to the human species and to none other. It is Napoleon himself, and not a select number of his attributes, who belongs to the human species, or "genre."

The hierarchy of genres

In highlighting the various frames of reference that determine the constitution of different generic categories, we have shown that they are based on variable cultural referents. But typologies, by placing genres side by side, also overlook the existence of a hierarchy of genres in culture. Jean-Loup Bourget emphasizes that in classical Hollywood cinema all genres are not equal in terms of value. "Literary adaptations, dramas, films with grand spectacles, enjoy a striking prestige that is not accorded to comedies, horror films, or low-budget adventure films" (1998, pp. 12–13).

Economic factors, such as whether a movie has an A or B classification, explains, of course, this hierarchy of productions, but it would be naïve to suppose that economic logic does not reflect a symbolic and cultural logic according to which works and genres are placed in a hierarchy. As Bourget observes, the making of a historical film today imparts a respectability not conferred on science-fiction films. Evidence of this can be seen in the fact that Steven Spielberg received seven Oscars for *Schindler's List* (1994), the first in his career, whereas he received none for *Close Encounters of the Third Kind* (1977) or *Jurassic Park* (1993) (Bourget 1998, p. 13). As far as *E.T.* (1982) was concerned, he had to content himself with Oscars for technical aspects of the film (Sound Effects Editing, Visual Effects, Best Music, Best Sound).

The hierarchical status of film genres thus derives from more general cultural legitimacies or illegitimacies. This is well illustrated in France by the fate of comedy – a genre that has not traditionally been valued in French cinema. Even when they acknowledge that a film is successful, critics and reviewers temper their enthusiasm when dealing with French comic films. They condescendingly pen faintly laudatory or clichéd comments like "our pleasure is not spoilt," "the laugh-machine is working," or "an amusing film that allows one to have a good time." The genre, which is less disparaged if the film comes from outside France, is only accorded high status if it departs from the strict parameters of the comic, so that "the comedy generates a real feeling of malaise," or that "beneath the laughter is hidden emotion and despair."[12] More typically, French comedies are viewed as being either vulgar, mechanical, or bourgeois. This condescension and contempt for the genre, leaving aside the quality of the films, is a legacy of the illegitimacy of comedy in France over three centuries. Comic theater of the eighteenth century is marked by two contradictory influences. The first is that of farce and the *commedia dell'arte*, which elevate and value laughter. The second is the traditional view inherited from Aristotle, whose few lines on comedy in the surviving version of *The Poetics* characterize this genre as a low one:

> Comedy is, as we said, a representation of people who are rather inferior – not, however, with respect to every [kind of] vice, but the laughable is [only] a part of what is ugly. For the laughable is a sort of error and ugliness that is not painful and destructive, just as, evidently, a laughable mask is something ugly and distorted without pain. (Aristotle 1987, p. 6)

From the seventeenth century, then, playwrights were divided between a desire to produce plays based on laughter inspired by farce, and a wish to rid themselves of violent laughter in order to make comedy into a noble genre that does not merely provoke laughter, but also instructs. To take a notable example, the first tendency is manifest in Molière's *Les Fourberies de Scapin* (*Scapin's Deceits*), and the second in *Le Misanthrope* (*The Misanthrope*). That is why the eighteenth century, which favored comedy that was mixed with morality (as in the plays of Beaumarchais and Diderot), and afterwards the nineteenth century, consistently preferred *Le Misanthrope* to *Les Fourberies de Scapin*. So much so, that a superficial reading of the classic works of the eighteenth and nineteenth centuries could lead one to think that their writers had all wished to empty comedy of farcical laughter, crude or popular – an assumption that is far from the case, if one rereads these works carefully. It appears that classical authors and their successors wished to rid comedy of crude laughter (the laughter of the people) in the way that modernity would later stigmatize the "bourgeois laughter" of a Feydeau or a Labiche. Comedy in France is only an acceptable genre on the condition that it is not merely a comedy.

Finally, one should note that the preference given to one name for a generic category over another, when several terms are available, can reflect a hierarchal logic of differentiation. Thus, the *"kung fu* film" connotes a popular audience from the 1970s, and the "martial arts film" is a more general term. The journal *Cahiers du cinema*, however, prefers to use the term *film de sabre* (sword film), which has scholarly overtones because of its rarity.

The question of history

Typologies record the existence of genres, but by flattening their categories they do not provide a historical perspective. The history of genres also remains outside their classification. They juxtapose transhistorical categories (comedy or drama) and categories whose production is limited in the case of film to a particular moment in the history of cinema. One example is the burlesque, which survives on the screen after the 1930s only as a "tone," and not as a genre. Directors (some of whom were also actors, such as Blake Edwards, Jerry Lewis, or Woody Allen), actors (such as the Marx Brothers), and genres (such as the screwball comedy) make use of burlesque comedy, adopting the device of the gag, and imitating some of the mannerisms of the jumping-jack stooge favored by actors in this genre (Nacache 1995, p. 32). Moreover, generic classifications place genres belonging to different periods in the history of cinema alongside one another. The western, which has languished since the 1970s, sits next to the gore film, which developed in the 1970s and 1980s, in these typologies. "Living" genres are juxtaposed in the typologies with "dead" genres. This does not mean that the latter no longer represent anything, or that they lack meaning. Even though these categories have ceased to exert an active influence on the making of new films, they remain productive in the memory of cinephiles, and in film analysis. Finally, just as generic categories carry along with them the totality of the culture in which they are inscribed, they also bear a history. To be convinced of this, one need only look at the classification generated by Antoine Vallet in 1963 in *Les Genres du cinéma* (*The Genres of Cinema*):

1 Nature and man: the documentary
2 The life of the world: pages of history
3 History and legend: the epic
4 Reality and fiction: the adventure film
5 The world of souls: the psychological film
6 The human comedy: the comic film
7 Dreams and reality: the poetic film
8 Films about art
9 The animated film

As noted by François de la Bretèque, this is a transcendental vision of cinema, inspired by Henri Agel, who presides over this classification. It ascends from nature to the soul and dream, to end up with poetry and art (Bretèque 1993).

If we consider film genres as categories of classification, one can only note the vitality of generic activity at an empirical level, and the impossibility of organizing cinema dogmatically into a definitive and universal typology of genres at a theoretical level. Categories exist, but they are not impermeable. They may coincide at certain points, contradict one another, and are the product of different levels of differentiation or different frames of reference. They take no account of either the internal interactions between film genres, or the external interactions between film genres and other artistic and cultural productions. Finally, maps of genres ignore the geographic and cultural dimensions of films, even though these are generated by a relationship with a specific period, place, or given activity that is expressed in the cinema. This lack of attention to cultural and geographic specificity explains, in particular, the ethnocentric nature of many common European typologies that leave off their lists genres that are found only in exotic filmographies; for example, those of Japanese cinema, which is strongly structured in terms of types and genres. The illusion of a rigorous and comprehensive generic classification dissipates, leaving in its place a veritable jungle of genres in which categories and films, like the trees of a tropical forest, grow branches, roots, and vines that meet and intertwine.

Notes

1 Even though historians may disagree over how to attain an adequate definition of a period, the films made in the 1930s, or in 1990, or in any other determinate period are, from the outset, a concrete grouping.

2 This listing by genres, which still existed when the original French edition of this work was published, disappeared from *Pariscope* in 2004. However, *Pariscope* makes use of the same batch of generic categories to define films.

3 Although this discussion will be restricted to these two examples of guides, the present analysis could be extended to almost all generic classifications that aim to provide guidance to viewers – in newspapers, magazines that list television programs, and video clubs. However, an examination of categories offered in newspapers and magazines would need to take account of the specific sociological circumstances of their readership.

4 *Microcosmos* is a rather poetic documentary without any scientific commentary that films the inhabitants of a field in a scale of centimeters. The ecosystem is examined in its entirety and all its interactions, with its list of imponderables, efforts, setbacks, and successes. The film, which won the *Grand Prix* of the higher technical commission at the Cannes Festival in 1996, although less anthropomorphic, is not unrelated to *La Marche de l'Empereur* (*March of the Penguins*) (Jacquet, 2005).

5 For a comparison, see the entries included in *Dictionnaire du cinéma mondial. Mouvements, écoles, courants, tendances et genres* (1994), edited by Alain and Odette Virmaux, Paris, Éditions du Rocher, and in Vincent Pinel's *Écoles, genres et mouvements au cinema* (2000), Paris, Larousse-Bordas/HER, Comprendre/Reconnaître, which, moreover, incorporate categories with a different status in the same list. The criteria that determine movements and genres are not the same, and do not translate into a comparable basis of comparison for understanding the cinema.

6 For the concept of language-game, see Ludwig Wittgenstein (1953) *Philosophical Investigations*, Oxford, Blackwell.

7 Written note, dated January 17, 2002, distributed during a press screening of the film. In all the interviews given about the release of *1974, une partie de campagne*, Giscard d'Estaing develops the same argument.

8   For a definition of illocutionary and perlocutionary acts, see John
     R. Searle (1969) Expressions, meaning and speech acts, in *Speech
     Acts: An Essay in the Philosophy of Language*, Cambridge, Cambridge
     University Press, pp. 22–50.

9   For a detailed catalogue of the semantic elements of the western,
     see Jean-Louis Leutrat and Suzane Liandrat-Guigues (1990) *Les Cartes
     de l'Ouest. Un genre cinématographique: le western*, Paris, A. Colin,
     pp. 11–73.

10   The notion of splatter movie highlights the joyous dimension that
     does not appear in the gore film. See John McCarty (1984) *Splatter
     Movies: Breaking the Last Taboo of the Screen*, New York, St. Martin's
     Press.

11   The verb "to stalk" evokes, at the same time, the idea of a regular
     progress forward which nothing can stop and that of tracking. These
     two actions define the murderers in the stalker movie, like the Friday
     killer of *Friday the 13th* (Cunningham, 1980), or like Freddy in *A
     Nightmare on Elm Street* (Craven, 1984). See Philippe Rouyer (1997)
     Le Cinéma Gore: une esthétique du sang, Paris, Cerf, 1997, pp. 87–90.

12   The veil of opprobrium thrown over purely comic cinema in
     France seems to exclude aggressive and burlesque foreign come-
     dies. It is likely that if Italian comedies or the films of Jerry Lewis
     were well received in France, it is in part because of their exoti-
     cism and, in the case of Italian comedies, because their reliance on
     stereotypical Italianness protects them.

Chapter 2
Looking for the Rules
of Genre

Having been unable to clear the genre jungle with a few machete blows as strong as they were lethal, we have to think of ways of penetrating it. It is wisest not to engage as a guide the first definition of cinematic genre that we considered ("an empirical category that serves to name, differentiate between, and classify works on the basis of the recurring configurations of formal and thematic elements they share"). This is because even though it allows for the uses of genre as a classifying device to be high-lighted, as well as the contradictions and limits inherent in these efforts at classification, it is silent on the cultural and historical consensus (subject to variation) upon which the existence and recognition of genres depend. In order to clear a path, therefore, we will provisionally make use of a definition proposed by Francesco Casetti: "Genre is a collection of shared rules that allows the filmmaker to use established communicative formulas and the viewer to organize his own system of expectations" (1999, p. 271). It is necessary to emphasize that this second definition is neither definitive, nor perfect, nor incontestable. The term "rules" used in this definition strikes one as rather rigid, running the risk of turning genre into a canon – a model to be used for the making and viewing of films. It supposes an absolute agreement between film producers (in the loose sense) and viewers con-cerning the recognition of genres that is frequently contradicted by the facts. Finally, it glosses over differences in the various understandings of the word "genre" that have come to be accepted, relating as they do to diverse activities and domains. Rick Altman reminds us that the existence of these understandings refers to a range of meanings inherent in the concept of "genre" itself (1999, p. 17):

- genre as a *blueprint*, a formula that precedes, programs, and patterns industrial production;
- genre as *structure*, as the formal framework on which individual films are founded;
- genre as *label*, as the name of a category central to the decisions and communications of distributors and exhibitors;
- genre as *contract*, as the viewing position required by each genre film of its audience.

Nevertheless, the objections that one might legitimately formulate, which could be leveled at all generalized definitions of genre (given that such definitions necessarily mask contradictions), do not negate the *instrumental value* of Casetti's definition. It is for this reason, and this reason alone, that we have chosen it to open up our way forward. In actuality, this definition implicitly acknowledges the variability of generic categories because it posits genre as depending upon an agreement. Furthermore, it suggests that this agreement operates in four different spaces that are viewed in relation to one another. These spaces may be designated schematically as the world of film production, the world of reception, the films themselves, and the space of negotiation and communication brought into being by the encounter between the three preceding spaces. Consequently, even though this definition erases disagreements, one should also appreciate that it synthesizes two features of genericity. Conventions exist (rules, formulas) that occur repeatedly *in films* of the same genre. These conventions insert themselves *into a process of communication* extending beyond the films themselves, their thematic elements, and their formal properties. Each of these two aspects (the conventions that are embodied in the film itself, and the process of communication that extends outside it) relates to two different types of film genre theory, both of which have seen many developments over a span of more than thirty years:

- *Structural and textual theories* that seek to establish the characteristic features of genres, conceived in terms of textual structures, and as collections of filmic texts.
- *Functional definitions of genre*, which, while retaining a theoretical perspective, define genres in terms of their function (social, cultural, economic, communicative).

These two approaches conceive of cinematic genre as residing at different levels: in the actual film for structural and textual approaches, and in the interactions of film with their contexts of production and reception for functional approaches. In addition, with regard to the issue of genre, they reflect two different ways of thinking about and studying cinema: the analysis of works and close-reading on one hand, and the analysis of cinema as a multilayered sociocultural practice on the other. The distinction between the two approaches is not always so radically defined, given that there are structural theories of cinema that also speculate upon its functions (but always by deducing the latter from structures that they have revealed). Moreover, certain theorists have been working for several years to reduce the gap between these two approaches, by attempting, as we shall see, to "reconnect" film texts and their contexts by using a complex method of genre analysis. Nevertheless, out of a concern for clarity, I will devote this chapter primarily to textual or structural definitions of film genres, reserving examination of the functional definitions for the following chapter.

Looking for Genre's Formal Rules

Certain definitions of genre, in accordance with a deductive theory, posit formal rules that govern the formation of genres. For this reason, they tend to convert genre into a closed system of formal procedures that feeds itself, then wears itself out on account of its own variations, which enter into competition with new forms (other genres). These definitions can be described as "formalist," provided that this term is given a fairly general meaning based on logic. The term "formalist," therefore, in the use we are making of it, encompasses the historical school of Russian Formalists and its subsequent influences, but is not limited to them.

Russian Formalists and cinematic genres

Those referred to as "Russian Formalists" – first by their detractors, and subsequently by the scholarly tradition – were members of the Society for the Study of Poetic Language (the OPOJAZ), a group of researchers and Russian scholars founded in Moscow in 1915 who remained active until the 1930s. Their project was to define "art" in general, as well as each individual art in its specificity. According to the formula launched by Shklovsky, a work of art is defined as "the sum-total of all stylistic devices employed in it" (Erlich 1955, p. 70).[1] Critical analyses produced by members of this group (including those who were interested in cinema) emphasized formal aspects over content. Because their goal was to isolate the authentic laws of cinema, it comes as no surprise to find that rather than defining cinema genres according to narrative structures or thematic elements, they do so in terms of the properties that are unique to the cinematic image, *photogénie*, and montage:

> We shall call cinema genre a group of procedures regarding composition, style, and subject that are linked to semantic material with a specific emotional goal, falling entirely within a precise generic system relating to art, that of cinema. To identify cinematic genres . . . we shall therefore examine how the use of space, of time, of humans, and of objects function in different genres, from the point of view of montage and *photogénie*, the disposition of the parts of a subject, and the relations that

are established between different elements within a genre. (Piotrovski 1996, p. 144)

The defining criteria of cinematic genres, then, consist of the stylistic laws that the formalists consider to be specific to cinematic art, with each genre relying upon a number of rules that reflect a particular application of these laws.

From the outset, Piotrovski identified two genres that should be excluded from the list of genres existing during the 1920s: the "cinema-drama," or "staged cinema" (involving the simple translation of a theatrical work on to the screen, and also, more generally, all films that emphasize intrigue, dramatic action, developing confrontations between characters), and the "cinema-novel" (the adaptation of a literary work that preserves the conception and subject of the story, and also, more generally, all films that borrow their manner from narrative literature, notably from the psychological novel, and the short story). He did not consider these two genres cinematic because they adopt and adapt canonical works – dramatic in the first case, and narrative in the second – and do not use specifically cinematic means of expression. Cinema-drama, for example, by borrowing a dramatic mode from theater emphasizing the battle of human passions and making the human individual its essential material, neglects the photogenic quality of cinema that places the human being at the same level of perception as the object. Moreover, because cinema-drama favors a linear sense of time, looking to make the duration of the film coincide with what we would now call the duration of the diegesis, and because it uses space as a simple point of reference in the composition, it neglects the power and potential of montage. The result is that this genre, in Piotrovski's estimation, by imperfectly understanding the expressive qualities specific to cinema, impoverishes them. By way of contrast, he considered authentic cinematic cinema genres to be those that had developed from the very beginning by using techniques available only to cinema, their appearance having been made possible by the expansion of those possibilities. Such genres included "the American comedy" (what is now called the "burlesque"

31

genre), the adventure film, the lyric genre, and two genres that were then in a process of "gestation" – monumental heroism (illustrated by Eisenstein's *Stachka* (*The Strike*), 1925, and *Bronenosets Potyomkin* (*The Battleship Potemkin*), 1925), and the filmed manifestations of Dziga Vertov and the "Kinoks."

Burlesque is considered authentically cinematic because it presents an unusual and dislocated use of objects that replenishes the arsenal of laughter – particularly through the use of the head shot. One might think of the sequence in which Buster Keaton tries on hats at the beginning of *Steamboat Bill, Jr.* (Keaton and Reisner, 1928), or the dance of the bread rolls in *The Gold Rush* (Chaplin, 1925). The hero of the burlesque is also closely linked to the world of objects. In a way, he is turned into an automaton by his emblematic mask (Charlie Chaplin is, above all, a bowler hat and a cane, Harold Lloyd a pair of round glasses), and wide shots underline his conflicted or fused relationship with his surroundings. Buster Keaton becomes as one with his locomotive in *The General* (Keaton and Bruckman, 1926). When the storm in *Steamboat Bill, Jr.* causes the front of a house to fall upon him, he finds himself miraculously spared, body and limbs intact, with his feet in the opening of a window. Chaplin does not manage to extricate himself from the escalator in *The Floorwalker* (1916). Harold Lloyd remains suspended from the hand of a clock on a skyscraper in *Safety Last!* (Newmeyer and Taylor, 1923).

Whereas burlesque is a cinematic genre because it unites the human being and the object in a single photogenic gesture, the adventure film displays the expressive possibilities of cinema through a principle underlying its construction: a "composition by leaps." More than the story itself, it is a succession of episodes involving ever greater dangers that creates the tension and structure of the film. Piotrovski saw American melodrama, in the form given to it by Griffith, as the apotheosis of the adventure film, because of its structure involving "catastrophe, chase, and rescue." The use of montage invests this structure with a great emotional power, as in the final sequence of *Orphans of the Storm* (Griffith, 1921). Louise, one of two sisters, and the Chevalier de

Vaudrey are condemned to death. The shots of the preparation for the execution, in which the hand that will release the guillotine is filmed closer and closer, alternates with shots of the hooves of Danton's horse, whose rider is galloping through the streets of Paris to save them, and who will rescue them *in extremis.*

The lyric genre, illustrated in particular by the films of Epstein, Delluc, Clair, and L'Herbier,[2] concentrates its expressivity on moments that generate strong impressions – for example, the face of the dying Mathilde, filmed in negative then immobilized as a frozen image in *La Chute de la maison Usher (The Fall of the House of Usher)* (Epstein, 1928). Genre is thus liberated from the demands of the story in a celebration of movement and objects, as illustrated by the race, sometimes extremely frenetic, sometimes filmed in slow motion, that fills the entire second half of *Entr'acte* (Clair, 1924).

As far as the last two cinema genres are concerned – monumental heroism, and cinema manifestations (genres developed under the Soviet Union) – Piotrovski views them as genres without subjects that are based on "an arrangement of objects shown in a new and unexpected fashion, using editing strategies that are based not on the story, but rather on associations aroused by the cinematic image itself." *The Battleship Potemkin* or *The Strike* (Eisenstein, 1925) depict objects having a powerful emotional charge, such as the statue of the lion in the first, and of the siren in the second, that are strongly linked to other elements of the film. Finally, Eisenstein's principle of "montage of attractions," and even more so the Kinoks' laws of rhythmic composition, distance editing from its narrative function in order to reveal its specifically cinematic expressivity (Piotrovski 1996).

It is clear that the five authentically cinematic film genres are not all equally authentic. The comic film, on occasions when it turns into a comedy, sometimes tends to hybridize with a theatrical form, and thus becomes a cinema drama. Similarly, the adventure film, if it overly privileges the romantic story, loses its cinematic authenticity and tends to merge into the cinema-novel genre. The other three genres whose historical existence is attested by groups of films (but which seem to have been more in a stage of development than fully formed) are no longer defined by their subject at all, but exclusively by their form. This gradation, then, implies a hierarchy of cinema genres. The more they use specifically cinematic techniques, and the more they distance themselves from the requirements of the literary story and the theatrical drama, the more they approach the essence of cinema itself. Furthermore, the lyric genre, the monumental heroism genre, and cinema manifestations are more accurately designated by what are now called a school, or a movement: namely, the French and the Soviet Avant-Gardes of the 1920s. This confusion between schools and genres arises directly out of the theoretical approach of Piotrovski. By regarding the issue of genres as one that could be determined through reference to a definition of cinematic art, he was led to the conclusion that schools that had also sought to define cinema as an art by basing their practice on the expressivity and the forms proper to the seventh art, should also be considered as genres.

The Russian Formalists, therefore, define cinema genres in a way that does not depend upon the criteria normally used to identify a genre (thematic elements and narrative structures), but rather on properties that are unique to the cinematic image. In an article published in 1995, Tom Gunning – who had already been led by notions of attraction and *photogénie* to define a "system of monstrative attractions" lacking any narrative intention, alongside the "system of narrative integration" in early cinema,[3] – proposes a new way of thinking about the concept of cinema genre (Gunning 1995a). Without denying the efficacy of the semantic-syntactic models that are currently dominant, he wishes to see the analysis of genres concern itself with the stylistic aspects of film that derive from the specificity of film. According to him, even though the themes and plots of the fantastic and the horror story are common both to cinema and literature, the origin of the genre nevertheless derives from the ontological ambiguity of the cinematic image: an absent presence. And even though the anxiety felt by spectators at their first encounter with this "kingdom of shadows" and "phantom of life" – noted by Gorky after screenings by Lumière in Russia – has long disappeared, certain genres such as the horror film can reawaken a perception of this fundamental and disquieting ambiguity. The *Freddy* series, in which the killer has the distinction of hunting down his young victims in their dreams, illustrates this well. In the first episode, *A Nightmare on Elm Street* (Craven, 1985), several adolescents simultaneously dream about a man with a burnt face and claws of steel who is chasing them. One of the young girls, Tina, is so traumatized by her nightmare that she asks her friends to spend the night with her. The next morning, she is discovered savagely killed, and Rod, the boy who spent the night in her room, is imprisoned. After these events, another teenager, Nancy, continues to dream about the monster, and Rod is found hanged in his cell. Convinced that the killer of Tina is none other than the man of her nightmare, Nancy decides to make him come out of her dream in order to kill him. Her attempts are not fruitful until the moment when, caught by the monster who is about to kill her, she decides to refuse to believe in the existence of her attacker. Everything fades away at this point, and the young woman wakes up at the end of a long nightmare that had in fact begun with the first images of the film – and which will continue in the following episodes of the series. It is this integration of the ambiguous relation between dream and reality in a story, combined with an aesthetic characteristic of the gore genre, that makes the *Freddy* films part of the fantastic genre.

It is self-evident that not all of the films usually considered part of the fantastic or horror genre on account of their themes and the narrative models could be considered part of the genre if it were to be defined by its capacity to play with the ambiguity of the cinematic image as a means of provoking anxiety. Gunning therefore proposes to establish two distinct generic corpora: one based on a definition of genre according to its semantic and syntactic elements, the other on a definition of genre developed from stylistic strategies that are linked to the specificity of the cinematic image. In addition, all the common genres (as was the case with the genre theories of the Russian Formalists) would probably not be able to find their origin in an element specific only to cinema. Given this constraint, the definition of cinema genres proposed by Gunning leads to a description of genres as "ways of narrativizing and naturalizing primal fascinations present in cinematic form itself" (1995a, p. 60).

The notion of a theoretical genre

The Russian Formalists' cinema genres, like the genres that Gunning proposes to define, are theoretical genres. They result, in fact, from a process of deduction based on a theory about cinema. A distinction between *theoretical genres* and *historical genres* was introduced into the field of genre studies by Tsvetan Todorov, in the preface to his *The Fantastic: A Structural Approach to a Literary Genre*. Todorov begins by stressing the impossibility of basing a rigorous analysis on a preexisting empirical observation that is meant to cover all works. If the analyst were to attempt to be exhaustive, he would soon have to give way under the weight of books and films – always supposing, especially with regard to the latter, that the oldest ones had not been completely lost. Elsewhere, he refutes the kind of approach that consists of studying a sample in the first instance, and then using it to construct a general hypothesis that is subsequently validated by checking it against other examples. The number of works studied, although important, does not in itself legitimize the deduction of universal laws. Just as "it is not the quantity of observations, but the logical coherence of a theory that finally matters," a theory of genres has to founded on a theory of the work – literary for Todorov, cinematic for the purposes of this book (Todorov 1973, p. 4). While historical genres are inferred from the empirical observation of actual works, the generic categories deduced from this theory constitute theoretical genres. Francesco Casetti develops this idea in the synthesis of Todorov's works that he published in 1979:

> In the first case [historical genres], we have the formalization of
> a certain number of concrete givens, and then the construction

of a sort of proto-text, a standard text that summarizes the characteristics of all the other texts in a genre. In the second case [theoretical genres], we have, to the contrary, the articulation of a terrain that is considered in its general aspects, having been chosen in advance, and then the construction of a general table (based on all the possible givens) that includes, as a result, both types that have already come into existence, and also those that are only potentially in existence. (1979, p. 38)

Many theories of genre prior to that of Todorov were constructed through deduction from a theory of literature, and therefore propose theoretical genres. We have seen this with the Russian Formalists and their legacy, but the same observation can be made with respect to the *Poetics* of Aristotle, who is considered to be the founding father of theories of genre, having been widely read, commented upon, corrected, and adapted through 25 centuries of literary history. The first lines of the *Poetics* assert that the definition of poetry finds its extension in the definition of its kinds:

Our topic is poetry in itself and its kinds, and what potential each has; how plots should be constructed if the composition is to turn out well; also, from how many parts it is [constituted], and of what sort they are; and likewise all other aspects of the same enquiry. Let us first begin, following the natural [order], from first [principles]. (Aristotle 1987, p. 1)

Aristotle's approach is normative, as well as being descriptive and analytic. It limits poetic art (at least in the version of the *Poetics* that has come down to us) to the art of imitation in verse, thus excluding all prose and verse that is non-imitative. This theory defines poetic art as the art of representational poetry. The two series of criteria that allow Aristotle to construct his general paradigm, to pick up the rather anachronistic terms used here by Casetti, arise from this question of representation. As Gérard Genette (1986) has shown in a reading of Aristotle that aims to synthesize and systemize him, the first element of differentiation depends on the manner of imitation (that is, the mode of enunciation), and the second on the object that is imitated. In the

Table 2.1 (Genette 1986)

Object \ Mode	Dramatic	Narrative
superior	tragedy	epic
inferior	comedy	parody

Aristotelian system, poetic works can imitate through telling (narrative mode), or by depicting characters who act and speak (dramatic mode). At the same time, they can imitate the actions of characters who are of higher or lower status. This double distinction permits four kinds to be deduced, corresponding to the genres of poetic art.

For the sake of clarity, we should note how the table provided by Genette allows for this Aristotelian system to be established. In it, generic categories are forms that result from the crossing of the two criteria, and poetic genres are the contents of these forms (table 2.1).

No matter what theory of works a theoretical genre is derived from, it manufactures a kind of "non-place," an ahistorical space that is supposed to permit the analyst to invoke "scientific" criteria in order to escape from empiricism, and from the variability of the categories established by culture. This is both the apparent strength of the notion, and also, in equal measure, its Achilles' heel. In actual fact, theories of literature, like that of cinema, are situated in the history of the arts and ideas, and can only be elaborated by taking them into account. All attempts to define genres involve a choice of theoretical criteria that reflect a historically conditioned conception about the artistic object being studied. In making this observation, I do not mean to disqualify theoretical genres, but simply to emphasize that they themselves also embody a degree of historicity. The criteria Todorov adopted to define a theoretical genre of the fantastic, for example, are anchored in a structural conception of signifying works that is indissolubly linked to the structuralist model developed in the field of the human sciences in the 1960s and 1970s. In general, all theories of cinema genres, from the most formal to the least formal, are edifices that have a particular conception of cinema as their foundation, along with the analyst's own theoretical hypotheses and practical aims as their architecture. This gives rise to a question underlying all approaches to genre that has been articulated explicitly by Rick Altman: how does one evaluate objectively a subjective critique (1989, pp. 10–12)?

To finish this discussion, let us return for a moment to the theoretical genre of the fantastic as Todorov defined it in the field of literature, which has had a great legacy in the domain of cinema studies. The fantastic genre is characterized by an uncertainty, in the presence of an event that is apparently inexplicable, about the validity of two possible explanations that are available simultaneously: a rational one that respects the known laws of this world (that it is only an illusion, a dream, a hallucination, or a human machination particularly well contrived by a perverse trickster, etc.); and a supernatural one that reaches beyond the limits of ordinary human knowledge (it's a manifestation of forces from the Beyond, from God or the devil, from extraterrestrial spirits, etc.). Moreover, this kind of text must compel the reader to apprehend the diegetical world as if it were a real world, then to *hesitate* between a natural explanation and a supernatural explanation of the bizarre events taking place in it. Indeed, choosing either one of these interpretations would tip the work out of the fantastic into either the strange or the marvelous. Finally, the reader has to reject an allegorical or poetic interpretation in order to install this hesitation. This theoretical definition, which is largely derived from a criterion involving "point of view," encompasses a range of historical genres, such as the gothic novel, ghost stories, and fairy stories, for which it substitutes itself. But it also excludes works from the traditional fantastic category that clearly align themselves with the supernatural. Thus, transposed into the domain of cinema, it can replace thematic definitions that privilege a "fantastic atmosphere." It excludes from the fantastic genre all those films that lack this space of uncertainty carved out of a world that is supposed to obey the laws of nature. Cinematic fairy stories, such as *Peau d'âne* (*Donkey Skin*) (Demy, 1970), and futuristic science-fiction films do not correspond to any theoretical fantastic genre, because they take place in another realm in accordance with non-realist rules. This definition, then, departs from the usual nomenclature used by producers and spectators, who have often subsumed science fiction and the fantastic under the same term since the 1950s.

When one looks at the matter closely, very few films satisfy the requirements of the fantastic as theorized by Todorov in a strict sense, because works that prolong a state of hesitation from one end to the other are very rare. Most films that maintain uncertainty for a fairly long time finally choose a supernatural explanation, and thus tip over into the marvelous. Rosemary has not gone mad, her neighbors and her husband are actually sorcerers, and her baby, who is never shown on screen, is the son of the devil (*Rosemary's Baby*, Polanski, 1968). After a skillfully maintained period of suspense, we learn that the little boy in *The Sixth Sense* (Shyamalan, 1999) does indeed see dead people, and that the psychiatrist who tries to help him is also one of these souls in pain. Less numerous are films that opt for a rational explanation, and by this means liberate the subject matter from the inexplicable. *The Beast with Five Fingers* (Florey, 1946) provides an example of this. In this film, the hand of the pianist, Ingram, is not an evil member that haunts the manor after his death. It has been severed from his corpse by Ingram's librarian, who aims through this means to unnerve his heirs and murder the lawyer who is in charge of settling the inheritance, using the hand to leave fingerprints other than his own on his victim. In the second part of the film, the viewer comes to understand that the sequences in which he has seen the crawling hand adopt the point of view of the librarian, who has become mad in the course of executing his crime. Only a handful of films that leave the viewer free to reach his or her own conclusions are able to correspond precisely to Todorov's definition. Romero, the director, does not take a position on the real nature (mad, or truly a vampire) of his *Martin* (1977). There is no way of telling whether the birds in Hitchcock's *The Birds* (1963) attack through an accident of nature or with a malevolent intention that exceeds their ordinary animal state. Similarly, *Lost Highway* (1997) or *Mulholland Drive* (2001) leave wide open the question of their interpretation, because of the constant interpenetration of spaces and times that Lynch uses in rolling out their images (Vanoye 2001, pp. 26–28). With respect to the fantastic, then, one can clearly see the limited extent to which a theoretical notion of a genre can be applied to the concrete reality of phenomena, even if it has the merit of introducing an interesting formal criterion (i.e., the point of view that pertains to extraordinary events) into a landscape of commentary on the fantastic that is very preoccupied with themes.

Genre: An Intertextual Phenomenon

Faced with the difficulty of defining genres on the basis of stable and coherent thematic or formal criteria, the application of which can be exemplified in particular works, or of forging theoretical genres that might really be capable of accounting for concrete phenomena, semiological studies shift the terms of the question by seeking to describe and explain the generic relationship that unites one literary or filmic text with other texts.

Genre as an architext

Gérard Genette (1982) perceives this generic relationship within the very large sphere of what he calls transtextuality; that is, everything that places one text in relation to other texts. Genericity is, according to this view, a textual component – one of the modes of transtextuality – and generic relations are a group of reinvestments and modulations of this textual component.

Among the collection of transtextual relations, he distinguishes paratextuality (the links between a text and its external context – title, preface, etc.), intertextuality (the presence of one text within another as a result of citation or allusion), hypertextuality (the links between two texts caused by imitation or transformative adaptation, or between a text and a style), metatextuality (the links between a text and any commentary on it), and architextuality (the inclusive relationship that unites each text with its architect). These relations are, moreover, not mutually exclusive. For example, documentaries use archival footage in montages, like *Le Chagrin et la pitié* (*The Sorrow and the Pity*) (Ophuls, 1969), or *L'Œil de Vichy* (*The Eye of Vichy*) (Chabrol, 1993), maintaining not only intertextual relations with the films they cite, but also metatextual relations, since they offer a commentary – verbally, and through editing. They are also imbricated in a network of paratextual relations (with their poster, or with their trailer, for instance) and architextual relations (with the documentary genre, or the sub-genre of the montage film). Genericity, that is, the relation that links a text to "its" genre, is only one of the forms of architextuality. In fact, several types of architexts exist – not only genres, but also modalities of enunciation and types of discourse. While remaining a matter of textuality, the question of the definition of genres is thus partly transposed into one concerning the definition of the relationships that texts maintain with one another.

Even though such a theory of genericity offers the interesting possibility of considering genre in a less static fashion, involving a system of circulation between texts, it nevertheless replaces rules for genres with rules for the exchange between texts, and it leaves unaddressed the problem of the relation of a text to "its" genre, and of the genre to "its texts" – for two reasons, signaled by Jean-Marie Schaeffer (1986, pp. 195–197). In the first place, in contrast to the other forms of transtextuality that one can observe, which define relational pairings of texts that are real and concrete, an architext has only a metaphoric existence. Next, it is problematic to conceive of genericity in terms of a relationship of inclusion or belonging between a text and its architext. In fact, genre is not a model for the writing of the film, and once made, the film, through its variations, modifies its genre. Rather than the architext and the general model of transtextuality, it is the investigation of intertextual relations that has acquired a legacy in the analysis of cinema genres – as attested by the definition of cinematic genre given by Allan and Gomery: genre is "an intertextual filmic system," an "important intertextual background set that generates definite audience expectations" (1985, p. 85). One must always emphasize the reductive and summary consequences of transforming genericity into intertextuality – that is, by viewing it as a mere recycling of elements from one film to another that abridges the complex system of intertextual relations in a way that caricatures the actual phenomenon of intertextuality.

Genre: a continuous and infinite text

The semiological model proposed by Christian Metz in *Language and Cinema*, influenced, as in the case of Genette's works, by structural linguistics, provides a conceptual system in which genre is viewed as a unique, continuous text, unendingly open to its own prolongation. Genre becomes a "group of films" understood as "a single vast and continuous text," which carries a "textual system" within itself" (Metz 1974, pp. 121–126). This conception of genre arises from the thesis proposed by Metz that cinema is a "language without a language-system" (*langage sans langue*), involving a play of codes whose articulation takes the place of a language that is nowhere to be found. The text is conceived as a concrete object, a "discursive unity," in which each element (the messages) are manifestations of a code. The group of codes that are purposely employed in a given text define the particular system of that text. One ends up, therefore, with a double opposition:

- *Between concrete entities and abstract entities*. The text and the message (both concrete) are thus opposed to the code and the textual system (both abstract) that provide the principles of intelligibility that are inferred through analysis.

43

- *Between uniqueness and plural existence.* The text and the system have a unique existence, while the message and the codes recur in different texts, defining in each instance a unique textual architecture.

The intersection of this double opposition thus offers a conceptual framework that takes account of the play of repetitions and variations that are characteristic of a genre: genre is a unique text characterized by the regular recurrence of messages and codes.

In addition, Metz distinguishes three kinds of codes: non-specific, thematic, and cultural codes that are not exclusively cinematic, because they are expressed in other representational works; general cinematic codes, only found in the cinema, and shared, either actually or virtually, by all films (the code of editing, of camera movements, of cinematic punctuation, etc.); and, finally, specific cinematic codes that are unique to cinema, but which appear only in certain groups of films.

If each film makes use of these three types of codes, its affinity with a cinematic genre is guaranteed by the use of particular cinematic codes (Metz 1974, pp. 62–63). Thus, the classical western, like all films, mobilizes non-specific and general cinematic codes, but it is only a genre because it adds particular codes to those ones, both on the non-specific side *and* on the cinematic side: the codes of honor and of friendship, or the ritual of the gunfight, which are particular cultural codes that one can find in other forms of expression, such as novels and songs about the West; and the favored use of extreme long shots, or of panoramic shots, which are particular cinematic codes. This model has the merit of providing a solution to the problem of the mixing of genres and their interrelations – if two genres appear to intersect, it is because they share one or more particular codes, as, for example, the extreme long shots found in westerns or adventure films. Equally, it allows one to establish a relationship between, and differentiate, cinematic genres and non-cinematic genres – for example, literary ones – that share a common theme. The cinematic genre is organized in accordance with the same non-specific particular codes, but differs in its particular cinematic codes. Thus, *film noir* shares the same labyrinthine crime plot with the *noir* novel, but the use of black and white, and of lighting with strong contrasts, is a device that is specifically cinematic. Such a definition of genre in terms of its specific codes nevertheless leaves several problems unresolved. As Metz observes, only genres that are strongly encoded can be viewed as a vast, unique text: namely, the classic western, the classic musical, and the *film noir* (1940–55). The model, therefore, is unable to account for all cinematic genres. Moreover, it is hard to see what distinguishes genre from other groups of films that can be viewed as unique texts organized in terms of particular codes – such as styles, films from the same school, or films of the same "auteur."

Following Christian Metz, Marc Vernet (1980) has proposed to take into account the particular codes that manifest themselves at the profilmic level (everything that one puts in front of the camera), and at the filmic level, in defining a genre. *Décor*, for example, constitutes one of these groupings of particular signifying elements. It is inaccurate to assert, as Vernet does, that the musical is distinguished by stylized settings that are close to those of the theater, given that numerous musicals are shot in natural settings (one only needs to think of *On the Town*, Kelly and Donen, 1949, or *Oklahoma!*, Zinnemann, 1955). It strikes me as more accurate to say that the settings of the musical are concerned with the representation of spaces. Venice in *Top Hat* (Sandrich, 1935), with its canal and its gondoliers, is a fixed image, made of paste-board; Paris in *An American in Paris* (Minnelli, 1951) alternates between Parisian postcards, *trompe-l'oeil*, and, in the imaginary sequences, references to Toulouse-Lautrec. Musicals shot in the West, like *Oklahoma!*, make use of filmic stereotypes of the western. At the filmic level, genres are distinguished, for example, by a particular use of the code of colors: westerns offer a realistic treatment of color, musicals use a palette of vivid colors in a highly stylized manner, and the crime film, in France as in Hollywood, is characterized by a marked use of black and white long after the use of color had become dominant. In the same way, the use of the dolly is a particular code of camera movement found in the musical, while the use of rapid traveling shots and of a camera mounted on a crane characterizes the western. The incorporation of optical illusions and special effects that are not visible to the naked eye, but nevertheless perceptible (the viewer is uncertain as to whether a trick is taking place or not), is a mark of the fantastic and science-fiction genres.

In Search of the Structures of Genre

The different theories that we have just seen – the first group of which, for the sake of simplicity, we can label as formalist, and the second group as intertextual – derive their definitions of genre from either a theory of cinema or a semiotic model which should ideally be able to account for all genres. Other approaches, also seeking rules capable of transcending the particularity of each film, and of modeling the play of variations and repetitions that form the basis of genre, try to identify common structures in films of the same genre. Rather than working through theoretical deduction, they use, at least ostensibly, systematic analysis. To pick up the terminology of Todorov, their goal is to define a particular historical genre (the one being analyzed) in a rigorous manner; their project therefore aims to be exemplary, meaning that they never generalize their conclusions as applying to all genres. In considering these attempts to extrapolate structures, I will first focus on the creation of narrative organizations that synthesize the particular plots of each film, and will then contemplate the term "structure" in a contemporary sense that is fairly imprecise. Following that, I will investigate analyses of genres that have been inspired by the structural model for analyzing myths proposed by Lévi-Strauss, and I will then give to the term "structure" its specific technical sense.

Grand narrative structures

A great number of genre analyses, in order to free themselves from long subdivided and heterogeneous lists of thematic or formal elements, choose instead to identify various types of plots and narrative situations in films around which the genre is organized. With little exaggeration, one could even say that this identification has become the main dish in the menu of all self-respecting studies of genre, which devote a copious number of pages to the topic. Thus, Noël Carroll distinguishes two principal types of plot in the horror and terror film, each of which, in its own distinctive way, narrativizes a mistrust of science. The *discovery plot* develops its theme around the incompetence and ineffectiveness of science, its institutional representatives, and rational thought, while the *over-reacher plot* does so around the dangers of a scientific activity that is pursued without any limits (Carroll 1981, 1990).

The discovery plot, which is to be found in many stories such as *Dracula* (Browning, 1931), *Cat People* (Tourneur, 1942), *Invasion of the Body Snatchers* (Siegel, 1956) and its two remakes (Kaufman, 1978; *The Faculty*, Rodriguez, 1998), *Jaws* (Spielberg, 1975), and *The Exorcist* (Friedkin, 1973), progresses through four stages:

1 *The attack*: the presence of the monster (or of an unsettling phenomenon) is established, often through an attack.
2 *The discovery*: an individual or a group of persons discover its existence and come to realize the danger that it represents; they alert the authorities, scientific ones in particular, who refuse to believe them.
3 *The confirmation*: the characters who recognize the danger try to convince the others of the reality of the menace that it represents, and the necessity for action. This stage is often fairly long and plays to a large degree on suspense. Are people finally going to accept the improbable? Will precious time be lost? It develops a contrast between two types of knowledge: knowledge gained through experience, often bestowed on the grossly ignorant or adolescents through a discovery; and a rational, scientific knowledge that refuses to recognize the knowledge of experience. One can well understand why this kind of plot is favored in the numerous horror films aimed particularly at adolescents (teen pictures), such as

A Nightmare on Elm Street or *The Faculty*: they model the conflicts between young people and parental authorities. At the end of this conflict, the authorities finally admit the supernatural reality of the peril.

4   *The final confrontation*: everyone joins together, generally with success, to fight the monster.

The over-reacher plot, illustrated by the different versions of *Frankenstein*, of *Doctor Jekyll and Mister Hyde*, or of *The Island of Dr Moreau*, narrativizes its critique of science in four movements:

1   *Preparations for the experiment*: scientific preparations, philosophical considerations, scientific explanations, a discussion of the motives of the scientist, often mad, are mingled into the *mise en scène*.

2   *The technical success of the experiment*: its achievement increases the megalomania of the scientist.

3   *The moral failure of the experiment*: the experiment and its consequences escape from the control of the scientist, creating innocent victims – the archetypal victim being the kind young girl for whom Frankenstein's monster plucks a daisy by the side of a lake before drowning her (*Frankenstein*, Whale, 1931).

4   *The destruction*: the experiment is interrupted, the creatures brought into being are destroyed, either by a group (with which the scientist does or does not ally himself) or by the scientist himself.

The horror genre, then, according to Carroll, is determined by these two types of story that reflect mistrust of scientific thought – useless and limited in the discovery plots, and dangerous in the plots of excess.

The identification of recurring narrative structures in genre films tends to result in a substitution of an analysis of genre for the definition of it, as Carroll's analysis demonstrates. Therefore, the kinds of plot that are plain and clear are especially useful for defining sub-genres, leaving almost untouched the question of the name and distinctive criteria of the genre that they sub-divide. Furthermore, such an approach privileges the story outlines of films at the expense of their images. The inverse criticism could be made, however, of iconographic analyses[4] that define genres in terms of the recurrence of symbolic images that have the same meaning bestowed on them from one film to another: the galloping horse in the desert, or the face of John Wayne in the western, the saber and the kimono in the martial arts film, the overcoat of the private detective or the police inspector in the crime film, or the intergalactic spaceship in the science-fiction film, etc.

Finally, it is essential not to confuse this approach, which aims at identifying the types of narrative structures pertaining to particulars genres, with analyses that group films according to subjects, or by cycles. Even though the latter may organize the genre into sub-genres, sometimes with indeterminate limits, they take themes as their point of departure, not plot structure. This is the case, for example, with the partition of the western into six big cycles proposed by Jean-Louis Rieupeyrout (1953, 1987), with which specialists in this genre generally agree: settlement, Indian wars, the Civil War, cattle-ranching, the Mexican-Texan conflict, and the cycle of outlaws versus the law. The peopling cycle tells the story of the settlement of the pioneers (*Unconquered*, De Mille, 1947) and recounts the dangers encountered by the wagon-trains: the crossing of the Platte River, the Indian attack, and the burning of the prairie in *The Covered Wagon* (Cruze, 1923), turbulent rivers, the encounter with hostile Indians, the crossing of scorching deserts, or the traversal of precipitous mountains in *The Big Trail* (Walsh, 1930). While the cycle concerning the Indian wars is the subject of numerous films in which the Indians, at first the aggressors, progressively become the victims, as in *Cheyenne Autumn* (Ford, 1964), *Little Big Man* (Penn, 1969), or *Soldier Blue* (Nelson, 1970), the cycle of films on the Civil War forms a more restricted group: the conflict between the Northerners and the Southerners is continued in the West over the hoard of gold collected for the Union in *Virginia City* (Curtiz, 1940), it appears in the return of the veteran (*Run of the Arrow*, Fuller, 1957), or explains the decline of the gambler Hatfield in *Stagecoach* (Ford, 1939). The cycle involving cattle-ranching, beginning with *Red River* (Hawks, 1948), is organized around the driving of herds, and links up with certain aspects of the populating cycle. The Mexican-Texan conflict, represented in films dealing with the defeat at the Alamo, is included among the many films located in Texas. Finally, the law cycle deals with marshals and sheriffs, bandits, and bounty-hunters, and covers hold-ups, attacks on trains and stagecoaches, conflicts between justice and the desire for revenge, or between the law of the gun and democratic law, in numerous films such as *Stagecoach*, *High Noon* (Zinnemann, 1952), or *The Man Who Shot Liberty Valance* (Ford, 1961). These different cycles, which cross over and blend into one another in cinematic stories, are not constructed out of specific narrative structures, but pick up and reuse historical themes to which the films give expression.

The elementary structures of genre

The structuralist analysis developed by Claude Lévi-Strauss with respect to myths in the four volumes of his *Mythologiques* (1964–71) has exerted a great influence on the analysis of film genres, especially in studies pursued during the years 1960 to 1970 on the western. For Lévi-Strauss, myth is a fundamental mental category, to which an abstract and logical form of thought corresponds – mythic thought. This, operating through dichotomies and a series of oppositions according to a binary code, is capable of reducing reality to a simple table of binary oppositions. Structural analysis of myths is therefore preoccupied with these "fundamental, shared properties," the "hidden" structures, and not with the thousand events of an unforeseeable story (Lévi-Strauss 1966, p. 408).

Different myths are historicized forms in which various cultures systematically organize their vision of the world (their reality) into systems of oppositions and distinctions. While the myths repeat and resemble one another, it is not because they are seeking to express a truth, but because they are concrete manifestations of an arrangement of elements that interact among themselves. The different versions of a myth can be read as so many particular configurations of elements from this combination. It would not be possible, therefore, to have myths that were better, more exact, or truer than others, nor an original myth. One can well understand why cinematic genre, which presupposes repetition and variation across particular films, has appeared to be a category that is susceptible to being analyzed according to a Lévi-Straussian model of myth, even of being defined as a myth. I shall leave to one side, for the time being, the sociocultural dimension of this assimilation of genre to myth that emerges from the strict paradigm of structural analysis, and will return to it in the following chapter. Instead, I will focus on the definition of genre in terms of its basic structures – "revealed," like those of myth, through analysis.

For Lévi-Strauss, the structural component is always uppermost in all signifying works, structure consisting of "a system of oppositions and correlations, integrating all the elements of a total situation (1963, p. 182). To identify this structure in myth or genre comes back to viewing myths or genres as a vast collection in which one cannot isolate any one element. On this point, the definition of cinematic genre as myth is in accord with Metz's definition (see above, pp. 43–45), which is also a structural definition, being based on a structural theory of cinematic language. In addition, the Lévi-Straussian definition of structure leads to a de-narrativization of myths, and to their de-textualization. This results from a reduction of these myths to paradigms of isolated elements, formed of pertinent oppositions that have been searched out. To apply the structuralist method of analyzing myths to cinematic genre is, then, to extract from the sum of films a structure that organizes signifying oppositions, in the way that Kitses (1969) does with respect to the western. He identifies structural oppositions in the films, the content of which can vary from one film to another, but which all refer back to a fundamental opposition between Wilderness and Civilization. Different westerns, therefore, only give expression to an underlying structure: the conflict between Wilderness and Civilization when these are

51

brought into contact on a frontier. This opposition is an aspect of structure because it accounts for all the particular thematic oppositions used in westerns, as well as all the combinations of these oppositions. Fundamentally, the opposition between Wilderness and Civilization can also be correlated with three intermediary oppositions (Individual/the Community, Nature/Culture, West/East), which, in turn, are divided into a series of oppositions between terms that have a narrower compass and are still more specific. The vocabulary of the western does not preexist this dialectical relationship, it is created by it. The western can thus be described in terms of an atemporal table, consisting of pairs of oppositions that one could further subdivide, which is supposed to account for the whole meaning of the genre (Kitses 1969, p. 11):

Wilderness	**Civilization**
The Individual	*The Community*
Freedom	Restriction
Honor	Institutions
Self-knowledge	Illusion
Integrity	Compromise
Self-interest	Social responsibility
Solipsism	Democracy
Nature	*Culture*
Purity	Corruption
Experience	Knowledge
Empiricism	Legalism
Pragmatism	Idealism
Brutalization	Refinement
Savagery	Humanity
The West	*The East*
America	Europe
The frontier	America
Equality	Class
Agrarianism	Industrialism
Tradition	Change
The past	The future

One can see that such a table removes the whole historical dimension of the western, since it proposes basic structures in a synchronic model: historical evolution is only one particular aspect of the fundamental opposition between Wilderness and Civilization.

Still on the western, Will Wright (1975) identifies four types of plot, and for each one of these types he chooses to work, on the same basis as structural analysis, on three or four films, chosen for their success and the box-office and their representativeness:

- *The classical plot*: the story of a lone stranger who arrives in a troubled town and restores it to order; the films analyzed: *Shane* (Stevens, 1953), *Dodge City* (Curtiz, 1939), *Canyon Passage* (Tourneur, 1946), *Duel in the Sun* (Vidor, 1946).
- *The vengeance variation*: a variation on the classic plot; films analyzed: *Stagecoach* (Ford, 1939), *The Man From Laramie* (Mann, 1955), *One-Eyed Jacks* (Brando, 1961), *Nevada Smith* (Hathaway, 1966).
- *The transition theme*: an inversion of the classic plot (the hero is in society at the beginning of the film, and outside society at the end); films analyzed: *High Noon* (Zinnemann, 1952), *Broken Arrow* (Daves, 1950), *Johnny Guitar* (Ray, 1954).
- *The professional plot*: in contrast to the heroes of the classic plot, who are outside society, professionals are paid to fight; films analyzed: *Rio Bravo* (Hawks, 1959), *The Professionals* (Brooks, 1966), *The Wild Bunch* (Peckinpah, 1969), *Butch Cassidy and the Sundance Kid* (Hill, 1969).

Wright then breaks down each of these four groups into a list of basic functions (that is, functions where a single action or a single characteristic are expressed) that describe the interactions between three types of characters: the *hero*, the *villain*, and *society* itself. Thus, in his view, classic westerns can be boiled down into a series of 16 functions (Wright 1975, pp. 40–49):

- The hero enters into a social group.
- The hero is revealed to have an exceptional ability.

- The society recognizes a difference between itself and the hero; the hero is given a special status.
- The society does not completely accept the hero.
- There is a conflict of interests between the villains and the society.
- The villains are stronger than the society; the society is weak.
- There is a strong friendship or respect between the hero and a villain.
- The villains threaten the society.
- The hero avoids involvement in the conflict.
- The villains endanger a friend of the hero.
- The hero fights the villains.
- The hero defeats the villains.
- The society is safe.
- The society accepts the hero.
- The hero loses or gives up his special status.

In each of these types considered, the intersection of functions and characters reveals four basic oppositions that operate on several levels: Exterior/Interior, Good/Evil, Strong/Weak, and Wild/Civilized. Wright thus defines the western as a nexus of these oppositions that each plot type configures differently; for example, the hero of the classical plot ends by taking up arms in the name of values embraced by society, and by reentering society, whereas the hero of the variation on revenge is in society at the beginning, but then leaves it by taking up arms in the name of values that are not recognized by society, only being reintegrated into it once he has abandoned his weapons.

One can justifiably ask oneself whether it is necessary to propose such a weighty edifice to arrive at a conclusion that was already implicitly contained in the (completely empirical) characterization of the four types of western, and by the selection of films representing each type. Wright presents the classic type as the prototype for all westerns, and *Shane* as the most classic of the classic westerns. Because of this, we are obliged to make the same reservation with respect to these structural definitions of the genre-myth western that is often made about Lévi-Straussian mythological analysis:

> The method appears here like a transfigured and transposed expression of the basic characteristics attributed *a priori* to the object being studied. That is, there is never any risk of contradictions appearing to exist between the general postulate, the object studied, and the chosen method. Each one deduces itself from the two others, and therefore only exists because of them. (Dubuisson 1993, p. 151)

Semantic-Syntactic Definitions of Genre

The model that is currently dominant in the domain of genre theory is the semantic-syntactic model, inspired by the work of Rick Altman (1989) on the Hollywood musical. In particular, it provides a response to two problems that are recurrently encountered in the study of genre – the definition of the corpus of films in a genre, and the need to take into account the history of genres, and of genres in history.

The semantic-syntactic definition of genre

Rick Altman opposes two broad types of definition of genre. In the first kind – which encompasses the definition of Vernet (see above, pp. 45–46) as well as the lists of characteristics currently offered in genre encyclopedias – genre is defined by a list of semantic elements (traits, attitudes, characters, settings, technical cinematographic elements, etc.). In the second, it is defined by syntax, with certain constitutive relations between the different aspects of the text being advanced in order to discern the global meaning and structures of genre. The semantic approach is applicable to an important number of films, but it has only a weak

55

explanatory potential. The syntactic approach has a strong explanatory potential (because it identifies the specific signifying structures of a genre), but has a field of application that is often fairly limited in its coverage. Altman therefore recommends a semantic-syntactic definition that combines the two approaches. Genre possesses semantic traits and syntactic traits that organize the relations between these semantic traits in a specific way. Thus, the western defines itself *simultaneously* through characters, locations, the modes that are used to film these characters and places, and by an organization of these elements around a frontier between wilderness and civilization. In brief, these semantic givens are the content of the film, and the syntactic situation the narrative structure in which the content inserts itself. Or, in other terms, to use an architectural metaphor, the semantic elements are the different materials used in the construction of a building. They can differ from one type of construction to another: stones, bricks, tiles, slates, ceramics, reinforced concrete, girders, etc. One can therefore compare syntactic characteristics to the plan of the building, to the uses that the different materials fulfill (decoration, supporting the roof, joining the walls, supporting the weight of the construction) and to the visual effects that the use of the materials produces. Moreover, the differentiation established by Altman (1981) between semantic and syntactic resides in a theory of textual signification that distinguishes two levels of signification: the linguistic meaning of the components of a text, and the textual meaning that these components acquire in the internal structure of the text. In the western, for example, a horse has a first level of signification that refers to the concept "horse": it is an animal. But it also acquires at that level several particular textual meanings that provide structures in which the western causes the horse to be represented: in association with the solitary cowboy, it is a means of individual transport that contrasts to the wagons and coaches of social groups, or an animal companion that contrast to human cultural companions, such as the family. It is also, if it is placed in opposition to a railway, a means of transport from the past. Similarly, the musical gives a particular textual signification to music, dance, and song: playing music, dancing, or singing in it are not only professional or leisure activities, given that the syntax of this genre turns them into a sign for the experience of being in love. The distinction between semantics and syntax corresponds, then, to the distinction between linguistic signification and textual signification.

Such a concept of genre enables one to describe the existence of strong genres, like the western or the musical, about which there is general agreement, on account of the recognition of these genres, if not their definition. It also allows one to account for the existence of less stable genres, the general status of which is subject to debate by critics, such as disaster films, or films of cape and sword. The longest-lasting genres are those which have a specific syntax that is very coherent, with the rest relying essentially on recurring semantic elements without ever developing a stable syntax. Furthermore, the corpus of films in a genre defined by the semantic-syntactic method is basically a dual corpus, which avoids the plethora of inclusive lists, and the thinness of selective pantheons. Films do not always become attached to a genre for the same reason: some actively contribute to the development of a syntax for the genre, others pick up in a less systematic way the traditional elements associated with a genre. The double approach, semantic and syntactic, emphasizes the imbrication of these different traits, thus providing the possibility of defining, for a given genre, different levels of genericity.

Approaching the matter from this perspective, Altman defines the musical on the basis of five semantic parameters and five syntactic parameters, with each of the two levels openly cross-referencing one another. The two lists of parameters, if one considers them in isolation, lead to the establishment of limits that are rather different in the corpus of films in a genre (Altman 1989, pp. 102–110):

Semantic criteria

- *Format*: the musical is a story, which excludes from the corpus a good number of musical films – music-hall films like *Ziegfeld Follies* (Minnelli, 1946), films of concerts, like *Woodstock*

(Wadleigh, 1970), or an animated feature like *Fantasia* (Disney, 1940), since they do not subordinate their musical numbers or spectacles to a narration or a motivation.

- *Length*: the musical needs to incorporate several songs in the story, and only the form of the feature film generally permits this.
- *Characters*: the plot is constructed around a pair of lovers in a human society. Musical films that include children in the *mise en scène* are not wholly subsumed in the genre unless the children, like Shirley Temple, for instance, are used to "act the role of Cupid regarding an older couple." It is the same for animated films involving animals: those that transfer the courtship theme on to the animals, like *The AristoCats* (Reitherman, 1970), fulfill this criterion, while Disney's films of initiation, like *Dumbo* (Disney, 1941), are excluded from the corpus.
- *The performance by actors*: they combine realism (bodily movements *not* dictated by the music) with rhythmic movements (that *are* dictated by the music).
- *Soundtrack*: the musical mixes the sounds that make up the music with those that are outside the musical expression – which places a film like *Les Parapluies de Cherbourg* (*The Umbrellas of Cherbourg*) (Demy, 1964), which is exclusively musical, outside the genre.

Syntactic criteria

- *Narrative strategy*: the film proceeds through a process of alternation, confrontation, and parallelism between characters, or groups of characters, of the opposite sex, each one of them being the bearer of a distinctive cultural value. For example, *Gigi* (Minnelli, 1958) establishes, through the mouth of Maurice Chevalier, a distinction between men and women in the overture ("Bonjour monsieur! Bonjour madame!") that is sustained right through the rest of the film, with each scene delivering amorous verses for one of the lovers, turn and turn about. At the beginning of the film, Gigi is at home, with an aged parent, and is not in any hurry to turn up at her rendezvous. In the following sequence, it is the same for Gaston. But Gigi is defined by feminine preoccupations (putting on makeup, taking care with her appearance), and Gaston by masculine preoccupations (buying cars, indulging in politics). Further along, before the first rendezvous, one shot shows Gaston in front of his mirror in the process of choosing a jewel (wealth is a masculine attribute). This shot then gives way to an image of Gigi in front of her mirror in the process of getting dressed (beauty is a feminine quality).

- *Couple/story*: the musical places in parallel, or establishes a relation of cause and effect between, the successful formation of the couple and the success of events, whether this concerns a kingdom, as in *The Love Parade* (Lubitsch, 1929), or a show, as in the series of *Gold Diggers* (LeRoy/Berkeley/Bacon, 1933–8), choreographed by Busby Berkeley.

- *Music/story*: music and dance are active agents in the production of meaning. They express an individual or collective joy, as in the song and dance in the rain that gives its title to *Singin' in the Rain* (Donen/Kelly, 1952), and love, as in the celebrated duet "Cheek to cheek" or the final ballet "Piccolino" in *Top Hat* (Sandrich, 1935).

- *Story/musical number*: the musical creates a continuity between the spoken dialogues and the music, as illustrated by the American lesson given by Gene Kelly to Parisian children that progressively turns into a tap-dance number (*An American in Paris*).

- *Image/sound*: the musical inverts the hierarchy between image and sound in the classic story, thanks to the sound fade-out. Thus, the walking of the dogs in *Shall We Dance* (Sandrich, 1937) becomes a dance when Fred Astaire and Ginger Rogers start to regulate their steps to the tempo of the music. In the first number of *Top Hat* ("No strings"), Fred Astaire conducts a conversation with his friend, over a background of music from the orchestra pit, with singing and dancing, while shaping his phrases and gestures to the rhythm of this music. Before composing a melody on the musical theme with his taps, he, in time with the rhythm, replaces the top of a bottle of whisky, and dilutes his drink with a stream of mineral water.

An open approach to context

The semantic-syntactic definition of a genre does not resolve all the problems of theories of genre. In particular, one can see how the characteristic criteria of genre, which this definition organizes into two levels, depend on a prior analysis of the structures of genre determined according to the aims of the analyst. In the case of the musical, for example, the love plot is identified in advance as the semantic and structural center of the genre. It does not escape, therefore, from the recursivity of definitions of genre that infer the defining characteristics of a genre from films that are already deemed to belong to it – noted by Tudor (1995). Nevertheless, it has the double advantage of making explicit both this circularity and the premises of the analysis. As Altman explains it:

> In the sense that I am using the word genre, a group of texts may be recognized as constituting a genre if and only if they constitute a semantic type *and* if that semantic type is matched by a corresponding syntactic type as well. In other words, a group of films with a common syntax but lacking a shared semantics (or vice versa) would not be recognized as constituting a genre. A genre, then, in the strong sense which I hold to, is neither an artificially derived but historically unattested theoretical type, nor a theoretically unacceptable historical type. A genre does not exist fully until a method is found of building its semantics into a stable syntax. (1989, p. 115)

The appeal to two descriptive systems, semantic and syntactic, makes it possible not only to articulate the exchanges of material that occur between genres, but also to avoid blurring the distinction between certain science-fiction films and intergalactic westerns, and certain war films and tropical westerns. Instead, it explains the similarities between these types of films by show-ing how science-fiction films in the 1970s and 1980s, and the *mise en scène* of films about Vietnam, borrow syntactic forms from the western genre. Similarly, one does not view *Star Wars* (Lucas, 1977) as a martial arts film set in outer space simply because of the intrusion of semantic elements such as the combat with laser swords, or the mastering of the force by the Jedi knight. In addition, the semantic-syntactic theory is able to be recon-ciled with a history of genres. In the other theories that we have considered, the evolution of genres tended to become reduced to a matter of internal structural modifications, and to take the form of a suite of discrete elements. Thus, the semiologists use over-coding to describe the evolution of the western, identify-ing within it the twilight western, the mannerist western, and then the spaghetti western (Metz 1974, p. 152). In contrast, it seems that the semantic-syntactic model, precisely because of its duality, is capable also of accounting for genres in their his-torical continuity. For example, new semantic elements can combine with old ones and enter into the syntax of a genre, as is demonstrated by the succession of musical styles (operetta, swing, rock) in musicals. Similarly, the use of an equivalent syn-tactic structure (while the syntactic material varies) explains the ability to translate the remake of a genre film into a different genre. Thus, the Japanese who confront the hero of *Objective, Burma!* (Walsh, 1945), a war film, become, once the conflict is over, hostile Indians that the same director transfers to the Everglades of Florida in *Distant Drums* (1951), a western.

As we have seen, different structural theories of genre depend, in the search for the rules of genre, on a theory of cin-ema, of language, and of signification. That is, they all bear the imprint of the movements of thought and the historical periods that have given birth to them. If we are favoring the semantic-syntactic definition, it is because it provides a theoretical model that is sufficiently flexible to combine with a history of genres, or an examination of the relations between genres. But it is also, undoubtedly, because this theory is in harmony with current intel-lectual and scientific orientations. Thus, the semantic-syntactic

61

theory, revised by its author in 1999, is capable of integrating analyses of the reception of genres, of being amplified with a pragmatic, or practical, dimension, in which case it becomes a "semantic-syntaxic-pragmatic" approach to genre (Altman 1999). It is no longer preoccupied only with the play of semantic and syntactic traits in the films, but also deals with the variety of uses and interpretations of genre (by viewers, producers, critics, etc.). If, as we have seen, "a genre only fully exists from the moment that one puts in place a method for organizing its semantics into a stable syntax," it only exists socially – that is, outside the intellectual activity of the theorist of cinema – when a community agrees to recognize its semantics and syntax.

Notes

1   For a discussion of the Russian Formalists, see *Théorie de la littérature. Textes des formalistes russes* (1965), Tsvetan Todorov (Ed.), Paris, Seuil; and for their views on cinema, *Les Formalistes russes et le cinéma. Poétique du film* (1996), François Albera (Ed.), Paris, Nathan.

2   It must be emphasized that the categorization of the works of French avant-garde filmmakers of the 1920s – for example, the lyric cinema genre – is a classification devised by the Russian Formalists.

3   See, for example, Tom Gunning (1990) "The Cinema of Attractions: Early Film, Its Spectator and the Avant Garde." In Thomas Elsaesser (Ed.) *Early Film: Space, Frame, Narrative*, London, BFI, pp. 56–62. See also André Gaudreault and Tom Gunning (1989) "Le Cinéma des premiers temps, un défi à l'histoire du cinéma." In Jacques Aumont, André Gaudreault, and Michel Marie (Eds.) *Histoire du cinéma, nouvelles approches*, Paris, Presse de la Sorbonne Nouvelle, pp. 49–63; and Tom Gunning (1995) "Attraction, truquage and photogénie: L'explosion du présent dans les films à truc français produit entre 1896 and 1907." In Jean A. Gili, Michèle Langy, Michel Marie, and Vincent Pinel (Eds.) *Les Vingt premières années du cinéma français*, Paris, Presses de la Sorbonne Nouvelle, pp. 177–193.

4   See Edward Buscombe (1970) "The Idea of Genre in the American Cinema," *Screen*, 2, pp. 33–45; and Lawrence Alloway (1971) *Violent America: The Movies 1946–1964*, New York, Moma.

Chapter 3
What is the Purpose of Genres?

Classificatory or analytical logics, because they conceive of genre as a group of films displaying shared characteristics – whether or not these logics formalize the play of repetitions and variations they describe – by-pass the functional dimension of genre. However, as we have seen, a genre only exists if it is recognized as such by a community. To recapitulate the terms of the semantic-syntactic model proposed by Rick Altman, a genre comes into being and is recognized when it organizes a set of semantic features into a stable syntax – that is, when a filmic formula is put in place that is recognizable to a public audience, and to which films attach themselves through different levels of genericity. The establishment of a tacit agreement about this semantic-syntactic formula presupposes, then, that those who make a "genre film" (producers, directors, screenwriters, etc.) are able to conceive of it as relating to this genre, and that viewers are able to respond to it as such. Thus, it is necessary for an audience to recognize the genre in the film, identify it, and grasp the formula that is being offered in order for its success and lasting appeal to be assured. To understand the phenomenon of genre, therefore, one must pay attention to the "established formulas of communication" mentioned by Casetti in his definition of genre (which we accepted provisionally at the beginning of the preceding chapter). This, in turn, requires us to consider the economic, social, cultural, and communicative functions of genre.

A Production Tool

It is often asserted that genres give cinema an effective model for industrial production because they provide producers with a formula that precedes and determines what should be produced. By applying a tried and true recipe that will guarantee the success of a film to a new subject, producers minimize their risks and justify the production. This idea, currently fairly widespread, would seem to imply a rather low opinion of popular culture. It suggests that commercial or popular cinema, along with cartoons, television, or popular fiction, are only capable of endlessly and mechanically reproducing prefabricated models. Furthermore, this vision of mass culture is completely static: how could the changes and innovations that anyone can observe in reality possibly be born out of a system that is exclusively governed by a principle of repetition? This is why it is appropriate to invoke a dynamic conception of mass culture when dealing with the economic issues relating to genre – especially given that mass culture is afflicted by an internal contradiction between standardization, which allows for repetition and mass production, and innovation, which permits the system to renew itself, and allows "models" to be altered and varied (Morin 1962).

The standardization/differentiation dialectic

The production of film genres, which presupposes both a repetition of traits and a variation, takes place within a dialectic between standardization and differentiation. It is one of the combinations made possible by the interplay between a normative logic and an innovative logic that characterizes the production and consumption of the "cultural goods" of mass culture. This fact allows one to understand why the industrial organization of classical Hollywood cinema – which owes its success to its ability to integrate elements of differentiation, while simultaneously exploiting an effectiveness based on a normalization of production

– has produced a panoply of genres that are both varied and relatively stable. In effect, the "dream factory" is characterized by an industrialization of the cinematic mode of production: standardization allows for films to be produced more quickly and in a way that is more profitable, all the time observing a norm of excellence (a "standardized" product, well made), at the same time as innovation generates differentiated products by importing external elements and blending them into the standardized work. As Janet Staiger explains, at an economic level, a Hollywood film derives its competitiveness simultaneously from its conformity to a standardized norm and from its capacity to distinguish itself from other films (Bordwell, Staiger, and Thompson 1985, pp. 95–97). One should note that, from this point of view, the making, the conception, and the consumption of the "film-product" hardly differ from those of a non-cultural consumer good. When a firm plans to put a new washing machine on the market, it designs a machine that uses electricity, is manufactured at the least possible cost, and corresponds to certain technical criteria (electric norms, shape, energy consumption, programs for different washing cycles, efficiency, design, etc.). At the same time, it tries to create a machine that will distinguish itself, like a brand, from other makes of washing machines – by emphasizing the qualities that make its product different (a supplementary service, a choice of colors, a revolutionary system for eliminating creases, etc.). In Hollywood, then, genres are an efficient tool within a similar standardization/innovation dialectic – just as film stars are. Laurent Creton calls this dialectic a strategy of "progressive innovation":

> It is the expression of an approach that aims to avoid anything revolutionary, and to assure the preservation of the values that subtend the model, as well as its structures. Its success depends on how well the tradition/innovation dialectic is activated, and its capacity to embed, valorize, and integrate events that are different and unusual, and even contradictory. The recombination of existing elements and their reformulation thus forms part of this modality of progressive innovation. (2001, p. 40)

Genres, then, are only one of the possibilities of this system of progressive innovation. Other possibilities include cycles, series, national or transnational remakes, the reuse of successful scenarios, colorization, and – more recently, post-dating Hollywood classicism – technological retouching applied to older films, the insertion of new special effects, or of passages omitted from the initial montage into existing works, transfers from the small to the big screen, the invention of filmic stories for video games, etc.

In addition, during the era of classical Hollywood, the studio system presented an organization set up for rationalizing the production of genre films and minimizing their costs. With both the major companies and the lesser ones, their stores of sets, costumes, and accessories, and the contract system that tied actors, directors, screenwriters, and technicians to them – thus assuring a continuity of personnel, as well as a division of labor – facilitated a constant reinvestment of material, talent, and expertise in genre films. When all things are taken into consideration, none of the studios, whether large or small, can be properly said to have specialized in one genre alone. If Warner owes its trademark image to two genres (gangster films and social films), that fact should not obscure its contribution to musicals (with the films choreographed by Busby Berkeley in the 1930s), to war films, to adventure films (in which Errol Flynn was often the star, such as *The Adventures of Robin Hood*, Keighley/Curtiz, 1938), to *film noir* in the 1940s, etc. (Gomery 1986, pp. 112–118). For the B-movie market, which had occasioned the founding of small companies, Republic Pictures, established in 1935 and active until 1957, offered three categories of feature films: *Jubilees* (westerns shot in 7 days with a very low budget), *Anniversaries* (westerns, action films, or musicals shot in 14 days), and *Deluxes* (more varied genre films shot in 21 days). To them should be added *serials* – produced at the rate of one episode each week – that were at the heart of Republic's production between 1935 and 1950. They were divided into five generic categories: westerns (*The Lone Ranger*, Witney and English, 1938), exotic adventures (*Jungle Girl*, Witney and English, 1941), science-fiction (*King of the Rocket Men*, Brannon, 1949), detective stories (*Dick Tracy*,

James and Taylor, 1937), and costume dramas (*Ghost of Zorro*, 1949) (Gomery 1986, pp. 182–187). Even though no studio had a monopoly over any one genre, and all the companies produced films in a variety of genres, the big companies, with their organization into production units, nevertheless had the advantage of specialized structures in which work was rigorously compartmentalized in such a way as to make them suitable for devoting themselves to one genre. This was the case with the unit supervised by Arthur Freed, which produced, among other films, *The Wizard of Oz* (Fleming, 1939) and musicals directed by Minnelli, or by the duo of Stanley Donen and Gene Kelly.

If the standardization/differentiation dialectic undoubtedly finds its homeland in the studio system of classical Hollywood, it also underpins the production of genre films outside of any geographical and/or temporal limits, especially in places where a studio system operated. The British company Ealing, for example, displayed a similar inclination to mix standardization with innovation. Strengthened by the distribution system made available to it by Rank in 1945, this firm launched itself into the production of films in a variety of genres before concentrating on social realist dramas and comedies. This last genre earned high distinction for Ealing's productions, and to make his films, Michael Balcon, the head of production at Ealing Studios, surrounded himself with actors like Alec Guinness, along with technicians, directors, and screenwriters whom he employed in film after film. Thus, *Whisky Galore!* (Mackendrick, 1949), *Kind Hearts and Coronets* (Hamer, 1949), *Passport to Pimlico* (Cornelius, 1949), *The Man in the White Suit* (Mackendrick, 1951), or *The Ladykillers* (Mackendrick, 1955) could be considered as variations on a form of comedy standardized by Ealing Studios: English humor.

More generally, the production of a genre film, if other films in the same genre have already been successful, minimizes risk-taking and allows the company to ride the wave of a perceived ground-swell. The success of *The Quatermass Experiment* (Guest, 1955), then of *The Curse of Frankenstein* (Fisher, 1957), enhanced the specialization of the British company Hammer in the fantastic genre and led to a decade of horror films created by the same

67

directors, assisted by the same cinematographers (like Jack Asher) and set designers (like Bernard Robinson), shot with the same actors (like Peter Cushing and Christopher Lee), before the successful formula was taken up and modified in Italy, notably by Mario Brava (Binh and Pilard 2000). In this case, therefore, genre, through its play of conventions, is also a means of making films at the lowest possible cost – to the point where the notion of "genre film" ends up being confused, as soon as one steps outside the context of Hollywood, with the concept of a *cinéma bis*, a popular form of cinema producing series of very low budget films.

The avoidance of generic ascription by Hollywood studios

While it is fair to say that in Hollywood genres are both an *effect* of the rationalization of production and also an efficient tool for making films that will be successful at the box office, the publicity practices of Hollywood show, paradoxically, that ascribing a film to a genre is not considered a good promotional tactic. Genre, because it is in the public domain and can therefore be advanced by any producer to characterize his or her film, does indeed assist *production*, but it does not allow a studio to put in place a marketing strategy that will distinguish the film from its competitors. Thus, genres, once they have become established and shared by several studios, cease to serve the particular interests of the studio that created them. The studio, in advertising the film, will want to be able to emphasize what is unique to it: its stars, who are under an exclusive contract to the studio, its cycles, or its characters that are protected by copyright. In evaluating the economic effectiveness of genre, therefore, one must not see it as depending solely on the facts relating to production, but also as a discursive activity pursued by studios to see what uses they can make of genres in their attempts to reach their audiences.

This is what Rick Altman does by distinguishing two different "voices" in the discourses maintained by the studios about the films they produce. The first voice reflects the studio as a participant in the Hollywood system, and therefore does not hesitate to attribute simple generic descriptors to genre films. The second voice is that of the studio as a particular studio, concerned to defend its image and its interests. This voice seeks in its discourse to avoid everything that it shares in common with other studios in order to promote the aspects that make it distinctive (Altman 1999, pp. 200–222). This latter voice is often detected in the publicity, posters, and trailers of both the majors in the classical era and the large companies of today. In the classical context, when the majors controlled the distribution of first-run films on American soil (the equivalent, to a certain extent, of the advance screenings that are shown for several weeks in a circuit of the large urban theaters), the big companies seemed especially anxious to distinguish themselves from their competitors, as far as their prestige productions were concerned. After the double-program had become established and widespread (consisting of an A-grade prestige film and a relatively low budget B-grade film), studios more often than not reserved genre appellations for B films only. By way of contrast, small or independent companies, almost excluded from the system of first-run release in the prestige theaters, tried to identify their films clearly with a preexisting generic denomination in order to exploit the places available in the program and to speak directly to their potential clients (distributors and independent theaters).

The large Hollywood studios, just like their neo-Hollywood successors, preferred, then, in their marketing discourse, to rely on "brand names" in their exclusive possession as a means of assuring their audiences that they would encounter something relatively new, rather than a hackneyed genre that had become common property. This is what explains, in particular, the abundance of cycles in genre cinema. The first features about James Bond, *Dr. No* (Young, 1962) and *From Russia With Love* (Young, 1963), were presented by United Artists not as spy films, but as "the first James Bond film" and "the return of James Bond." A similar thing happens with the cycle of *Tarzan* films made by MGM from 1932 or *Raiders of the Lost Ark* (Spielberg, 1981) produced by Lucasfilms, which used a "labeled" character for their promotion

(Tarzan, Indiana Jones), taking care not to evoke explicitly the genre of the "adventure film."

If companies only seem to promote a generic denomination when they can put forward a star, a character, or a cycle (that is, a resource uniquely possessed by the studio), they also seek to avoid restricting their audience, in mentioning a genre, to those who enjoy genre. Rick Altman has magisterially shown this by comparing the publicity prepared for the near-contemporaneous release of two biopics, *Dr. Ehrlich's Magic Bullet* and *The Story of Alexander Graham Bell* (1999, pp. 57–58). The first film, made by Dieterle in 1940 and produced by Warner, recounts the life of the man who discovered the remedy for syphilis; the second, made by Cummings in 1939 and produced by Fox, depicts that of the inventor of the telephone. The success of two preceding productions, *The Story of Louis Pasteur* and *The Life of Emile Zola*, made in 1935 and 1937 by the same Dieterle, under contract with Warner, explains why the firm had chosen to exploit the biopic vein with Dr. Ehrlich. But if indeed it is the constitution of a biographical genre that makes possible the production of this third film – in accordance with the standardization/differentiation logic that we have seen earlier – neither the title nor the poster of the film foreground the work of the doctor (because of the delicacy of the subject), or the grounding of the film in the biopic genre. The "bullet" of the title is there to appeal to a masculine audience, the word "doctor" attracts the female audience, and the word "magic" completes the audience by suggesting a *tertium quid* that is not imbued with gendered sociological expectations. The text of the poster confirms this desire to address three different audiences: the first column refers to "the laughter of children . . . The love of a woman . . . the hope of a thousand men," while the second column, which foregrounds the face and name (in large letters) of the principal actor, Edward G. Robinson, does not mention the genre at all. Rather than circumscribing its subject (and potentially its audience) by including a generic designation, Warner Studios preferred to "cast a wide net" by saying nothing specific about the film.

Fox adopted the same strategy in *The Story of Alexander Graham Bell*. Warner's publicity constantly mentions the names of the characters Zola and Pasteur (Dr. Ehrlich is "another Zola" in certain posters where his name follow those of Pasteur and Zola in large letters printed in an identical typeface). The purpose of this is not to invoke a common genre, but to associate the film with a Warner cycle. In contrast, Fox, which did not have the benefit of such a cycle, had to specify the generic roots of *The Story of Alexander Graham Bell* in order to cash in on the success of the biopic trend. To do so, Fox compared the film to other explicitly named "unforgettable" films made by a number of studios, including Warner's *The Story of Louis Pasteur*, *The Citadel* (the story of a London doctor) (Vidor, 1938), *The Life of Emile Zola*, *Anthony Adverse* (LeRoy, 1936), and *The Count of Monte Cristo* (Lee, 1934).

Once created, a genre offers a limited commercial interest for the studios. A competitive situation that compels companies to distinguish themselves from one another by offering novelties while simultaneously mastering proven recipes establishes a standardization/differentiation dynamic in the commercial uses that producers make even of the notion of genre.

The Social Functions of Genre

If genres exist, that is, if films with shared semantic and syntactic characteristics are perceived as such by an audience and are produced in quantity over a relatively long period, it is because these films are successful, and because the audience is responsive to the genre. For that to happen, as Jean-Pierre Esquenazi signals, "a phenomenon of resonance needs to be generated between the world that pertains to a genre and the world that pertains to an interpretative community" (2001a, p. 43). This observation prompts very divergent hypotheses on the nature of this resonance. For some, genre expresses the desires, aspirations, and beliefs of the audience; for others, conversely, genre is a repressive structure of ideological containment that shapes and formats its viewers.

Genres and the production of stereotypes in contemporary culture

This opposition between the idea of cinematic genres as *"cultural ritual* – as a form of collective expression"* (Schatz 1981, p. 13) – and genres conceived of as manipulative and reductive reflects a more fundamental split between two positions in contemporary culture – one valorizing mass production in popular culture, and the other devaluing such products as impoverished and alienating. These two attitudes give rise not only to two antagonistic conceptions of the social function of genre (the expression of social "truths"/constraining ideological enclosure), but also, as we shall see further on (see below, pp. 87–95), two ways of envisaging genre as a process of communication (a useful form of mediation/a blocking of interpretation). In other words, these attitudes reflect an essential ambivalence surrounding stereotyped products of mass culture.

One knows that the contemporary period is both the era of the stereotype, involving both the embracing and also the denunciation of it, and the era of its massive industrial distribution. In this context, art, for example, to be viewed as such must distance itself from the banal by distinguishing itself from it, while mass culture – from the serial novel to televised soap operas, Harlequin romances to commercial films, major cinematic genres to advertising pictures and slogans – sustains itself with stereotypes and collective forms. At the same time as the technical, ideological, and political conditions for a mass culture emerged in the West during the second half of the nineteenth century, the relationship between the *already said* and the *already seen* changed considerably. Commonplaces, which were formal categories of general argument integrated into *inventio*, stripped of all pejorative overtones before the end of the eighteenth century, became transmuted into stereotypes, in forms that were fixed, reductive, and reproducible. As Ruth Amossy signals, a "stereotype" is above all "a standardized product that is the outcome of mass distribution and consumption," leading to the design, in a cynical manner, of a "mechanization of cultural production" (1991, pp. 25–26).

In 1922, the notion appeared in the field of the social sciences with *Public Opinion* by Walter Lippman, who gave it a more neutral meaning that has remained fairly current since then ("pictures in our heads"). Arising out of this, analyses of stereotypical forms, including cinematic genres, have tended to pursue either of two opposed routes (Moine 1999). On one hand, analyses that adopt a pejorative conception of the stereotype attempt to demystify collective representations that serve to naturalize and promote power relationships through the dissemination of simplistic and repetitive images. Seeking to expose the *doxa* latent in the recurrent traits and banal images of these representations, such analyses make apparent the encoding, the hidden scripts, and the ideological hierarchies that are implicit in stereotypes. On the other hand, a study of the logic of stereotypes, even though it does not necessarily rehabilitate them, avoids investing them with a pejorative value. Instead, it focuses both on their usefulness (however partial or biased they may be) for explaining social factors, and also on their ability to provide interpretive cues for readers of a text or viewers of a film that help to make the work intelligible.[1]

This ambivalent sense of the stereotype partly explains why many critics prefer to restrict generic designations to commercial films, and why, with respect to genre films made by filmmakers who are viewed as auteurs, they seek to show how the latter exceed or transgress the genre, how they exploit it in a way that is at some distance from the usual rules, clichés, and stereotypical motives of the genre, and how they pay homage to the genre, etc. I am not denying that some directors seize upon a genre in order to rework it in a parodic or original way, leaving viewers in no doubt about its divergence from the stereotype, rather than simply circulating it. This practice of incorporating or hijacking stereotypes is fairly characteristic of artistic creation since Flaubert. It is simply a question of emphasizing here that stereotypical practices (banal narrative outlines, impoverished clichés, simplified and conventional images of the world), unless they are carried out with a clearly signaled secondary intention, or in an individual style, cause the work and its creator to be relegated to the field of mass production.

An instrument of ideological repression

Genre can be regarded as an effective instrument for ideological containment that imposes on viewers, through recurrent stereotyped stories, solutions that conform to social norms. The regular showing of genre films serves the interests of the dominant classes, of which the cinema industry is a representative and an agent, because of the ways in which it lulls the public, leading it to share their own ideological positions. Genre thus guarantees a social and political status quo by reaffirming normative social values. Identification of this repressive and reactionary function of genre has been inspired both by the works of the Frankfurt School on media and cultural industries, and by Marxist reflections on ideology:

> An ideology is a system (possessing its own logic and rigor) of representations (images, myths, ideas or concepts according to the case) endowed with an historic existence and role in a given society. Without entering into the problem of the relationships of a science with its past (ideological), let us say that ideology as a system of representations is distinct from science and that its practico-social function overpowers its theoretical function (or function of knowledge) . . . [The systematically organized representations] for most of the time are images, sometimes concepts, but it is primarily as a structure that they imposes themselves on the great majority of people, without passing through their "awareness." They are perceived-accepted-suffered cultural objects and act functionally on people through a process that is unconscious . . . In ideology, the real relationship [to the world] is inevitably invested in an imaginary relationship: a relationship that expresses a desire (conservative, conformist, reformist, revolutionary), even a hope or a nostalgia, that it might describe a reality.
> (Althusser 1966, pp. 238–243)

Viewed from this perspective, cinematic genres are carriers of an ideology to which their systems of representation give a form. This thesis, particularly invoked in cinema studies with regard to Hollywood genres, makes genres into structures through which the dream factory can transmit its messages and values in a concealed way in order to deceive the viewer. For this reason we will not draw upon ideological readings here on particular individual genres, from America or elsewhere, but only on functional theories that regard a repressive function as being at the heart of, and as the pretext for, a genuine, normative system of genres.

One frequently reads, even though critics do not make explicit reference to neo-Marxist analyses, that musicals or adventure films are genres of evasion that divert viewers away from daily reality and social problems by drawing them into an imaginary or exotic world. Like Mia Farrow in *The Purple Rose of Cairo* (Allen, 1985) who forgets her social and emotional misery by returning incessantly to see the romance of the same name screened in the cinema, the viewer finds consolation in the magical spectacle of cinematic representation. Acceptance of the conventions of genre, which allows the audience to substitute a generic reality for an actual reality, and which licenses reverie and fantasy, explains this (temporary) fixation with stories of the marvelous.

It is, however, more interesting to focus on the displacement that is at work in genres which base their stories on "real" problems originating in other conflicts. The emergence of the fantastic film in Germany during the 1920s, or in the United States at the beginning of the 1930s, can be seen as resulting from a comparable desire (more or less conscious) to evacuate social and economic problems by transferring them to an imaginary level. The monster, under different guises, from *Nosferatu* (Murnau, 1922) to *Dracula* (Browning, 1931), incarnates, crystallizes, and deforms sociological and ideological fears and tensions. Thus, *King Kong* (Cooper and Schoedsack, 1933) constructs itself around a double displacement of the Great Depression. At the beginning of the film, Carl Denham, a famous director, is searching through the streets of New York to find a young woman to play Beauty in a film of *Beauty and the Beast* he hopes to shoot on an island that has not yet been explored, on which lives a giant ape, Kong. He waits in front of the entrance of a refuge for women where unemployed young women are queued in line, and then intercepts a young, pretty thief, Ann, in the act of stealing an apple from a shop display. While he comes to an agreement with the grocer to settle for this theft, Ann, weak with hunger, just about faints. Her face is then filmed in close-up and anchored in the subjectivity of Denham. The sight of this fainting fit, which is a symptom of starvation turned into an aesthetic object, convinces the director to hire the young woman.

The rest of the film presents the story of an expedition into a *terra incognita* that takes the human characters out of the geographically and historically identifiable real world. The ship chartered by Denham penetrates into a more and more distant "elsewhere," increasingly wild, and ever more remote in time: the ocean, then Kong's island, where one first discovers "primitives," and then a jungle populated with dinosaurs over which the giant ape rules. The film thus converts social danger (the crisis) into a sexual danger (the representation of the crisis exclusively involves a woman – Ann is a thief before becoming the catalyst for Kong's amorous passion). At the same time, it empties historical time of its actual culture (New York in the 1930s) in order to replace it with a mythical and imaginary world (the kingdom of Kong). It is not surprising that commentators and critics have often seen in the irruption of King Kong in New York the return, terrifying and phantasmagorical, of the repressed – whether psychic (the Other, desire, the all-powerfulness of impulses, etc.), or social (the Great Depression, the effects of which are quickly shown and evacuated at the beginning of the film, returning in the form of a monster that destroys everything in its passage) (Ishaghpour 1982, pp. 83–103).

Similarly, Anne-Marie Bidaud argues that the development of the disaster film in the 1970s should be seen as the staging of "diversionary fears that exorcise the fears of the public by placing the causes of them at a remove, outside of history" (1994, p. 220). The embroilment in Vietnam, the Watergate crisis, and the recession are thus hidden within, and displaced into, disasters that are caused by the natural elements: water in *The Poseidon Adventure* (Neame, 1972), fire in *The Towering Inferno* (Guillermin, 1974), earth in *Earthquake* (Robson, 1974), wild animals in *Jaws* (Spielberg, 1975). Moreover, in apocalyptic films, just as in their science-fiction first-cousins that create futuristic worlds born of a nuclear explosion (for example, *Logan's Run*, Anderson, 1976), extreme destruction and danger often open out into hope or a rebirth. Not only is the ideological and political crisis in America during the 1970s replaced by other dangers, but a solution is also found for these displaced dangers that confirms and reinforces dominant social values and institutions.[2]

Judith Whright, in an article published in *Jump Cut* in 1974, an American journal that presented ideological readings during this period, successfully generalized this reactionary function to include all genres. She saw its aim as being to maintain the social status quo:

> These films came into being and were financially successful because they temporarily relieved the fears aroused by a recognition of social and political conflicts; they helped to discourage any action that might otherwise follow upon the pressure generated by living with these conflicts. Genre films produce satisfaction rather than action, pity and fear rather than revolt. They serve the interests of the ruling class by assisting in the maintenance of the status quo, and they throw a sop to oppressed groups who, because they are unorganized and therefore afraid to act, eagerly accept the genre film's absurd solutions to economic and social conflicts. When we return to the complexities of the society in which we live, the same conflicts assert themselves, so we return to genre films for easy comfort and solace – hence their popularity. (Whright 1995, p. 41)

Whright shows that four Hollywood genres – the western, the science-fiction film, the horror film, and the gangster film – dramatize conflicts that are not political, within a frame that is distanced from the social present, and in a micro-society that is reduced to a structure that is simplified to the extreme. In this carefully marked-out fictive space, each of these genres focuses on a central conflict for which it provides a solution. The western deals with violence and the conditions in which force can become legitimate; the horror film with the conflict between scientific rationalism and traditional beliefs; the science-fiction film with problems posed by otherness, conceived of in this genre as a mode of intrusion; and the gangster film with the conflict between fear and the inherent desire to achieve social and economic success. From this last genre, for example, emerges the lesson that anonymity (that is, the common lot of the viewers) guarantees happiness. Success makes one vulnerable, by turning anyone who reaches the top into the enemy of all those who are also trying to succeed.

For Whright, the gangster film shows, then, that a pronounced elevation in the social hierarchy has catastrophic consequences. It justifies and confirms class boundaries. Her analysis starts with the observation that the world of gangsters, organized in a pyramidal structure in these films, is a true reductive model of the capitalist world (Whright 1995, pp. 47–49). A single man rules at the summit, and the films describe the rise, signposted with crimes and murders, of a man towards this coveted position. Rico in *Little Caesar* (LeRoy, 1931) eliminates all his rivals and takes total control of the gambling dens and black market in the city. In *Scarface* (Hawks, 1932) the young and ambitious Italian, Tony Camonte, becomes a body-guard of the gang-leader in the district of the south of Chicago, in 1920, dispatches all his rivals, and seizes both the position and the mistress of the boss. In *The Godfather: Part II* (Coppola, 1974), one follows the parallel rise of Vito Corleone, the old godfather, and of his son and heir, Michael Corleone. But these heroes pay a heavy price for this success. Rico is betrayed and killed by the police. In the first part of *The Godfather* (Coppola, 1972), Vito Corleone survives the attempted murder perpetrated against him by other members of the Mafia, but is greatly diminished. In the second part, his son Michael is left by his wife, has to cut down his own father, and must continuously defend himself against the enemies who surround him, the government, and the police. Death, solitude, and an endless struggle to stay alive and retain the position of godfather are the price he has to pay for success.

The character of the gangster embodies a dilemma: failure is a kind of death, but success reveals itself as dangerous and impossible. Moreover, gangster films implicitly maintain the capitalist system by making the gangster a tragic figure. Genre does not relate this dilemma to social causes (the capitalist law of the jungle that also rules in the world of crime), but tends to make it a consequence of the psychological character of a hero who is unstable and devoured by ambition. This explains the string of "psychotic gangsters" such as Tom Powers (James Cagney) in *The Public Enemy* (Wellman, 1931) who for no apparent reason crushes half a grapefruit into the face of Kitty, or shoots the stuffed head of a bear during the hold-up of a warehouse of furs. For Judith Whright, the spectacle of a gangster film removes from us the necessity of placing social hierarchies in question, conditioning us to believe that we should not leave our class for any price, and that we should remain content with our lot in life: it is better to survive, even though it may entail frugality and anonymity. The only alternative is to be a tragic hero.

A collective cultural expression

Other functional theories, diametrically opposed to the preceding one, assert that genres offer, via their fictive stories, solutions to real social problems and inherent cultural tensions. These theories, inspired by Lévi-Strauss's analyses of myth, often extend structural analyses of genre (cf. chapter 2, pp. 46–55) to make cinematic genre a form of collective cultural expression that enables the dramatization of the common values and fundamental cultural oppositions that structure a society, as well as more coincidental conflicts.

Genre films, then, are viewed as being like other versions of a myth, in that they express the particular system of oppositions and correlations that structure a culture. According to this hypothesis, a genre's success (the essential condition of its being) depends on its ability to reshuffle the trump cards of the culture and its social organization without changing the game, or, as Cawelti says, to produce "formulas" that give expression to cultural ambiguities and conflicts while proposing harmonious solutions for them (1976, p. 35). Just like myths, which exist in a range of versions in any given culture (formed of repetitions, variations, and innovations around a single structure, with the same relationship between characters, the same spatial dispositions, etc.), genre films are engaged in a synthesizing activity – the product of a collective imaginary that puts the world and its elements into some kind of order.

Genres, conceived as myths or formulas, therefore, offer specific configurations that materialize structuring oppositions in characters, situations, and culturally significant, historically determined places. This can be seen in the western when it organizes its geographical and social space around a frontier that separates Wilderness from Civilization. Genre films thus create a narrative structure that materializes the mental structure of a social conceptualization (Wright 1975, pp. 185–194). Thomas Schatz, for instance, divides up the map of classical Hollywood genres into two structurally different groups in which each genre does no more than encode specific conflicts between fundamental cultural values through particular narrative structures (1981, pp. 27–30). In his view, the western, the gangster film, and the detective film delimit, within a space of particular actions, a "symbolic arena" governed by conventions, and by conflicts that are linked to the order and the control imposed by this space. In contrast, the musical, screwball comedy, and melodrama dramatize interpersonal tensions in non-specific spaces: how to reconcile one's views with those of another? How to integrate oneself into a community? The genres in the first group dramatize struggles to dominate, organize, and impose order on a space, which explains the large number of iconographic conventions they employ, while genres in the second group are centered on conflicts that are more psycho-sociological than physical, and which are usually gendered. Each of these genres thus mediates particular cultural tensions. We need, however, to signal a major problem posed by this model. By making the specific social functions of genres derive from a divided classification, it simplifies each genre (the relations between men and women, for example, can play a role in the western), and it ignores the mixing of genres (how are the conflicts in musicals set in the

West organized?). Moreover, its explanatory value is singularly limited by the fact that it simply leaves to one side many Hollywood genres, such as adventure films, the biopic, the horror film, etc.

Adopting a more overtly myth-based perspective, the anthropologist Lee Drummond (1996) analyzes successful American genre films produced from the 1960s to the 1990s. The movies he selects are all fantasy movies, which he defines as "non-realist" films. These involve "space operas" (films with extraterrestrial beings), films with super-heroes, horror films (which are only fleetingly dealt with in his book), and films in which the main character is an animal. The fantasy movie category encompasses, then, all genres that explore, outside of reality, relations between human beings and creatures that are in- or non-human and traverse the shifting and complex limits of humanity. For Drummond, these films do not owe their success exclusively to the economic determinism of a powerful commercial strategy, but to the fact that they, like myths, provide a mechanism for defining human identity in its variability.

Contemporary fantasy movies present a world of virtual experiences to our view that are organized according to three semiotic dimensions. They correspond to continuous axes, determined at both ends by contradictory concepts, around which contemporary American culture structures itself and problematizes its representations of humanity. The first dimension consists of two poles, "Animal" and "Machine," and pertains essentially to fantasy film. The second dimension, involving a tension between "Us"/"Me" and "Them"/"the Other," generates relations of affinity, inclusion, identity and kind, exclusion, and alterity. Finally, the third dimension is organized around principles of creation and destruction, expressed as "Life Force" and "Death Force." Fantasy movies, from James Bond to *E.T.*, passing through *Jaws* and *Star Wars*, depict actual relations of conflict between men and machines (seen as ever more present, useful but alienating) by proposing *virtual models of relations* with machines.

Thus, James Bond, for Drummond, is before anything else a double-agent of the capitalist system in which one possesses and employs machines. In fact, even though 007 makes use of machines, he exploits them. Unlike us, he is also the Master, since he controls or destroys them in the course of extraordinary adventures – as the mechanized pursuit-sequences in the prologues to each film demonstrate. An incomparable lover, he is also a technician of passion, thus displaying the prowess to successfully unite contraries (sensuality/technology). The *Star Wars* trilogy presents another variation on the relationship between men and machines. It includes in the *mise en scène* robots that are androids, but nevertheless a little bit human, robots that have a non-human appearance but which are rather more human, Masters of machines, fabulous animals, and creatures that combine human and mechanical aspects in their bodies in various ways. Luke, the hero, embodies different states of relationship with machines in the course of the episodes and his combats. Completely human at the beginning of the saga, little by little he becomes a Master of machines before "mechanizing" himself in his turn. The "light side" and the "dark side" of the Force, leitmotivs of the cycle (relating to the third "Life Force"/"Death Force" semiotic dimension), tend to converge to the degree that Luke's body, more and more repaired, comes to resemble that of his father Darth Vader – totally mechanized. The success of *Star Wars*, the third episode of which abandons the epic of machines in order to focus in a more conventional way on a family epic, also derives from the trilogy's imaginary exploration (both detailed and contradictory) of the distinction between human ("Us") and non-human ("Them" and "Sexless creatures" – *It*). Finally, in *Jaws*, the shark is an animal that is wholly animal, unequivocally ranked in the group of "Them" adversaries, an inhuman predator that endangers the family of one of the protagonists, a destructive beast to hate. But this animal is also presented as a killing "machine." As a distanced and mechanized creature, it prefigures the cruel dinosaurs of *Jurassic Park*, the stars of a new biotechnological world – that nevertheless recover their animal nature when they reveal themselves, against all expectations, to be capable of procreating.

A conception of cinematic genre as myth leads inevitably to the attribution of a ritual function to the viewing of a genre film. By offering a representation of a society's value system codified in rules and functions that are known by all, a genre helps viewers to recognize themselves as members of that society. It thus permits the audience to share together both the common values and references that it offers, and also, at a symbolic level, mediations that can have the effect of resolving conflicts, thus assisting society to maintain itself. The regular consumption of films of the same genre is explained not only by the fact that a community sees itself in the genre, but also by the fact that it provides a periodic rendezvous capable, like rituals, of uniting a group through the shared pleasure of recognizing common values together. In this way, the repeated experience of watching westerns contributes to the construction of a national identity. This particular genre emerged in the United States at the beginning of the 1910s in the context of an Americanization of cinema in the USA that accompanied the larger development of a "New World" national identity (Abel 2002). Since this era, westerns have contributed to the formation of a "national imaginary community" by establishing symbolic representations of things to be included, and things to be excluded (Anderson 1991, p. 4). For decades, the American western has permitted "Americanness" to be clarified for diverse populations who had no opportunity to live through the actual winning of the West. These films establish a relationship of familiarity between recent immigrants and the past. Constituting a myth of origins that celebrates national roots and values, westerns thus become a commemorative ritual that puts a twentieth-century American in touch with the pioneer spirit of the past. For those who believe in the mythic and ritual function of genres, the appeal to a sense of community and the resolution of conflicts in the space of the western are neutral cultural operations, while for those who adhere to the view that the discursive strategies of the film industry have an ideological function, this appeal is a form of manipulation.

The limits of ideological and ritual functions

The main objection that one could formulate against the conception of genre as an ideological yoke, encircling the audience in the normative, soothing constraint of Hollywood's rhetoric, is that it presupposes a passive spectator who unquestioningly accepts the ideological prescriptions. Genre, in this conception, seeks to impose a univocal, universal reading upon those who view it, with viewers being regarded as a homogeneous group who are constrained to accept the interpretation thrust upon them. Serving as a true opium of the people, genre is presumed to anesthetize, as if by nature, all readings that are subversive, critical, or divergent, and all possibilities of multiple receptions.

The approach to genre as ritual presents an analogous problem. To say that a genre sorts out contemporary problems or cultural conflicts at a symbolic level, and that, in so doing, it responds to an audience expectation which is addressed in the form of a ritualized spectacle, is to postulate a homogeneous audience for this genre that shares the same values, and is aware of the same issues. One could certainly object that the audiences of Hollywood genres are targeted by gender, or that they are aimed at a young audience, like horror and science-fiction films after the 1950s, and that viewers, since they form a segmented audience, form a community that is united by similar cultural models. But the cultural world of viewers is also ordered by other determinants (for example, ethnic or social ones), which, for this reason, are liable to shift in their applicability to a particular genre. The definition of genre as ritual, therefore, is an ethnocentric explanation, insofar as it postulates the ritual function of a genre on the basis of filmic texts alone, neglecting the experience, the investments, and the interpretations of particular viewers. Even if genre is a structure that articulates a social sense, there are many different ways – the fruits of multiple decisions – in which this sense can be invested with meaning. How else to understand the success of Hollywood genres overseas – that is, outside of American culture? Viewers from France, Hong Kong, and America – to propose a selection which, in my view, is still too homogeneous – undoubtedly do not recognize themselves in the same way in a western or a martial arts film.

It is equally important to stress that it is mainly the analysis of Hollywood genres that has given rise to these two antagonistic social functions and brought them into prominence. This preoccupation with Hollywood is prompted by the powerful presence of genres in this cinema, which has motivated attempts to devise general systematic explanations that can explain this presence. Nevertheless, without wanting to be too schematic, I would suggest that the economic organization and ideology of the Hollywood film industry, the cultural spearhead of capitalism, undoubtedly explains why Hollywood genres are instruments of control and ideological repression to a greater extent than in other cinemas that are less comprehensively structured into a unique system. Because Hollywood cinema is an industrial cinema funded by large groups of financiers, it is obliged to serve their economic and ideological interests. Finally, one should remember that American ideology is a non-conceptual ideology that insinuates itself through myths (Bidaud 1994, pp. 14–15). These myths make it possible for a vision of the world that is historically and politically conditioned to emerge from history and become naturalized.

This last point explains how ideological normalization and collective cultural expression can work together in genre films, rather than forcing a compromise between the two social functions. In fact, while myth proclaims the order of a social world, and ritual unites its participants around the values of this society in a codified collective ceremony, their worth and communicative functions also serve the interests of social permanence. Myth articulates an order that ritual works to sustain, with both expressing and assuring values in the same operation (Balandier 1988). By finding and imposing collective imaginary responses to real issues, myth depoliticizes and purifies conflicts in contemporary societies, rendering them harmless. Myth is not, therefore, a neutral category, a simple effect of structure. As Barthes (1957) demonstrated, myth is inscribed in an ideological intention.

One can, then, agree with Rick Altman that the success of a Hollywood genre results from a conjunction of the ideological interests of the studios and the cultural expectations of the viewers. The formula resulting from this reciprocal adaptation of Hollywood's pressing aspirations and the desires of the public – a semantic-syntactic equilibrium that stabilizes a genre – has the effect of masking the ideological framework (Altman 1989, p. 99). One can better understand, then, how genre films authorize their viewers to experience cultural transgressions vicariously in the course of the film, and to derive pleasure from doing so. The gangster film or the horror film, for example, allow the enjoyment of a generic, codified, culturally inadmissible pleasure by giving access to the witnessing of crimes and murders, while at the same time reasserting the cultural, social, and moral values of the law *in extremis*. The gangster or the monster go a little too far, they commit a heinous crime, and they end up being caught. Similarly, as Altman shows, the counter-cultural pleasure of the viewer in the musical *Top Hat* is at its height when Ginger Rogers, driven to distraction at night by the noise of the tap shoes of Fred Astaire (who is dancing in the room above), after having seen the manager of the hotel, goes herself in a state of undress to accost the perpetrator of the annoyance. In order for the film to fulfill the conventions of the genre, and for the amorous comings and goings to get under way, it is necessary for this meeting to take place, whereas morality would dictate that Ginger should again telephone the manager of the hotel from her room. Because she ascends to the room of her neighbor, she mistakes Fred Astaire, who has simply been invited there, for the hotel guest. The following day, she discovers that the man who has rented the room is none other than the husband of her best friend, whom she has not met before. The transgression of the code of propriety is necessary for activating a confusion surrounding the identity of the male protagonist (since Fred Astaire is not really the husband of Ginger's best friend). This confusion allows the film to present over an hour's worth of romantic misunderstanding, during which the pleasure of the genre completely overpowers any respect for social conventions. Even though she hesitates, Ginger ends up dancing with Fred under a kiosk, then by dancing romantically "cheek to cheek" with him at a ball, under the eyes of her best friend! But all these transgressions are erased at the end of the film when the misidentifications are clarified. Morality is preserved, the infringements of good manners forgiven, and the pleasure of the genre made culturally harmless, since the whole business concludes with the marriage of the two principal protagonists.

Burlesque film employs yet another strategy to recuperate the ideological transgressions that are presented. Even though the laziness of the heroes of slapstick treads on the toes of the work ethic, and their larcenies and the damage they cause affront propriety, their inventiveness, their lack of restraint, and their acrobatic talents can beguile viewers. Nevertheless, their marginal status, their violence, and their inability to fit in with the world ensures that they cannot be accepted as models. One laughs heartily not only at their victims (policemen, matrons), but also at the transgressive heroes themselves. Burlesque disorder, carefully contained in this way, authorizes a counter-cultural pleasure without generating any social danger.

The Communicative Function of Genre

The communicative function of a genre is determined by the conventions according to which it is constructed and recognized. This means that in order for a film to be related to a genre, it needs not only to be classified – whether the generic designation be proposed by producers, critics, or viewers – but also to be "read" and interpreted. An awareness of the generic identity of a film allows its viewer to recognize "an established formula for communication" that serves to "organize its system of expectations," to use Casetti's terms (cf. chapter 2). To appeal to a generic category for the purpose of proposing, receiving, or thinking about a film, is to invest it with a "horizon of expectation," defined by Jauss as a "system of references capable of being objectively formulated," which, with respect to each work at the moment in history when it appears, relates to three main factors: the audience's experience of the genre to which the formulation refers, the form and thematic preoccupations of earlier works of which it is presumed to be aware, and the opposition between poetic language and practical language, and between the imaginary world and daily reality (Jauss 1978, p. 53).

Generic "rails"

The assignation of a film to a particular genre, whether signposted or self-evident, is designed to trigger in the viewer a memory and awareness of the genre – to which he or she is disposed by regular viewing of genre films, or even, to a certain degree, because of a diffused cultural knowledge surrounding the genre. Genre constitutes a space in which experiences occur that determine the nature of the expectations and interpretation that the film is designed to elicit. As long as one considers it a communication pact, a promise, or an interpretive contract, genre organizes the frame of reference in which the film is viewed. Genre does not function, therefore, as a classificatory category, but as a familiar structure that is identifiable because of its play of conventions. This play of conventions makes possible the film's reception, and, consequently, its success. Moreover, in determining the expectations of the viewer, a genre intervenes in the anticipation that governs the perceptual and cognitive activity of the viewer. To produce a genre film, therefore, is to furnish the audience with a context for the interpretation of the film; to see a genre film, with an awareness of its generic origins, is to interpret the film in this context. But, in determining the interpretive framework for understanding the film, genre both opens and shuts various possibilities for appropriation and comprehension. That is why theorists sometimes emphasize the ability of a genre to help make the film intelligible, and sometimes its propensity to short-circuit interpretation by predetermining it. Thus Barthélemy Amengual violently condemns genre films because they extort a "blank check" from the viewer, a "blank sheet of paper that they sign without determining the content," which offers them a "crutch," thinking for them, and setting them traveling down "rails" (1993, p. 202). The generic "rails" along which genre films roll can be considered either as useful guides or as an obligatory route that constrains the viewer. It is not surprising that this latter conception unites critics who, like Amengual, repudiate genre works (which, in their eyes, are the source of a mediocre consumerist pleasure) in favor of auteur works, and most of those who see genre as having an ideologically enclosing function (cf. see above, pp. 71–75).

A genre film proffers (or imposes) genre indicators to the viewer, which the latter receives and activates by relating them to his or her memory of the genre. These indicators, which are responsible for arousing generic expectations by exemplifying the established conventions of the genre, are not merely disseminated in the text of the film. They signal the communication of the film even before it is viewed. Reviews of the film, and the promotional discourse surrounding it, can emphasize one or more of its generic intentions, thus influencing not only the choice of the viewer, but also his or her attitude. Trailers, advertising posters, and the jackets of video-cassettes serve equally as indicators. Thus, during the past fifteen years, posters for French comedies have frequently presented several characters, most often dressed in vivid or contrasting colors, who stand out against a white background. Familiarity with this composition and this choice of colors, then, activates a specific generic expectation among viewers. The credits and the opening sequences also mark a contractual moment of entry into the fiction through which the genre film proclaims its affiliation. Thus, the graphic characteristic of the letters in which the title of *Rio Bravo* (Hawks, 1959) is written evokes the West. The name of its director, Howard Hawks, and the names of its stars, John Wayne and Dean Martin (who are closely associated with the western), the music, and the wide shot of a wagon train and horses advancing into the depths of a canyon are also emblems of the genre that condition the expectation of the viewer. Similarly, *Les Trois frères* (*The Three*

Brothers) (Bourdon and Campan), one of the greatest hits at the French national box office in 1995, arouses a comic expectation right from the opening credits by foreshadowing in writing that the work will be "a film about the Unknowns." For French viewers, this recalls the team of three comics nicknamed "The Unknowns" (*Les Inconnus*) who were very popular, first on stage and then on television, at the beginning of the 1990s. Because viewers would not necessarily realize the connection between the film and "The Unknowns" from the names of the actors/ directors (Bourdon and Campan) alone, the film advertises its comic nature more directly by presenting and foregrounding "The Unknowns" as a label. The first three sequences of the film confirm its genealogical links with this comic trio, since the three main characters (the three brothers) are acted by the comedians who formed the team of "The Unknowns" on the stage and on television. Inherently, then, these sequences immediately confirm the comic intention of the film. The three brothers do not yet know one another, and they are each shown in their respective professional activities. One of them, having an ornate hoop with a pink bow on his head, is illegally hawking his wares, and extols the merits of a miraculous stain-remover that gets rid of, as he stutters, the "caca-, the cata-, the catastrophes." Another one of the brothers, a "suit," arrives with a smug air and false nonchalance at the business where he works, where all men are called "my chook," conversing familiarly among themselves with a hypocritical absence of hierarchy, kissing one another as a mode of greeting, and sporting ponytails. The third works under the orders of his future father-in-law operating the video-surveillance system in the shop, gluing his eyes on the women who are getting undressed in the changing rooms as soon as his boss turns his back. These three expository scenes thus clearly proclaim the generic intention of the film, which is to offer a comedy of manners. In the case of Hollywood films, the use of indicators that insistently draw attention at the opening of the film to its generic affiliation is part of a deliberate strategy: if a generic interpretive frame is firmly put in place early in the work, a wager is then laid, as Jacqueline Nacache signals, that "the viewer will lose all awareness of the conditions under which the film is being experienced, owing to this narrative fluidity which delivers a Hollywood transparency" (1995, p. 17).

The metaphor of generic rails has the disadvantage of placing too much emphasis on the repetition and predictability of genre films. One knows that certain genre films, although strongly encoded (as, for example, the horror film or the thriller), like to frustrate the expectations of their viewers by offering unanticipated variations, as much for the sake of continuing to arouse fear in the viewer as to lead him or her through breathtaking unexpected or unforeseen twists in the action. Furthermore, as Casetti (among others) has emphasized, genre is only able to bind the spectator to the film through a *preliminary* communicative pact – a pact that opens up a space for negotiation when the film introduces new configurations and changes to the relationships in the system of conventions of the genre with which the viewer is already familiar (1998, pp. 29–36). The spectator is then led to "renegotiate" the generic communicational frame in which the film has been offered to him or her, and in which he or she is disposed to view it. If viewers are able to reconcile these departures with the "law of the genre," if they regard them as an attribute of the semantic or syntactic systems of the genre, or if they update the generic communicative pact in the light of these changes, they continue to read the film in a generic perspective that is modified in due course. That is why, rather than speaking of a contract or pact which firmly binds the two main parties (the producer and the viewer), one can accept the proposition of François Jost, who views audiovisual genre as "a promise that brings expectations with it to the viewer, which the vision of the program [or of a film] puts to the test" (1997, p. 16). Such a conception, without denying the predetermination of the interpretation that generic anchoring imposes on a film, relativizes that very interpretation: promises only engage those who make them, or those who believe in them.

It is also necessary to emphasize that genre is not simply a static interpretive framework, but that a dynamic generic process accompanying the reception of a film can facilitate the integration of exogenous elements. The semantic-syntactic arrangement that characterizes a genre film and gives it an interpretive context can reveal itself as an agent of integration. This function helps to explain, for example, the success of directors who have come from Hong Kong to the new Hollywood. Thus, in *Face/Off* (Woo, 1997), the codified texture of the encounter of a virtuous policeman and a psychopathological criminal, which can only end with the death of one of the protagonists, presents a generic frame familiar to western audiences in which the choreography and characteristic effects of Hong Kong swordplay films can come to be written. This integration is facilitated, furthermore, by the penchant of American cinema for exoticism, from *The Lady from Shanghai* (Welles, 1946) – from which *Face/Off*, moreover, imitates the famous mirror scene – to *Chinatown* (Polanski, 1974).

Generic mediation

The communicative functions of genre have often been studied with respect to genre films – that is, with respect to stable semantic-syntactic formulas that follow a predictable schema. This approach considerably reduces the scope of the notion of genre, and fails to account for its effective uses, given that critics use the same generic designations for films by auteurs. Such an outcome derives chiefly from the way most studies regard producers and filmic texts as the only agents entrusted with registering a generic intention, to which the interpretations of viewers are supposed to conform. But, as Jean-Marie Schaeffer observes with respect to literary genres, a "readerly regime relating to genericity" also exists, which is present in all acts of reception – insofar as all reception implies an interpretation that could not take place without reference to a generic horizon (1989, p. 151).

In other words, a film's horizon of generic expectation is determined by two regimes of genericity: an authorial regime that proposes, and a spectatorial regime that disposes. Sometimes, however, the spectatorial regime does not coincide with the authorial regime. In the case of generic expectations, the frustration of those expectations makes interpretation of the film impossible unless they are replaced by another interpretive system. For example, some viewers of *The Thin Red Line* (Malick, 1998) – which appeared on the screen shortly after the success of the war film *Saving Private Ryan* (Spielberg, 1998) – expected to see a genre film (a war film) because of the temporal proximity of one film to the other, and because the advertisement and theme of the film gave them reason to think so. As I myself was able to judge from the discontented and impatient reactions from those in the theater (the expected action had not eventuated), followed by the departure of many viewers, the management of the authorial and spectatorial regimes, which had been inadequate, had not been able to ensure that this alternative interpretive system could become established.

That is why one should define genre as one of the mediations that renders a film intelligible by permitting an audience (that knows and recognizes the generic category) to receive and understand it. It is probably the case that with genre film, generic mediation, which anticipates the pleasure of the genre, is one of the most important forms of mediation. But there are other "ferrymen," such as the auteur, the stars, and even the type of theater in which the film is projected, who can play the role of mediator between the film and its audience. Genre is thus one of the possible ways of accessing a film, one of the possible conditions of its intelligibility, whether or not the film manifests a generic intention in other ways. This partly explains why we do not all ascribe the same film to the same genre, and why we are able to see *Stagecoach* as a western, as a John Wayne film, or as a film by John Ford, etc.

It also happens that generic mediation can lead to an interpretation that carries with it a precise, careful reading of a film. The system of expectations imposed by genre can be so oppressively laden with meaning for the viewer that it provokes him or her to reject what it proposes. This is what Jean-Pierre Esquenazi demonstrates in comparing the literal description of the fifth sequence in *Vertigo* (Hitchcock, 1958) – in which we first encounter Madeleine, whom Scottie the detective must follow, in the restaurant – with descriptions given by commentators on the film (2001a, pp. 122–125). The camera, after a traveling shot that moves toward the outside of the door of the restaurant, then a fade-in shot of Scottie's face, swings around in an arc that makes an angle of 60 degrees in the direction of Scottie's gaze. This reverse traveling shot is accompanied by a panoramic shot towards the left, which causes the detective to disappear out of the frame. In the far distance there then appears a clear glimpse of a bare back in the field, on which the camera accelerates its reframing before moving forward, to the accompaniment of a slow, romantic musical theme, as far as the young blond woman with the naked back (Madeleine). After this shot, which lasts 40 seconds, Hitchcock returns to the gaze of Scottie, who is not alongside, but almost opposite. It becomes clear, then, that it is only the camera that is looking at the naked back of the Hitchcockian heroine, whom Scottie cannot physically see. Five shots later, we focus on the elegant profile of Madeleine, well set-off against the dark red décor of the restaurant, before returning to Scottie who is seated at the bar with his back turned to the young woman. Even though his face expresses a trace of emotion, it is still not possible for him to have seen the image of Madeleine that the camera has presented to us. Hitchcock, then, does not show us what the detective sees, since he twice separates the gaze of the camera from that of the character, even though he lets the effects of Madeleine's presence on Scottie be seen. Even though it is impossible to attribute the sight of the naked back and the profile of the young woman to the detective, all commentators situate these images within the subjective gaze of Scottie. As Esquenazi explains, this interpretation is only possible because it is constructed out of a habitual expectation that occurs in Hollywood cinema and, more particularly, in *film noir*. Indeed, in films of this genre, the *femme fatale*, imaged as a sublime, unattainable woman, appears and is immediately taken in charge by the male gaze of the hero, who will possess her by the end of the film. From *The Maltese Falcon* (Huston, 1941) to *The Woman in the Window* (Lang, 1944), *film noir* thus presents the same "primitive scene" which links the fascinated gaze of a man to the body of a woman offered for display. Generic mediation, while it allows us to understand Scottie's fascination for the image of Madeleine, prevents us from seeing that in *Vertigo* he is preoccupied with an image that resides completely within the imagination of his character.

Two observations suggest themselves at the conclusion of this examination of the functions of cinematic genres. First, cinematic genre, whatever function one imagines it has, is both a good and a bad object. While it is useful for the industrial manufacture of films, this alone is not a particularly good selling point in the marketing of films. The ritual function of genres and their celebration of the values of a community are also a form of ideological repression. While they assist the viewer to form an expectation that makes the film receivable, they predetermine and block interpretations. On the other hand, while one can theorize the effects of genre on a viewer, each genre and each generic reading must be considered in its context of production and reception. While one recognizes an economic, ideological, ritual, or communicative function for genre, it only takes shape in historical and social contexts, and in the context of particular instances of reception.

Notes

1   See, for example, "Narrative Structures in Fleming," the lecture on James Bond published by Umberto Eco (1984) in *The Role of The Reader: Explorations in the Semiotics of Texts*, Bloomington, Indiana University Press, pp. 144–174.

2   On this subject, see Hélène Puiseux (1988) *L'Apocalypse nucléaire et son cinéma*, Paris, Cerf, 7ième Art; Ignacio Ramonet (1980) "Les Films-catastrophes américains. Des fictions pour la crise," in *Le Chewing-gum des yeux*, Paris, Éditions Alain Moreau.

Chapter 4
The Generic Identities of a Film

The generic identity of a film is far from being a constant given. Whatever the degree of consensus on which their uses are based, genres are not neatly distinct boxes in which films can be placed. In actuality, cinematic genres are neither frozen categories, nor essentialist models to which films conform by imitating them, nor *a priori* textual structures. Moreover, films do not place themselves into putative generic boxes – which brings us back to the fact that producers, viewers, and critics construct maps of genres, and sometimes attribute different generic identities to the same film. Finally, genre is not only a classificatory category, but also an interpretive category. In this regard, genre only finds meaning in the interactions between works, and between works and their contexts of production and reception, as we saw in chapter 3. That is why, rather than talking in terms of the relation of a film to "its class," we now need to consider the places in which the generic identity, or identities, of a film are negotiated, along with the ways in which this negotiation is conducted.

The Relations Between Film and Genre

Studies devoted to a genre are often constructed, more or less consciously, according to two different types of analysis. On one hand, by looking at a relatively large body of works, critics offer an analysis of the structures and semantic features of the genre in question, as well as its history. On the other hand, because of the needs of particular sections or chapters, they restrict themselves to dealing with works that are considered the highpoints of the genre, or filmmakers who have established its credentials by realizing its expressive possibilities in idiosyncratic terms.

Such studies try to harmonize two approaches that are contradictory, in my opinion – through attempting to account for the whole group of works in a genre by referring only to a range of select examples that are extremely varied. In fact, the chosen strategy necessarily separates the two approaches by focusing on auteurs who cease to be representative of a genre because they constitute outstanding exceptions: for example, John Ford, Howard Hawks, or Sergio Leone for the western, Vincent Minnelli or Douglas Sirk for melodrama, Minnelli again for the musical, Dino Risi and Mario Monicelli for Italian comedy, etc. The study of genre proper, then, gives way to an examination of the style of "the Fordian western," of "the musicals made by Minnelli for MGM," etc. My aim here is not to revive or confirm hierarchical distinctions between "minor" genre works and "major" works (of whatever genre), but to stress that the two approaches correspond to two different cultural uses of genre on the part of commentators, reflecting different levels of genericity that are not comparable. On one hand, they invoke the genre of the "genre film," conceived of as an infinite variation of the same formula; on the other hand, they focus on the genre of the "auteur film," viewed as a field narrower in scope than that of cinema as a whole, involving the uniqueness of an auteur as reflected in an individual style and a personal vision of the world. At the opposite end of the scale, an equally numerous body of books or articles, often centering on the question of genre *per se* rather than on any particular genre, narrow their examination of the "notion of genre" to isolated examples of genre films, or else use a selection of examples as the basis for their generalizations. In doing so, they overlook the fact that generic designations are used very differently to characterize virtually the whole production of cinema – as a reading of literary, journalistic, or scholarly criticism confirms. It is important, therefore, not to reduce the field of a genre to single commercial films, nor to single groups of sequels. Equally, one should not persist in ignoring the fact that the question of the generic identity of a film poses itself in a number of ways, since it interacts with other criteria of judgment, differentiation, or classification that are used to conceptualize the cinematic field. The relationships of a film to a genre or genres, then, are not always of the same kind, and this plurality owes as much to the different ways of interpreting films and attitudes influencing their reception, as to their modes of production or their textual structures.

Generically modeled films, and generically marked films

The notion of genre is not useful simply for accounting for the making, structure, and reception of genre films; it also serves to identify, in a more general way, a group of filmic productions. The term "genre" does not always have the same meaning – it can refer to films that are produced and consumed in accordance with a specific generic model (genre films), or it can fulfill a simple descriptive and classificatory function that aims to situate and identify a film (the genre of films). That is why, for example, Steve Neale proposes a distinction between *generically modeled films*, whose production and reception are conditioned by genre, and *generically marked films*, in which genre certainly provides an indispensable basis for the making and the interpretation of the film, but without entirely determining it (2000, p. 28). The latter practice can be observed, for example, in parodies or pastiches in which the notion of genre itself plays an essential role. Parody, when it is applied to a genre, picks up and underlines its semantic and syntactic traits. Its caricatured conventions still serve the development of the story, but they are informed by a comic intention, as in the case of the rotten fish that causes the crew to perish in *Airplane – Flying High* (Abrahams, Zucker, and Zucker, 1980), a famous parody of disaster movies. Generic pastiche, which is often mixed with parody, imitates and reworks the parameters of format, shot, the framing, lighting, editing, music, etc. that pertain to a genre. But in doing so, they make them obvious. Woody Allen, for example, created a pastiche of the biographical documentary film with *Zelig* in 1983, in which real archival images are alternated with fake ones, with most of the archival sequences accompanied by a commentary delivered through a voice-off, and (more rarely) on screen. Archival images also alternate with interviews attesting to the qualities of "Zelig the man," or analyzing "the case of Zelig." The pastiche is intensified at the end of the film with the insertion of fake sequences from an American B movie in which a different actor – distinct from Woody Allen who embodies Zelig in the false archival footage – re-enacts an episode in the life of this character. The pastiche of the biographical documentary therefore contains, in a film within a film, a pastiche of the fictional biographical film. Similarly, all the films that "revisit" or "pay homage" to genre films – to pick up two expressions that are recurrently used by critics – are considered to be films that are "generically marked': as, for example, neo-*noir* films, from *Chinatown* (Polanski, 1974) to *The Man Who Wasn't There* (Coen brothers, 2001).

The genre film

By referring to a "genre film" (or "generically modeled" film), one often means, as Barry Keith Grant does, "those commercial feature films which, through repetition and variation, tell familiar stories with familiar characters in familiar situations" (1995, p. xv). Genre thus serves to indicate a form of seriality, and the generic identity of a genre film depends on an industrial mode of production that is characteristic of mass culture. A genre film is constructed out of a limited repertoire of techniques that can be viewed as common property, which allows a large audience to become established that remains enthusiastic about the genre. Bearing these facts in mind, Rick Altman (1999, pp. 24–26) proposes to define Hollywood genre films in terms of seven characteristic properties (sometimes redundant) in which the reader will recognize some of the aspects of genre that we saw in chapters 2 and 3:[1]

Dual protagonists and dualistic structure
Genre films regularly oppose cultural values to anti-cultural impulses that are often embodied in a pair of protagonists. Musicals are constructed around a sexual dichotomy, on which a secondary thematic and cultural dichotomy is superimposed (as, for example, work/entertainment), and they progress across a series of twinned segments that place leading masculine and feminine roles in parallel, and in opposition, until the final resolution of the antagonisms in marriage. In horror films, the dangerous and antisocial *libido sciendi* of the mad scientist and his acolytes is countered by the traditional wisdom of society, as, for example, in *Frankenstein* (Whale, 1931), in which the experiences of the famous doctor are set against the intended marriage and family that his father the baron has planned for him. In westerns, the hero confronts a villain in a gunfight, ranchers fight against rustlers, the pioneer family is threatened by a horde of cruel Indians, etc. More generally, it is true to say that in genre films the fiction is constructed around a conflict of values and alternatively focuses the attention of the viewer on one or the other of the characters who embody them. Romantic comedies, for example, describe the (improbable) meeting of a man and a woman who are *a priori* ill-matched in terms of their social position, their character, and their view of life. Within this genre, the screwball comedies that flourished on American screens from 1933 to 1943 place their heroes in contradictory settings, and in this way frequently inscribe the amorous encounter under the double sign of a conflict of gender and of class. The female in these screwball comedies, who is either a rich heiress or a poor young woman, is always eccentric and determined, imposing her decisions and rhythm on the man, who is presented as an antihero. For example, the young, rich, capricious, and willful Ellie Andrews in *It Happened One Night* (Capra, 1934), who has fled from her gilded cage in order to marry the aviator

of her dreams despite the opposition of her father, is seduced by the frankness, insolence, and spontaneity of an unemployed journalist, Peter Warne, whom she meets on a bus during her escapade. At the completion of this amorous journey, which consists of many hectic events, she ends up by renouncing her aviator upon becoming fully aware of her love for Peter, whom she sets off to find at the end of the film. The "walls of Jericho," a blanket that the traveling companions had strung between their twin beds in the hotel (which symbolizes the gap between the two characters), can now come tumbling down.

A repetitive nature

Genre films make use of the same materials, and subject them to an identical cinematic treatment, which has the effect of establishing an iconography for the genre (for example, the wide shots in westerns showing a desert in the West eroded into deep canyons or scattered with rocky mesas, or the night clubs in which *femmes fatales* appear, poorly lit streets, offices where the slats of venetian blinds cast patterns of shadow and light of the *film noir*). They resolve the same conflicts through identical means, and thus give the impression that when the viewer has seen one of them, he has seen them all.

A cumulative economy

Repetition is not only an intertextual phenomenon in genre films, but also marks the narrative of each individual film. In the horror film that piles up scenes of fear and violent death, the monster that is believed dead reappears around the bend of the road, as in the different episodes of *Alien*, where the creature that the hero and viewers think is dead or expelled into space reveals itself after a deceptive respite. Burlesque films present gags. In the musical, spectacular numbers in which love, joy, and happiness are expressed in singing and dancing succeed one another in a cascade, etc.

Predictability

Films are made predictable by intertextual repetition and intra-textual accumulation, along with the effects of the star system

101

that associates certain actors with certain roles. The pleasure of a genre does not derive from prolonged suspense, but rather from the reaffirmation of conventions that the viewer knows and recognizes in the film. From this point of view, the suspense in genre films is a false suspense, since the end is certain.

A heavy use of intertextual references
A propensity to cite or allude to other films in the genre, the history, or the roots of the genre is evident in genre films. This explains the nostalgia that is frequently nurtured in westerns, for example, as well as in genre films made after the classical Hollywood era. This same inclination towards intertextuality is observable in the discourse of the *aficionados* of a genre, who engage fairly systematically in a form of generic self-referencing by comparing a new film in a genre to other older ones.

A symbolic usage of key images, sounds, and situations
Genre films present a symbolic usage of key images, sounds, and situations that is more important than their referential value. Whatever the realist ambitions of westerns or gangster films may be, the wagon trains that cross the prairie or the churches under construction in the former, and the excesses of the criminals in the latter, have a symbolic value that exceeds their historically referential function.

A social function
Genre films allow for cultural or hypothetical conflicts that society cannot, or does not know how to, deal with to be raised and resolved in fiction (cf. chapter 3, pp. 71–78).

Such a definition of the Hollywood genre film, which, moreover, could furnish a model for approaching the genre films of other cinemas, nevertheless places a lot of stress on different aspects of a structural repetition that is inherent in genre films. However, the "familiarity" with the stories, the characters, and the situations that makes the narrative of genre films predictable also requires the viewer to have had a preexisting experience of the genre. The genericity of a genre film thus originates as much from an "institutionalization" of reception (which causes the generic interpretation to take place prior to the textual interpretation) as from an "institutionalization" of production. That is why Bernard Perron (1995), in examining the perceptual and cognitive processes that structure the comprehension and reception of genre films, emphasizes how they privilege a top-down descending mode of perception. Taking his cue from the notion of a perceptual cycle proposed by Ulrich Neisser (1976), who organizes perception according to two interdependent modes – descending and ascending – Perron argues that the top-down descending mode directs the perceptual cycle when the audiovisual information given by a film coincides with a preexisting schema of generic knowledge. Conversely, the bottom-up ascending mode governs the cycle, while looking for an appropriate interpretive structure, when the information does not ally itself with the usual variables proposed by a generic schema because of its novelty. While the descending mode is dominant with genre films, it is still active in the perception of all sorts of films (there is no comprehension and interpretation without anticipation) and can confidently hand over the reins to the ascending mode.

This happens, for example, when a genre film renews itself through unexpected surprise effects – because the pleasure of genre film does not derive exclusively from a reaffirmation of conventions, but also from the value that the viewer accords to its variations. The more familiar one is with a genre, the more one is in a position to appreciate its mutations, its evolution, and its diversity. The same phenomenon occurs when a viewer who is poorly acquainted with a genre does not employ a preexisting generic schema, and because of this does not interpret the film as a genre film. Two films in the fantastic genre that were released only a short time apart, *The Sixth Sense* (Shyamalan, 1999) and *The Others* (Amenabar, 2001), whose events end up with a similar final revelation, illustrate both the collaboration that is possible between the descending and ascending modes in the perception of genre films, and also the constitutive domination of descending processes in the generic economy. Effectually, *The Sixth Sense*, which furthermore develops its disturbing plot in

103

accordance with a universally recognizable schema used by the fantastic genre, presents a final unexpected plot reversal that the descending mode does not permit one to anticipate (or only belatedly) – the psychiatrist helping the child who is perturbed by the vision of the dead people is himself dead, but does not know it. By way of contrast, Amenabar's film, because it exploits the same recipe (troubling events that the mother and her two children encounter are explained in the final scenes by the fact that they no longer belong, without knowing it, to the world of the living), hardly surprises the viewer who has seen *The Sixth Sense* and therefore anticipates, in a descending mode of perception, the final twist in the narrative. This motif of the denouement that retrospectively explains what has gone before, after it is known, subsequently becomes part of the genre's repertoire of conventions. Finally, it should be noted that the practice of mixing genres, often considered dominant in contemporary cinema, makes modes of perception more complex because it involves the crossing of different generic schemata and a multiplication of the possibilities for variation.

Genre and auteur

One should not overlook the relationships between genre and auteur when contrasting genre works with auteur works. This is especially dangerous if genre is associated with an industrial production that is completely governed by a principle of reiteration, and auteurship with an artistic creation that is completely freed from the constraints of the social and cinematic milieu. Indeed, this schematic distinction (based essentially on an ideological cleavage between popular culture and legitimate culture) totally ignores the fact that auteur films do not spring fully armed out of the head of an artistic Jupiter who is placed above or at a distance from modes of production and aesthetic, stylistic, cultural, cinematographic, and (more particularly) generic conventions.

An auteur film, even if it expresses the personality of a filmmaker, is often also a generically marked film. Given that artistic qualities in contemporary culture are always viewed as differential, one needs to abandon all subtle qualifications and affirm unequivocally that the personality and the uniqueness of an auteur can only be expressed and recognized as such in the specific conditions of their context – to which generic conventions belong. It is possible for films at one moment to enter into the corpus of a genre, or to function as if they were generically marked films, and then at another moment to constitute a self-contained work that is unique to the filmmaker. This occurs as a result of the critical perspective a commentator adopts in situating a film, or as a result of the mediation (generic or authorial) that the viewer activates in order to interpret them. Thus, *Senso (Livia)* (1954) is both a film by the auteur Visconti, and also a melodrama – because of its theatricality, its use of romantic music, its semantic elements (the passionate and self-destructive love of the Countess San Serpieri for a contemptible and feckless young Austrian lieutenant, for whom she sacrifices her patriotic ideal), and its syntactic elements (the string of successive betrayals, both amorous and political). Similarly, while *2001: A Space Odyssey* (1968), *Barry Lyndon* (1975), and *The Shining* (1980) are films by the auteur Kubrick, they are also, respectively, a science-fiction film, a historical film, and a horror film.

Without entering into the details of the history of the notion of auteur and of the famous "politics of auteurship,"[2] it is appropriate to recall that contrary to the practice current in the 1950s of reserving the term "film auteurs" to a fairly small number of directors who had exercised absolute control over the production and making of their films, the politics of auteurship aims to show that real artists, whose *mise en scène* expresses a distinctive filmmaker's vision, can reveal themselves even in the studio system. Institutional and generic determinants, therefore, do not systematically exclude the emergence of auteur works. This notion allowed the critics of *Cahiers*, in particular, following the example of Chabrol and Rohmer in their *Alfred Hitchcock* (1957), to demonstrate that the master of suspense, who devoted a part of his career to the adaptation of detective novels, was not an adroit journeyman, but an auteur in the full sense of the word

– a veritable "father of a metaphysical school." However, we should emphasize that the identification of certain filmmakers in a commercial or popular cinema as auteurs (Hitchcock, Hawks, Lang, but also Becker, Pagnol, Guitry, etc.) tends to underestimate the artist's inventiveness in the face of the web of constraints, influences, and conventions within which he makes his films. Indeed, to label a filmmaker as an auteur can have the effect of removing him from these determining influences (Esquenazi 2000, pp. 17–19). In analyses that place great store on the *mise en scène*, the aspects that make auteur films comparable to other films are often passed over in silence. It is assumed that genre films can only be auteur films if their generic component is evacuated through the conjuring tricks of the director's artistic and creative genius. The defense of Hitchcock as an auteur given by Alexandre Astruc well illustrates this point:

> When a man over the course of thirty years, and across fifty films, almost always tells the same story – that of a soul fighting against evil – and maintains through the length of this unique output the same style, which is created in an exemplary manner by stripping characters bare and plunging them into the abstract world of their passions, it seems difficult, to me, not to admit that for once one is in the presence of that rarest of things in what is an industry: an auteur of films. (quoted in Baecque 2001, p. 43)

It is difficult to find any allusion in this short extract to the generic markers of the detective film that characterize the films of Hitchcock, given that generic considerations have been effaced by an interest in a *mise en scène* that deals with a metaphysical conflict. The same desire to replace the empirical determinants of genre by ahistorical categories (indisputably more elevated and legitimate!) is found again in studies of John Ford that overlook the symbolic Americanness of the landscapes of his westerns in order to insist upon their sterility and tragic abstraction – through which a biblical quest is depicted (representative of all human beings marching towards the West as symbolizing the mythic promise of a lost paradise) and a philosophy of nature.[3] Auteurist readings (without any pejorative overtones) and generic readings seem mutually exclusive, and it is rare that critics genuinely try to entertain or unravel the paradox of "auteurs of genre." In addition, just as the politics of auteurship embraces Giraudoux's axiom that "there are no works, there are only authors," all the films of a filmmaker, from the moment he is recognized as an auteur, become auteur films, whatever might be their fidelity to a particular genre in other respects. One can see this in the case of several Mexican melodramas, like *Susana demonio y carne* (*The Devil and the Flesh*) (1951), which Luis Buñuel shot in Mexico at the end of the 1940s and at the very beginning of the 1950s. Finally, beyond any explicit reference to the politics of auteurship, studies of auteurs tend most often to detach the auteur film from its generic roots in the course of showing how it "surpasses," "transgresses," or "transcends" the limits of genre.

In his book devoted to *Vertigo*, Jean-Pierre Esquenazi (2001a) sets out to reconsider the notion of auteur in order to get out of this dichotomy that leads to the films of a genre auteur being viewed either as the anonymous products of a milieu endowed with codes, conventions, and an aesthetic, ideological, and economic system of production, or else as works that express the personality, style, and worldview of an artist. The auteur is a "network of interactions" between the milieu and the individual person, between the different milieux that he or she has traversed (and to which he or she has adapted), and between the different roles that make up his or her personality. These interactions have thus formed "a network of constraints, dependencies, prior judgments, institutions, chance happenings, etc., which have led to the creation of the film" (2001a, p. 220). By selecting the example of Hitchcock and *Vertigo*, Esquenazi shows how the Hitchcockian film (which is probably the only instance in which a director's name is attached to a genre) is born out of an amalgam that is derived from other genres. The genres used by Hitchcock include English crime fiction, the meaning and structure of which Hitchcock modifies by turning the mystery surrounding a "MacGuffin" into a narrative pretext. Apart from augmenting the story with a MacGuffin, he also draws upon

Hollywood comedy by adding a meeting between a man and a woman to the mystery of the detective film. This has the effect of placing the meeting under the double sign of coincidence and constraint, from which the pair must be liberated in order for their story to become a plausible love story. Finally, Hitchcock draws upon *film noir*, from which he retains the basic semantic and syntactical attributes of the *femme fatale*, but turns her into the characteristic "Hitchcockian blond" of his American films, thus feminizing this stock *noir* character as a result of his contact with the Hollywood milieu (Esquenazi 2001a, pp. 73–77). Esquenazi's analysis of *Vertigo* is neither one that is limited to the effects of Hollywood conventions in the film, nor one that conceives the film as being an individual expression of Hitchcock the artist, but one that concerns specific relations between the milieu of Hollywood (its style, its star system, its genres) and a singular personality, itself constructed from diverse influences and encounters.

The Uses of Generic Identity

The generic identity of a film is not given once and for all, nor is it inscribed into filmic texts, owing to the fact that genre is not a causal category explaining the essence of texts. Moreover, producers, critics, and commentators frequently redefine generic designations in response to new uses. This practice – abundantly illustrated in Rick Altman's book, *Film/Genre* – relates to the way genre serves as a means of classifying films. It also relates to the further fact that producers, auteurs, and viewers can choose whether or not to make reference to a generic mediation in presenting the film to the audience, or in their reception of the film.

Generic redefinitions

One of the reasons for changes of generic identity over the course of history is the fact that new generic categories emerge, causing films from the past to be retrospectively viewed in a different light. Thus, Lubitsch's *The Love Parade*, which we would describe today as a musical, was considered to be a "light opera" when it appeared in 1929, because the very notion of the "musical" had not yet been formulated, and was not in use (Altman 1999, p. 32). *The Great Train Robbery* (Porter), often presented as "the first western," was clearly not regarded as such in 1903 (the term only surfaced around 1910). Charles Musser (1984) shows how its first part makes use of the railway variant of the journey film, a very popular genre during this period, and how its second part draws on the criminal films that had been successfully imported from England several months earlier. Similarly, the analytical perspectives adopted by academic works devoted to a genre, because they simultaneously determine the corpus studied, as well as the content of the notion of genre being studied, end up by bestowing a generic identity on a film – or withholding it, as the case might be. This is the case, for example, with "easterns" (such as the different versions of *The Last of the Mohicans*), sometimes integrated into the corpus of westerns by studies that privilege the syntactical element in their understanding of genre (the frontier, the opposition between wilderness/civilization), and at other times excluded from the western and given the label of "adventure films" by those who define the western in terms of its historical and geographical referents.

Equally, films can change their generic denominations in the course of passing from one culture into another, the classificatory categories into which each culture assigns film being far from strictly identical – both in popular discourse and also in that of scholars. For a long time, the names of genres have been much more numerous and varied in the United States, for example, than in France. This flourishing of genres in America can partly be attributed to the great number of films produced by the national film industry, prompting the professional press to invent specific labels for the purpose of more precisely identifying particular films among the general mass of those produced. In addition, this multiplicity of appellations attests to the continuous development of cycles in American cinema for the sake of exploiting successful formulas (cf. chapter 5, pp. 150–153). Also, certain films, defined either wholly or partially by an American term that has no equivalent in France, must of necessity change their generic title in crossing the Atlantic. *Lethal Weapon* (Donner, 1987) is located in the generic tradition of the buddy film, but it could only be received in France as a comedy, an action film, or an action comedy. Similarly, it is unlikely that any French viewer would think of describing as "buddy films" Francis Veber's trilogy, *La Chèvre* (*The Goat*) (1981), *Les Compères* (*ComDads*) (1983), and *Les Fugitifs* (The Fugitives) (1986) – three films that were subsequently remade by Hollywood in fairly faithful adaptations as *Pure Luck* (Tass, 1991), *Fathers' Day* (Reitman, 1997), and *The Three Fugitives* (Veber, 1989). Although these three French films depended on the comic pairing of Pierre Richard and Gérard Depardieu, and on the contrast between the two actors/characters – just as in their Hollywood remakes – they are solely identified in France as "comedies," because the category "buddy film" (or, in French, *film de copains*) is totally absent from French vocabulary. Big caper films, which depict extraordinary "heists" undertaken by a team of professionals reunited for the purpose, such as *Du Rififi chez les hommes* (*Rififi*) (Dassin, 1954) or *Ocean's Eleven* (Soderbergh, 2001), merge into a larger generic category in France – that of the gangster movie, or the police film.

It also happens that producers change the generic identity of films in their catalogues for commercial reasons. Rick Altman explains how Universal released *Creature From the Black Lagoon* (Arnold) in 1954 under the label of "science-fiction," although the aquatic creature is only a monster that is a human/fish hybrid. Horror films, which had included films with monsters up until then, were relegated to the B series in the 1950s, and Universal, a company too small at that time to promote a film without referring it to a generic category, aimed at profiting from the vogue for science-fiction films. Furthermore, the press kits sent to theater proprietors when *Creature From the Black Lagoon* was released presented the film as a new story about creatures out of science-fiction, in the tradition of *The Phantom of the Opera* (Lubin, 1943), *The Hunchback of Notre Dame* (Dieterle, 1939), *Frankenstein*

(Whale, 1931), *Dracula* (Browning, 1931), *The Mummy* (Freund, 1932), *The Wolf Man* (Waggner, 1941), and *The Invisible Man* (Whale, 1933), etc. (Altman 1999, pp. 28–29). The creatures of the horror movie, many of which owe nothing to science in the strict sense, thus began to leave the horror film, which had waned in popularity during the 1950s, to occupy the more marketable territory of the science-fiction film. We should also observe that the boundaries between the horror film (an Anglo-Saxon label currently overtaking the term "fantastic" in France, which is reserved more for literature than cinema) and the science-fiction movie became much more fluid from this time onwards.

Two examples: film noir *and the woman's film*

Journalistic and scholarly critics are not always content with discussing genres and defining new generic descriptors within the fairly narrow circle of cinephiles, students of cinema, and university academics. The learned and well-reasoned generic categories that they propose certainly have practical value in the community of their readers, but it sometimes happens that their descriptors emerge out of this closed sphere to become the object of a much larger consensus, as is demonstrated by the example of *film noir*. This term appeared for the first time in an article by Nino Frank (1946) published in *L'Écran français* during the summer of 1946, which was devoted to a discussion of *The Maltese Falcon* (Huston, 1941), *Double Indemnity* (Wilder, 1944), *Laura* (Preminger, 1944), and *Murder My Sweet* (Dmytryk, 1944). Frank saw in these films the expression of a new tendency in the Hollywood crime film, mirrored also in the writings of Dashiell Hammett and Raymond Chandler in American detective fiction. The word *noir* was picked up three months later by Jean-Pierre Chartier in *La Revue du cinéma*, but this time for the express purpose of describing films (Frank was proposing to designate them as "crime adventures"). His article, entitled "Les Américains aussi font des films '*noirs*'," comprised an analysis devoted to three films: *Double Indemnity*, *Murder My Sweet*, and *The Lost Weekend*

111

(Wilder, 1945). Like Frank, Chartier underlined the importance of sexual attraction in the plots of these films, notes the use of a first person narrative, and identifies their somber and despairing atmosphere (despite the happy ending of *The Lost Weekend*) to justify the descriptor "*noir*" (placed in quotation marks in the title). In addition, as the title suggests, this designation is comparative:

> We have been speaking of a French school of *films noirs*, but *Le Quai des brumes* (*Port of Shadows*) or *L'Hôtel du Nord* at least had overtones of rebelliousness, love was present in them like the mirage of a better world, an implicit social reclamation opened the door to hope and, even though the characters in them may have been despairing, they elicited our pity or empathy. There is nothing like that here – these are monsters, criminals, or ill people whom nothing can excuse, and who act as if they do so solely because of the predestined evil that resides in them. (Chartier 1946, p. 70)

Here, as in all writings from this period on films, it is a comparison with poetic realism that produces the descriptor "*noir*."[4] This term was then regularly adopted until it lost its quotation marks – as is illustrated, for example, by Henri-François Rey's article published in 1948, "Démonstration par l'absurde: les *films noirs*," which again emphasized the perturbed atmosphere and the very somber picture that marked contemporary American films such as *Double Indemnity*, *The Lost Weekend*, *The Woman in the Window* (Lang, 1944), and *Scarlet Street* (Lang, 1945) – a remake of Renoir's *La Chienne* (*The Bitch*) (1931). The almost simultaneous release of these films on French screens after the war, following an absence of American films for more than four years, undoubtedly created the effect of a corpus that allowed critics to perceive more clearly a unity of tone and treatment, and, bit by bit, to make a genre out of this group of films. Thus, *film noir* as a generic category gradually replaced the appellations under which the films had been released in France. In addition, even though the readings initiated by Frank or Chartier pulled these films towards the crime detective genre, not all of them had originally been assigned to the police genre. *Double Indemnity* had been described as a "criminal melodrama," and in France *The Woman in the Window* had at first been identified by Jacques Bourgeois (1946) as a bourgeois police tragedy. The establishment of the new genre was confirmed in 1955 by the appearance of the book by Raymond Borde and Étienne Chaumeton, *Panorama du film noir*, and after that the adjective *noir* ceased in the world of French cinema during the 1930s to refer exclusively to the specific mood found in American detective movies. In the preface, Marcel Duhamel links the term *film noir* to the collection of detective novels published by Gallimard from 1945 entitled the *Série noire*, in which were included, in particular, American authors whose novels had been adapted in *films noirs*. Since that date, the expression *film noir* has been imposed on both sides of the Atlantic as a generic category – without being translated into the term "dark movie." Its definition has been elaborated and discussed (notably at the narrative and visual levels), and numerous Anglophone studies, inspired by gender studies, have placed a particular emphasis on the figure of the *femme fatale* and the crisis of masculinity expressed in this genre.[5]

Neither the use of existing generic categories nor the definition of new genres are neutral operations: discourses about genres and about films are ideologically situated discourses. The generic identities attributed to a film, therefore, also reflect particular points of view on cinema and its history that generic variations allow to be invoked. This is illustrated, for example, by the way that the notion of a "woman's film" has been taken up, defined, and rehabilitated by feminists since the 1970s.[6] Women's films are films that place one of the female characters at the center of the fiction, and address a feminine audience. This specification of films and genres according to gender, almost non-existent in French cinema, was widely practiced in the context of Hollywood, in which many genres (up until the 1960s at least) were sexually marked. Publicity produced by the studios attests to this, even though one cannot properly speak of a conscious, rationally organized system for segmenting audiences. Adventure and action movies, gangster films, westerns, and war films are addressed to male viewers; dramas, melodramas, romantic comedies, and musicals are addressed to female viewers; historical films, burlesque comedies, and journey films constitute *a tertium quid* where children and older people, especially, can be found. The term "woman's film," without being identified with one particular genre, appears in the press from the 1910s to describe series and serials celebrating the image of a New Woman, modern and active, who contrasts with the Victorian woman (Neale 2000, p. 191).

The expressions that designate a film as a work aimed at women were heavily loaded with pejorative overtones during the 1930s, 1940s, and 1950s (often being referred to as "weepies," dramas that induce tears "in the way women like"). Feminist critics, in picking up the term, have emptied it of all pejorative connotations, and have extended its field of application well beyond its original usage (which referred to a melodrama that had a female star in the top billing). For them, "A woman's film is a movie that places at the center of its universe a female who is trying to deal with emotional, social, and psychological problems that are specifically related to the fact that she is a woman" (Basinger 1993, p. 20). Films that would be traditionally identified with other genres thus enter into the woman's film alongside melodramas – with characters ranging from mothers who sacrifice themselves, like *Stella Dallas* (Vidor, 1937) to fallen women, like *Blonde Venus* (Sternberg, 1932). The woman's film crosses the path of the western with *Johnny Guitar* (Ray, 1954), of the biopic with *Madame Curie* (LeRoy, 1943), of the gothic film with *Dragonwyck* (Mankiewicz, 1946), and of the road movie with *Thelma and Louise* (Scott, 1991). Because of this, the woman's film is sometimes viewed as a variant of melodrama, a kind of sub-genre (which is explained by the particular attention paid to this genre by feminist critics in the 1980s); sometimes perceived as a tendency that crosses a range of genres (since it is not defined by specific semantic and syntactic traits); sometimes presented as a cinematographic genre. In this last instance, the woman's film incorporates films previously related to other genres into a new shared generic identity.

Genre, series, auteur: categories of interpretation

As the example of the woman's film shows, the generic identity of a film is also a matter of interpretation. Different genres simultaneously reveal and propose interpretive perspectives through which films are both received and understood. But given that genre is not the only category that can be used for interpretation, critics, like viewers, can choose whether or not they will make use of generic mediation to understand a film. That explains, in particular, how a film can end up receiving several different ascriptions concurrently, depending on the nature of the viewers' responses: a generic identity, or an authorial identity, or an identity as one film within a series, or an identity based on cinematographic techniques, etc. Thus, as Jean-Pierre Esquenazi (2001b) shows through an analysis of the reception of *Alphaville, a Strange Adventure of Lemmy Caution* (1962), this film has been understood as a film by Godard, as an allegorical film, or as a science-fiction film. As a result, one critic can say that he hates all the films by Jean-Luc Godard (viewed from the perspective of authorial mediation), while at the same time declaring that he loves *Alphaville*, which remains faithful to the rules of science-fiction. Conversely, the identity given to *Alphaville* as a film in a series – its subtitle reads "a Strange Adventure of Lemmy Caution" (a hero who recurrently appears in popular French cinema in the 1950s, acted by Eddie Constantine) – generally misleads viewers. Even though the character is played by the same actor, the Lemmy Caution of *Alphaville* does not engage in adventures that are typical of the detective and secret agent as portrayed in the films of Bernard Borderie: *La Môme vert-de-gris* (*Poison Ivy*) (1953), *Les Femmes s'en balancent* (*Dames Don't Care*) (1954), or *Lemmy pour les dames* (*Ladies' Man*) (1961). The generic divide between *Alphaville* and these gangster movies is too great for the Lemmy Caution series to serve as a good mediation. In the other direction, generic identity can be obscured behind a series identity, frequently used by Hollywood studios to label a film for the sake of exploiting the enthusiasm that viewers have demonstrated for particular productions. The names alone of James Bond, Rambo, or Rocky are sufficient to provide their fans with an interpretive framework that transcends any mention of genre, just as with the opening words in the titles of the English comic series of *Carry on* . . . films in the 1950s and 1960s.[7] Similarly, with cult films (which function as a community ritual in and through which a group finds and defines itself), the social function of the cult-object, even if it owes its status to grounding in a genre, overtakes the social function of the genre. *The Rocky Horror Picture Show* (Sharman, 1975), seen in video by an ordinary viewer, is a musical, a horror film, or the parody of a horror film; viewed in the cinema, in the context of extremely ritualized conditions of projection, it assumes its identity not from the textual determinants of the film itself, but from the festive *mise en scène* involved in its enunciation.

The Mixing of Genres: Pluri-generic Attributes

It is not only the contents and structures of a filmic text that give it a generic identity, but also interpretive contexts, partly determined by institutions (producers, critics), and partly produced by cinematic viewing habits. In other words, the reception of a film also determines its generic identity and the importance of this identity in the interpretive process relating to the film. A consideration of the divergent practices and usages surrounding genres helps to clarify a phenomenon that disconcerts all those who are obsessionally fixated on taxonomy (including many cinephiles): the mixing of genres.

The myth of the pure genre

The mixing of genres, often alluded to in the post-modern era, is a longstanding phenomenon that is much more general. It even appears that "pure" genre films may be more rare than "mixed" genre films – a difficulty encountered by anyone who has ever raised the question of what genre to attribute to a film, or of how to define the corpus of a specific genre. That is why it is more interesting to analyze the causes and particular conditions of various states of hybridity, than to try and augment the defining criteria of a genre in order to make simple an object that is not simple.

One of the merits of the semantic-syntactic model for analyzing genres (cf. chapter 2, pp. 55–62) is its ability to account for the mixing of genres. Rick Altman, for instance, shows that the Hollywood musical, while it exploits a set of themes, musical forms, dances, and settings that are traditional in, or emblematic of, America, is able to combine with the western, for example, without losing the stability of its formula. It borrows semantic elements from the western that are then inserted into its own syntax. This tendency to mix genres increased with World War II, which saw the production of musicals in which folklore themes exalted patriotic sentiment. The usual syntax of a genre, under the effect of the insertion of this new material, becomes slightly modified: singing and dancing remain the joyous expression of an amorous encounter, but the music and the formation of a couple, which the films align in order to create a spectacle, are here associated with the feeling of belonging to the same community. The union of the protagonists illustrates the bond that unites the groups from which each of them has come, confirming their ties to the land in which they live. This blending of an amorous union and the celebration of a community, achieved through music, is characteristic of a sub-genre that Altman baptizes the "folklore-comedy." He sees its boundaries as extending well beyond a mere mixing of the musical with the western, reflected, for example, in a more "natural" transition from realist moments to spectacular moments – the singing and dancing are no longer the exclusive domain of professionals, but the voice of a community that finds the wellsprings of musical expression in its relationship with nature and in its daily activities. A local song passes from one mouth to another in the opening of *Meet Me in St. Louis* (Minnelli, 1944), and the farm work in Oregon of *Seven Brides for Seven Brothers* (Donen, 1954) or the action of grooming horses in *Riding High* (Capra, 1950) inherently contain the germs of the rhythm and movements of dance. Finally, we should recall that western songs are already present in the "non-musical" western, from songs in the credits to saloon songs. Marilyn Monroe, for instance, sings the title song of *River of No Return* (Preminger, 1954) at the end of the film. The ubiquitousness of western songs undoubtedly facilitated the hybridization of the western with the musical, unifying the formulas of the two genres involved.

Five complementary explanations can be advanced to account for the practice of mingling genres in film.

One of the reasons, to which we will return at greater length in the next chapter, is linked to the history and genesis of genres. Genres are always categories that are created *a posteriori* to take account of resemblances between a group of films, and the origin of the genre (i.e., that which precedes awareness and recognition of it) consists of the crossing of preexisting forms and their derivatives, until a formula crystallizes with a semantic-syntactic equilibrium that is often identified as the "nucleus of the genre." It is self-evident that this metaphor, which annuls any diachronic perspective, makes a center out of the stable formula of a genre; in departing from it, films become more and more distant cousins, located in a circle that inevitably leads them back into an intersection with others. We should stress that such a generic nucleus, which often allows a genre to be defined, is only a momentary snapshot of the genre and that this moment in no way constitutes an origin for the genre, but is rather a stereotypical reduction of it.

To that can be added heterogeneity as a second factor – that is, the coexistence of several generic categories, on which we have already insisted several times in the course of defining generic determinants as labeling games, interpretive categories, or mediations. The idea of a generic mixture is intrinsically tied to all types of generic logic that depend upon a classificatory system applied, after the fact, to created objects. The intellectual project relating to genres, which aims to identify self-contained groupings of films, in fact produces intersections, because films cannot be a mechanical reiteration of categories that are not their causes. That is why genres that are defined according to a single characteristic, such as their tone (for comedy) or their semantic constitution (as in the case of science-fiction), lend themselves particularly well to hybridization. In addition, the idea of a mixing of genres arises out of the use of designations that have been formulated at different times, or from different ideological or analytical perspectives. Thus, rather than saying that *Mildred Pierce* (Curtiz, 1945) is in certain respects a melodrama, in certain respects a *film noir*, in certain respects a woman's film, and in certain respects a mixture of all three, it is more appropriate to say that it is *viewed as being* a melodrama, a *film noir*, or a woman's film. In other words, even though the mixing of genres can be detected in filmic texts, it is also an effect of interpretation, and of the variability of interpretation.

Genres are not, in the actual reality of films, impermeable categories. Influences and interactions occur between films "of different genres." Thus, the musicals produced by RKO from 1933 to 1938, starring the duo of Ginger Rogers and Fred Astaire, embody certain relations with the contemporaneous screwball comedies of that time. Just as Ginger and Fred provoked one another in ironic duets, and quarreled until the end of the movie which, finally (!) celebrated their erotic union, the couple of Claudette Colbert and Clark Gable in *It Happened One Night* (Capra, 1934), or Katharine Hepburn and Cary Grant in *Holiday* (Cukor, 1938), or in *The Philadelphia Story* (Cukor, 1940), fought and provoked each other through the whole length of the comedy in order to disguise their manifest attraction. The two genres each displace sexual energy into rhythmically paced arguments and trenchant dialogues in a comparable manner. Sex, which is the preoccupation of both musicals and screwball comedy, resurfaces, in response to the tightening of censorship imposed by the Hays code, in a polemical form; the attraction between the protagonists grows commensurately to the conflict between them (Sarris 1978).

A change of tone in the course of a film can also tip the story from one genre into another. *An Affair to Remember* (McCarey,

1957) begins like a sentimental comedy in which erotic union and sexual consummation are deferred in a spirit and tone that is fairly similar to that found in screwball comedies, until the visit of Nickie's very aged grandmother throws a melodramatic veil over the story, which intensifies itself to the point of occluding any comic dimension with the tragic accident of Terry. Terry and Nickie had decided, at the end of the cruise during which they had met, to put the sincerity and solidity of their love to the test by not seeing each other for several months. They were supposed to meet one another, if their feelings had not changed, at the top of the Empire State Building. The big day arrives, their feelings have not changed, but the young woman is knocked over at the foot of the skyscraper. Nickie is unaware of the real reason for her absence at the rendezvous and thinks that she has changed her mind. Terry, who has survived the accident, remains alone and paralyzed . . . until the final happy ending. The union of the leading couple is at first, then, delayed by the conventions of the romantic or screwball comedy, and then by the devices of melodrama.

The fourth reason is an economic one. A single genre, by allowing the film to be pigeon-holed, can potentially restrict its potential audience. The crossing of several plots and several genres can have the effect of attracting a greater number of viewers. That is what happens, for example, with the action comedies that have become especially numerous since the middle of the 1980s, in which an actor like Arnold Schwarzenegger, originally known for his performances as a body-builder, has enjoyed a second career with *Kindergarten Cop* (Reitman, 1990) or *True Lies* (Cameron, 1994), a remake of Claude Zidi's film, *La Totale!* (*The Jackpot!*) (1991). The economic strategy for mixing genres can equally be paired with an attempt to fuse contradictory ideologies within the same film. This is particularly evident in the Hollywood films of the late 1970s that Robin Wood (1986) calls "incoherent texts," such as *Taxi Driver* (Scorsese, 1976), or *Looking for Mr. Goodbar* (Brooks, 1977). *Taxi Driver*, which was the product of a liberal director, Scorsese, and a scriptwriter who was openly conservative, Paul Schrader, was interpreted by the American middle classes as a "horror film," in which Travis, a Vietnam veteran, violently kills in cold blood a stickup man and some hippy pimps who did not deserve such an extreme punishment, while the white working-class audience viewed the film as an "urban western." They saw Travis as an avenging hero who justly plucks the young prostitute away from her pimps, in the same way that Ethan in *The Searchers* (Ford, 1956), played by John Wayne, organizes the massacre of Scar's tribe to avenge the murder of his brother's family and to bring his niece, Debbie (Natalie Wood), who had been kidnapped by the Indians, back home after this slaughter. As Noël Burch observes, the fusion of genres in *Taxi Driver* allows the film to reach two audiences that are mutually exclusive, by accomplishing a kind of "grand ideological synthesis." The double meaning reflects a vast cultural conflict: "with working-class groups of those who are white, masculine, chauvinist, racist, security-minded, identifying with the character played by De Niro, versus trendy middle-class groups who hang on every word of the dull Betty, the volunteer employee of a Democratic candidate, who makes a brief appearance in the film in order to withdraw immediately in disgust, before briefly returning at the end, vaguely fascinated nonetheless" (Burch 2000, p. 103). Similarly, of more recent date, *Thelma and Louise* (Scott, 1991), a film that divided feminist critics just as *Alien* (1979) by the same director had done, can be seen as a road movie or as a buddy film, in which a couple of male friends become a couple of female friends. While it can be interpreted as an extension of traditionally masculine genres, but with female heroines, it also displays elements of the woman's film by examining from a feminine point of view issues relating to sexual violence and the conflict between family life and the joys of an adventure lived by two friends outside the home. This mixing of genres is largely responsible for the ambiguity of the film: is the journey of the two women – which begins as a weekend of freedom, followed, after the attempted rape of Thelma and the murder of her assailant, by a flight that ends in aimless wandering – a story that denounces sexism and violence against women? Or, to the contrary, by showing women who become

121

independent and take possession of masculine instruments of power (a gun stolen from a soldier), does the film embody a male fantasy of the avenging female who is finally punished, since the last image of the film shows the suicide of the two friends, who launch themselves into the void with their vehicle rather than surrender?[8]

Finally, the mutation of cultural modes of creation under the influence of post-modernity is frequently advanced as an explanation of the prevalence of composite generic forms in the contemporary era.

Post-modern augmentation of genre-mixing

Within a post-modernist perspective, it is often argued that contemporary cinema registers and translates a more general taste for hybridization, born out of the loss of determinate indices, universal references (or universalizable), and metanarratives. It is assumed that each film recombines, in its own way, and not without a certain inclination towards reflexivity, semantic and syntactic elements from different genres. In this view, the social function of genres is, then, essentially a "pseudo-memorial" function, through which a genre does not so much mediate actual or symbolic conflicts, as activate an awareness, strongly marked by intertextuality, of codes, conventions, and significations in genre films from the past (Altman 1999, pp. 188–192). The films of Tim Burton, the Coen brothers, or Tarantino are representative of this tendency, just like the *Blade Runner* (1982) of Ridley Scott which takes up the codes of the detective film (more precisely the thriller) and transposes them into a futuristic science-fiction world and setting, while multiplying the allusions to *film noir*. Thus, at the beginning of the film, Deckard makes Rachel undertake the test that allows one to identify the "replicants" of humans. The young woman appears, with a fatal and cold beauty, dressed in a suit cut in the style of the 1940s, smokes a cigarette during the experience in a manner recalling the female characters of *film noir*, and the lighting of the scene, which had been brightly lit at the beginning of the sequence, is dimmed into shadow at Deckard's order (the test apparently being easier to conduct in semi-darkness). Awareness of the genre is transformed into a memory of the genre, and the viewer's investment in the film oscillates between first and second degree. This augmentation of genre-mixing in New Hollywood, as in the large national productions that rival the American blockbusters, also has an economic motive (to attract varied audiences) and is partly explained by a constant refinement since the 1960s of the instruments for measuring and evaluating the different categories of audience. Confronted by an audience that is segmented into groups that are smaller and more numerous (divided by age, sex, ethnicity, social milieu, level of education, type of leisure pursuits, sexual orientation, etc.), producers and marketing managers have proposed mixed formulas that provide for the interests of each group. In France, the action comedies produced by Luc Besson illustrate this phenomenon well. *Taxi* (1997), for example, is a film directed by Gérard Pirès – who became well known for comedies he made during the 1970s, *Fantasia chez les Ploucs* (*Fantasia among the Squares*) (1970), *Elle court, elle court la banlieue* (*The Suburbs are Everywhere*) (1973) – and written by Luc Besson, who also produced the movie. It is therefore the work of two men who represent two different periods of the cinema, and two different genres: the French sociological comedy and the American action film. This duo is mirrored in the film by another duo, the two main characters who form a strongly contrasting couple who complement one another. Emilien is a rather introverted police inspector, who has not learnt how to drive, who is shy with girls, under the thumb of his mother who gives him prepackaged meals for the week; Daniel is a former pizza delivery man who has become a taxi-driver, does not like representatives of order, is always committing traffic offences, is an extrovert, a peerless driver, has a girlfriend, and is detached from any familial connections. One of them lives in the old city, the other in a kind of warehouse in the suburbs; the one does not succeed in seducing his colleague and making her his lover, the other has a lover from the beginning of the movie,

123

but unforeseen events continually interrupt their lovemaking after the preliminaries. His Arab identity is both apparent (because of his interpreter, Samy Naceri, and several remarks made by the racist commissaire) and also erased – since he calls himself Daniel. These two characters form a team, the one in order to avoid a suspension of his license, the other to have a good chauffeur at his disposal, with the aim of breaking up the German Mercedes gang. The film does not abstain from making racist allusions to the Germans (viewed as the "schleus,"[9] descendants of the invaders of 1940, by the commissaire, whose actions and remarks make for a wicked caricature of the French middle class). The film therefore exploits a traditional comic recipe from French comedy: the pair of heroes who are contrasted psychologically and sociologically, as in *La Chèvre* (*The Goat*) (Veber, 1981) or *Les Visiteurs* (*The Visitors*) (Poiré, 1992). But it is also an action film, since car chases, scenes with pile-ups, and armed confrontations between police and gangsters embellish the whole film. This, then, allies dialogues and a plot borrowed from comedy with a "visual punch" derived from spectacular scenes filmed in a way that is strongly reinforced by subjective camera movements, as is typical of contemporary neo-Hollywood action films. Because of this, the mixing of the two genres establishes a double mediation. The viewer can interpret the film as a comic film or an action film. In this form of representation, the comic pair can be related to at least three genres that each addresses a different audience. They include:

- A comic pair from the comedy of manners, allowing a confrontation between social and psychological types. The presence in the film of a stereotyped image of Marseille, in which a working-class Marseille crossed with the North is placed in contrast with middle-class Marseille and the petit bourgeois of the South, and in which grandfathers with a strong accent read the paper, and Notre Dame de la Garde appears several times as an authentic icon, assures this national generic anchoring, and therefore authorizes a reading of the film as an updated *pagnolade*.[10]

- A comic pair from French comic action films, given that since the 1960s comedies like *L'Homme de Rio* (*That Man From Rio*) (de Broca, 1963) or the *Fantomas* films (1964, 1965, and 1966) had imported elements from the American action film.

- A comic pair characteristic of the neo-Hollywood action comedies, a genre developed in the 1980s by American cinema following *Die Hard* (McTiernan, 1988), starring actors like Bruce Willis or Arnold Schwarzenegger in the second part of his career (*Terminator II, True Lies*). This generic marking corresponds to another face of Marseille in the film, translated into another culture and stripped of all its regionalism: the leading and supporting characters do not have accents, which are reserved for the extras, and the landscape transforms itself (during nearly half of the film) into motorway interchanges, emblematic of a universal modernity, where speeding vehicles confront one another.

In addition, changes in the "formation" of filmmakers – who might have passed through film schools, or have been exposed to critical perspectives – have given them a familiarity with the historical forms of cinema genres which is translated into citations of, homages to, or the hijacking of genres. *Le Pacte des Loups* (*Brotherhood of the Wolf*) (Gans, 2001) is an extreme example of the desire to reach different communities of viewers in a superproduction, and to display, through maximizing the possibilities for hybridization, Gans's own awareness of cinematic culture – he was a film critic before becoming a filmmaker. The film is in the fantastic genre, in the tradition of the monster film of the 1930s, because of the attacks and nature of the Beast of Gévaudan. It is also a gore film because the attacks of the Beast, right from the early sequences, give way to very bloody sequences that show violence, wounds, and death. It is also a historical film that recreates the Lozère, a remote region in the Massif Central, in the time of the nobles and peasants at the end of the eighteenth century and imitates, in the interior scenes, the lighting of *Barry Lyndon* (Kubrick, 1975). It also elects to give a political explanation for the misdeeds of the Beast of Gévaudan, a creature manipulated by particularly reactionary nobles for the sake of creating a climate of terror aimed at justifying a takeover of the kingdom, and to prevent any possibility of a liberal evolution of the monarchy. Kung-fu scenes which, curiously, are enacted by an Indian – a friend of the hero who has returned with him from America – complete the ornamenting of the story. They refer less to the martial arts films of Asian cinema than to the integration of this combat genre into contemporary Hollywood cinema. *Le Pacte des Loups* exploits, then, the devices and the technical arsenal of American blockbusters and displaces neo-Hollywood genres into a frame of reference that is simultaneously national, geographical (the Massif Central), historical, and cultural (the French Revolution), by making the Beast the instrument of a conspiracy. This action reattaches the film still more strongly to a place in the national memory associated with the first revolutionary troubles, which the story has described in a flashback by a narrator who has witnessed the events. One can therefore consider *Le Pacte des Loups* as a grafting of a form and of neo-Hollywood genres onto a national topic and a genre (the costume film) that strongly express French national identity.

Parody and pastiche

Parody and pastiche are fairly specific agents of the mixing of genres. These two practices construct cinematic stories by imitating the characteristics of earlier films with a comic or burlesque intention. The parodic film presupposes, then, both in its conception and in its reception, an awareness and knowledge of the object being parodied. That is why all identifiable narrative structures, all codified objects, like successful films, mythic themes, recurring heroes, or genres, form the raw material of parody and pastiche. In the case of genre, parody works through repetition and manipulation of generic conventions, and it is rare that a genre has not had its films parodied. Let us point, for example, to *Airplane – Flying High* for the disaster film, *Mars Attacks!* (Burton, 1996) or *Galaxy Quest* (Parisot, 1999) for science-fiction,

Les Barbouzes (*The Great Spy Chase*) (Lautner, 1964) for the spy film, *Dance of the Vampires* (Polanski, 1967) or *Frankenstein Junior* (Brooks, 1974) for the horror film, *O.K. Nerone* (*O.K. Nero*) (Soldati, 1952) for the toga film, *L'Étroit Mousquetaire* (*The Three Must-Get-Theres*) (Linder, 1922) or *Monty Python and the Holy Grail* (Gilliam, 1974) for the historical adventure film, *Lo chiavamano Trinita* (*My Name is Trinity*) (Clucher/Enzo Barboni, 1970) and its sequels for the western, *Dead Men Don't Wear Plaid* (Reiner, 1982) for the *film noir*, etc. Parodies and pastiches, when they are clearly recognized as such by the viewer, offer a second-degree reading of a genre: the spectator can thus enjoy both the pleasure of the genre and the specific pleasure of the parodic enunciation of it. It is easy to understand, then, why television program guides that are aimed at a sophisticated and knowledgeable audience – such as *Télérama* – describe many genre films as parodic. Applying a cultural "logic of differentiation," they bypass ordinary generic labels, choosing instead to identify films in terms of fanciful genres (that is, ones that have no currency in popular usage). The more general meaning given by these magazines to the term "parody" extends this practice to any conscious reuse of narrative schemata, even though the work may lack a specific comic intention. The imputation of a parodic intention, therefore, gives a kind of legitimacy to the genre films under discussion by pointing to the filmmaker, and by inviting the viewer to adopt a distanced, ironic perspective. Without debating here whether or not the terms are well founded, we will simply note that the terms "pastiche" or "parody" tend to be mentioned when a genre film has been produced at the end, or after the end, of a period that has witnessed a flourishing of the genre.

If parody and pastiche are to be invoked in terms of their strict meaning, it is only possible to view a parodic film as having a mixed generic identity, given that it transposes the semantic and syntactic traits of another genre into a comic register. Is it possible to view parody as a separate genre in its own right? It seems to me that the answer to this question differs, depending upon whether one answers it in a theoretical manner, or in a historical fashion. From a theoretical point of view, the practice of parody, which one can discern in the history of both cinematic genres and also those relating to other modes of expression, is a mode of writing, a mode of enunciation, and also a mode of reading. This explains, in particular, why certain viewers, like the *Télérama* critics of whom we spoke earlier, are able to interpret as parodies films that were not conceived as such. Parody is therefore not able to constitute a genre, since it operates on the same level as genre. Parody and pastiche compete with, and disturb, the generic identity of films. Seen in a historical perspective, the equivalence of parody to a genre is more debatable. If the current tendency to engage in parody (which can also be observed during the past twenty years of cinematic production) and the inclination by viewers to interpret films as parodic are confirmed, it is foreseeable that even if a grand parodic genre does not eventuate, at the very least new generic designations might be formed in which the parodic dimension would have a part to play – along the lines, for example, of the LaughingScreaming movies that William Paul (1994) identifies in American cinema since the 1980s. The films involved are those in which carnivalesque and festive spectacle combine horror with laughter, and anxiety with comic pleasure, as in the series of *Freddy* or *Scream* (Craven, 1997) movies, and those that followed them. More generally, Paul notes a current tendency in Hollywood cinema to infuse a touch of terror, even if very fleetingly, into comic films, or to give a comic touch to the horror film.

At the end of this chapter, it would seem indispensable to substitute a dynamic conception of genre for essentialist definitions. The generic characteristics of a film, like generic appellations, far from constituting fixed and immutable points of reference, are the effects of constant (re)compositions and (re)interpretations to which producers, critics, and spectators contribute. The generic identity of a film is not given to it once and for all, and is not enclosed within the text of a film. The preexisting agreement that allows a genre and a genre film to be recognized is an unstable balance, a crossroads where cinema practices, ideological perspectives, and various interpretive approaches intersect and encounter one another. To examine the relation between films and genres is, therefore, not so much a matter of determining what film(s) one is going to place in which generic box(es), as of reflecting, first, on who is doing the putting, why, and in what context, and, second, on the multiple historical and sociocultural cinematic interactions in which films and genres are created, exist, and are received. Instead of a simple generic denomination – one that uses dictionaries and programs for purposes of classification – it is better to adopt a pluralist conception, and to speak of multiple generic identities.

Notes

1 These pages refine and amend the account of the characteristics of genre films that Altman had proposed a dozen years earlier in *The American Film Musical* (1989), Bloomington, Indiana University Press, pp. 330–334.

2 See, for example, Antoine de Baecque (1991) *Les Cahiers du cinéma, Histoire d'une revue I and II*, Paris, Éditions des Cahiers du cinéma, as well as his anthology of writings published in *Les Cahiers du cinema* from 1954 to 1997: *Politique des auteurs* (2001), Paris, Éditions des Cahiers du cinéma.

3 See, for example, the chapter devoted to Ford's landscapes in the book by Jacques Mauduy and Gérard Henriet (1989) *Géographies du western. Une nation en marche*, Paris, Nathan.

4 On European influences, particularly French ones, on the genesis of *film noir*, see J. Morgan and D. Andrew (Eds.) (1996), *Iris*, 21, "European Precursors of Film Noir/Précurseurs européens du film noir."

5 See, for example, *Women in Film noir* (1978), E. Ann Kaplan (Ed.), London, BFI; Frank Krutnick (1991) *In a Lonely Street: Film Noir, Genre, Masculinity*, London, Routledge; and the texts compiled and translated by Noël Burch (1993) in *Revoir Hollywood. La nouvelle critique anglo-américaine*, Paris, Nathan, pp. 153–219.

6 Rick Altman (1999, p. 72) dates the revitalization of the woman's film from the appearance of the book by Molly Haskell (1974), *From Reverence to Rape: The Treatment of Women in the Movies*, Chicago, University of Chicago Press.

7 For European film series in the 1950s (English *Carry On . . .* movies, Italian melodramas, and German *Heimatfilme*), see Pierre Sorlin (2000)

"Ce qu'était un film populaire dans l'Europe des années 50." In Jean-Pierre Bertin-Maghit (Ed.) *Les Cinémas européens des années cinquante*, Paris, AFRHC, pp. 19–46.

8 For a detailed analysis of the ambiguities of action films (a genre that is traditionally masculine) that place the female characters at the center of the film, see Yvonne Tasker (1993), "Criminelles: *Thelma et Louise* et autres délinquantes." In Ginette Vincendeau and Bérénice Reynaud (Eds.) *CinémAction*, 67, pp. 92–95.

9 This is a traditional, extremely pejorative slang term used since World War I to stigmatize the German enemy.

10 A *pagnolade* is a story told in the manner of the plays and films of Marcel Pagnol.

Chapter 5
How To Conceptualize
the History of a Genre?

Cinematic genres are not rigid formulas fixed for all time, but, as we have seen, *a posteriori* categories that are subject to redefinition. This simple fact is sufficient to anchor them in history – by which "theoretical" genres formulated analytically are just as constrained as "historical" genres (cf. chapter 2). The history of genres, however, is a complex phenomenon that concerns both generic designations and the grouping of films. It involves two dimensions that are merged, but which cannot be confused with one another. To construct the history of a genre is to take account of the birth of a generic appellation (a necessary precondition for the awareness and recognition of the genre), of the modifications it has undergone, of its obsolescence, and of its eventual disappearance; it is also to focus on the variations of the genre – that is, to explain its syntactic and semantic modifications, to understand the periods when it was successful and the times in which it was less popular, and to analyze the reasons for its demise or its disappearance from screens. For this reason, the play of repetitions and variations that constitute a genre is not to be seen as an ahistorical collection of maps and rules – contrary to the assumption of certain structural and textual analyses that use a synchronic approach to extrapolate rules from the corpus of films with which they are dealing, or to reveal the logic that determines its combinations. Rather, this play is to be viewed as a constitutive element that is enacted and realized in historical time.

The aim of this chapter is to propose a frame of reference in which one can think about the history of a genre, its development, and eventually its disappearance. Because of this, the reader should not expect to find a collection of the histories of particular genres, nor a universal history of genres – it is more a matter of understanding the factors that govern, determine, and permit the birth and development of a genre.

To Put an End to the Theory of Generic Evolution

The idea that genres evolve in accordance with a trajectory that is fixed and foreseeable, often revived with respect to cinema, originates in generic theories that view history as the field in which the essence of genres is deployed. This essentialism, present from the time of Aristotle, is also found in theories developed in the nineteenth century, which sometimes view the history of genres from a teleological perspective.

Organicism and evolutionism: the genre's destiny

Hegel (1998), in his *Aesthetics*, proposed an explicitly teleological system of genres that has had a major influence on literary theories of genre in the twentieth century.[1] In this closed system, which is simultaneously essentialist and historicist, distinctions between the arts (architecture, painting, sculpture, music, and poetry) and between three forms of art (symbolic, classical, and romantic) correspond to historical distinctions. To the empirical historicity that accounts for temporal succession, Hegel opposes a systematic historicity that obeys a conceptual necessity – the unfolding of the determinations of Mind. From this perspective, which leads to the thesis that art will end, the essence of literary genres (poetry) is retrospectively determined by three generic "moments" (that of the epic, of lyricism, and of dramatic poetry), with each being embodied concretely in three forms of art – the symbolic, the classical, and the romantic.

At the end of the century, and from a different perspective, Brunetière was inspired by the evolutionary model developed by Darwin, whose *Origin of Species* (1859) he cites on several occasions.[2] The evolution of literature in general, and of genres in particular, is explained (in terms of biological evolution) as an incessant struggle "for life" between neighboring forms, eventuating in the survival of the most adaptable forms and the disappearance of the others. While this general framework, in which genres are treated like species in accordance with Darwinian doctrine, avoids any reference to the notion of progress, a teleological inclination resurfaces, as Jean-Marie Schaeffer has observed, when Brunetière deals with the internal evolution of genres (1989, pp. 61–62). A genre, endowed with a life of its own, is born, flourishes, declines, and dies in an invariable cycle of which the high point is determined by its internal nature. Brunetière thus transforms the biological model which serves as his point of reference and considers genre not as a species (as conceived within the evolutionist paradigm), but as a biological individual whose fate is to be born, grow up, mature into adulthood, grow old, and disappear.

A more obviously evolutionist perspective (although it does not refer explicitly to the biological model, and lacks any teleological aim) was adopted by the Russian Formalists (cf. chapter 2, pp. 30–36) for whom artistic evolution occurs through a self-propelled dialectical production of forms. An original creation evolves towards a canonized dominant form (a genre) that perpetuates itself through automatically repeated actions until it ends up withdrawing before the arrival of, and under the pressure of, a new innovative form, which in its turn becomes canonized, etc.:

The new work appears in opposition to other works (either earlier ones, or else works that appear simultaneously). It then defines the "skyline" of a literary era through the success of its form, and soon gives birth to imitations that become progressively stereotyped. Finally, it gives rise to a genre that exhausts itself and ends up by surviving, once the next form has imposed itself,

133

only in the banality of literature written for popular consumption. (Jauss 1978, p. 70)

In the following decades, a comparable schema was often used, explicitly or implicitly, in the study of films. Genres knew a "golden age" (a recurrent expression in monographs devoted to a single genre) in which the essence of the genre was expressed, preceded by a more tentative phase of experimentations drawing upon diverse influences, and followed by a period of decadence. Such a notion of the history of a genre in fact privileges a "classical" stage in the evolution of the genre, in which it is supposed to embody, momentarily, a pure and stable form.[3] The position adopted by André Bazin on this subject in an article on the evolution of the western published in 1955 in *Cahiers du cinéma* is fairly representative of this mixture of evolutionism and essentialism. Discussing westerns shot after World War II, Bazin sets out to distinguish a classical perfection achieved during the years between 1939 and 1940 with *Stagecoach* by John Ford or with *Northwest Passage* by King Vidor:

> The western attained a certain degree of perfection on the eve of the War. The year 1940 marked a point beyond which a new stage of development inevitably had to occur – an evolution that the four years of war had simply delayed, then modified, without determining the form that it would have. *Stagecoach* (1939) is the perfect example of this maturity of a style that had attained its classical form. John Ford achieved a perfect equilibrium between social myths, historical evocation, psychological truth, and the traditional themes of the western mise en scène. None of these fundamental elements was realized at the expense of any other. (1995, p. 229)

Choosing to explain the evolution of the genre by examining the genre itself, he proposes to call westerns produced after 1945 the "super-western" (*sur-western*). This appellation, which covers a range of phenomena, designates a western "that would be ashamed to be only itself, and therefore seeks to justify its existence by including a supplementary interest: of an aesthetic, sociological, moral, psychological, political, erotic (etc.) order . . . in brief, through including some value that is extrinsic to the genre, and which is supposed to enrich it" (Bazin 1995, p. 231). Hence, the lavish spectacle and melodramatic plot of *Duel in the Sun* (Vidor, 1946), the love argument of *Shane* (Stevens, 1953), and the manner in which Stevens consciously picks up the mythology and iconography of the western are, in Bazin's eyes, the mark of a genre which, having become aware of itself, transgresses beyond its classical purity, or, conversely, turns in upon itself in order to practice self-citation. For example, in dressing its hero in white, *Shane* makes the color of the costume not a sign of virtue and courage, but a symbol of the western itself. Recognizing that the term "super-western" is not appropriate for characterizing all the films in the genre produced during the 1950s, given that not all of them display a tendency towards what we would now call reflexivity, Bazin nevertheless identifies westerns of this period as "modern" westerns, characterized by romantic enrichment. Even though Bazin does not deny the influence of the world conflict taking place at the time on the transformation of the genre, it places this transformation at some sort of secondary level by presenting "decadence" and "transgression" as inherent in the destiny of a genre that has passed the high point of its classical form (1995, p. 233).

Such a conception of the evolution of genre does not totally get rid of historical factors, but it subordinates them to a general schema that assumes an inescapable development from classical equilibrium towards decline. Thus, for Jane Feuer, the Hollywood musical evolves towards a progressively deepening reflexivity, as witnessed after the War by MGM productions such as *The Barkleys of Broadway* (Walters, 1949), *Singin' in the Rain* (Donen and Kelly, 1952), and *The Band Wagon* (Minnelli, 1953), the stories of which alternate imperfect performances with performances that enjoy an instant success with the intra-diegetic audience (Feuer 1995). These reflexive films allow the codes of the genre to be perpetuated by activating the memory of them: they borrow music from other films, include allusions to earlier musicals, and imitate famous shots and sequences – like the opening shot of the feet of the star-couple in *The Barkleys of Broadway* that reproduces the opening shot of *Top Hat* (Sandrich, 1935). They nostalgically celebrate the stars of the past – fictive ones in *Singin' in the Rain*, or "real" ones in *The Bandwagon* (Astaire) and *The Barkleys of Broadway*. They insistently enact or express in song the various myths (of spontaneity, of the integration of the individual into a group or into a couple) that are created by the "musical" genre itself. In doing this, they reaffirm the power, the excellence, and the efficaciousness of the musical in a world that is no longer that of the prewar period. For Feuer, the plot of *Singin' in the Rain*, by presenting the sung film as a response to the crisis posed by the transition of silent movies into talking pictures, indicates that the musical can still be relied upon: firstly, in the face of upheavals resulting from the introduction of new technologies (caused, in particular, by the convergence of television with other forms of entertainment), and secondly, in the face of the changing expectations of an audience that has become aware of the conventions of the genre. Despite their success, these films are the prelude to a tendency even more marked than reflexivity: they announce the decline of the genre. Although certainly accompanied by socioeconomic factors, this decline remains, above all, the consequence of the inexorable laws of genre, with the musical being condemned to repetition, parody, and than contestation. Years later, the melodramatic form of the musical film in *Dancer in the Dark* (2000) by the Danish filmmaker Lars von Trier oscillates between homage to the world of the musical and its contestation. Selma, a poor Czech immigrant in the United States, the solo mother of a young boy threatened with blindness by a hereditary sickness from which she herself suffers, works hard and lives in terrible conditions to save the money necessary for an operation on her son's eyes. Her only happiness is to watch musicals in the cinema, and to find herself in an imaginary space for the duration of the musical numbers that punctuate and lighten what is a fairly dark film – in a way that totally contrasts with the harshness of her existence, the pathos of the plot, and the "reality" of the America that Lars von Trier depicts surrounding his heroine.

Applying this cyclical developmental schema to the whole group of Hollywood genres, Thomas Schatz even proposes a rule according to which *all* genres proceed from transparency to opacity: genre films cease progressively to present stories and evolve towards a conscious formalism (1981, p. 38). The spectator is then led not to look at a story through a form (the conventions of the genre), but to appreciate this form in its own right. For Schatz, the story tends to intervene as it were an accident along the way that prevents certain genres from achieving their destiny in the "genesis/classicism/formalism" cycle. In contrast to the musical, the western, or the melodrama, the gangster film does not undergo the reflexive phase because the threat of censure prevents any formalist prolongation of the genre.

The limits of historical determinism

Several objections can be made to this model, which presupposes that the evolution of a genre is a predetermined process divided up into successive cycles in which a period of formation gives way to a classical age, followed by an inevitable decline marked by parody, reflexivity, overwriting, formalism, mannerism, etc. While such a scheme of development has the merit of illuminating the inevitable self-reflexive effects produced by the play of repetition and variation, it reserves them for the "end of the genre," even seeing them as a characteristic of the decline of a genre.

This view of genre does not survive the test of the facts. More than half a century before *Buffalo Bill and the Indians* (Altman, 1976) or the Italian ("spaghetti") westerns, a vein of satirical and parodic westerns had existed since the 1910s – illustrated, for example, by the films with Douglas Fairbanks, such as *Wild and Woolly* (Emerson, 1917). More generally, as Jean-Louis Leutrat and Suzanne Liandrat-Guigues observe with respect to the 1920s, "the margin between a genre and a satire of it is very small," even if it is "not always easy to distinguish humor from ingenuity, and clumsiness from negligence" (1990, p. 113). Gallagher (1986) also insists on the generic "hyperconsciousness" of the early westerns, and recalls that the reflexivity attributed to westerns made during the 1960s and 1970s should not lead us to forget that the "supposed naïveté" that is now detected in *Stagecoach* disguises a play of allusions, a recycling of conventions, characters, and motifs that are "consciously revisiting not only the old West, but old westerns as well." Even though they may be invisible to contemporary viewers, the presence of generic elements in *Stagecoach* was undoubtedly perceived by spectators in 1939, who were closer to, and more familiar with, the westerns of the silent era.

To this empirical objection, which, moreover, does not apply only to the western, we must add more theoretical reservations. Indeed, models for the evolution of genres that postulate a period of decadence following a classical age often turn the classical one into a period in which one can isolate a pure form of the genre. Accordingly, they see the essence of the genre in this pure type, whereas a genre always takes shape on a cinematic terrain where it crosses other forms and other genres with which it perpetually interacts, often hybridizing with them. It is not surprising, then, that such models are primarily interested in the internal history of a single genre (or consider the evolution of each genre individually when they are examining the development of several). They also overlook the fact that a cinematic genre can be recognized because a semi-stable formula has become established and embedded in the films that maintains a balance between semantic and syntactic traits. This is not to say that this formula represents a unique point of perfection that cannot be exceeded, but, to the contrary, that it is, in a given era, and in a specific cinematic and cultural context, only one moment of possible equilibrium in the genre's potential configuration, which is temporary and changing. Indeed, one configuration can eventually be succeeded by another configuration, as we shall see later on in this book with the science-fiction movie and the woman's film (cf. below, pp. 164–166). Finally, these theories, by making a determinist principle the key to the evolution of genres, relegate to the ranks of the coincidental the whole history of changes affecting the social, cultural, and political contexts of films, the modifications that occur to the economic and aesthetic system of their production, and changes in the nature of audiences and their expectations. While this model might be useful for appraising classical Hollywood genres, despite its systematizing nature, it is not very relevant to an understanding of genres after the studio era, or those that flourished in places other than Hollywood.

Thus, from its first appearance with *Blood Feast* (Lewis, 1963) or *The Night of the Living Dead* (Romero, 1969) the gore film defined itself in terms of its repetitive structure and its taste for excess (murders and violent effects). As Philippe Rouyer observes, the accumulation of blood (within one film, or from one film to another) ends up by detaching the situations depicted from reality, creating a "distancing" that is "an essential component of the gore film," being particularly evident in a propensity for a tone of wry or comic detachment (1997, pp. 170–171). The "classic" gore films (to use the terminology of those adhering to a theory of generic evolutionism) – that is, American or European films made during the 1970s – adopt the same serial structure, display the same sense of excess, and play simultaneously on the twin effects of horror and laughter. In *Reazione a catena* (*Bay of Blood*) (1971), for example, Mario Brava piles up 13 murders in 90 minutes and depicts an entomologist who passes his time observing insects captured in the bay – a diegetic figure representing the filmmaker and the viewer observing the slaughter of characters trapped within a closed milieu. The image of a fisherman nailed to a door recalls that of an insect pinned on a display board, head-shots and zooms on lacerated bodies and faces evoke the scientist's microscope. This horrific story ends with a jocular remark by two children who have just accidentally killed their parents: "Look how well they're playing the part of dead people!" It is difficult indeed not to describe this "classical" gore film, which is also a crime movie (*giallo*), as formalist, parodic, and reflexive.

Towards a complex history of genres

Organicist and evolutionist models, then, whatever their virtues, fail in their ambition to bring the history of a genre back to an

139

evolution that is inseparable from genre as a phenomenon. Instead of proposing a single, all-encompassing model for genre *per se*, we shall be content for the time being to identify various factors that have had a determining influence in the history of a range of specific genres. It is neither possible for this history to be reduced to an effect of structure, as we have seen earlier, nor for it to be described as the simple translation of extra-cinematic phenomena or the reflection of social and political changes in films. In the first case, the evolution of the structure of genre obscures its roots in history; in the second, the exclusive emphasis placed on circumstances exterior to films that are assumed to have influenced their discourse does not take account of the specific formula that constitutes a genre. Between these two pitfalls, the semantic-syntactic definition (cf. chapter 2, pp. 55–62) offers interesting perspectives. Its twin approaches allow one to account for the circulation between genres, and to integrate semantic ruptures (introduced by non-cinematic modifications) in a syntax that is specific to a genre. We have already seen a striking demonstration in the Hollywood musical of folkloric themes borrowed from westerns (cf. chapter 4, p. 118). An identical observation can be made with regard to certain war films, such as *All Through the Night* (Sherman, 1942) or *Sherlock Holmes and the Voice of Terror* (Rawlins, 1942), which "transfer to a new set of semantic elements [the enemy Germans] the syntax of the righteous cops-punish-criminals genre," as characterized by gangster films beginning with *The G-Men* in 1935 (Altman 1989, p. 117).

Putting it succinctly, to trace the history of a cinematic genre is to trace the history of a generic film formula that is susceptible to change and development, in its various contexts. Finally, because all histories of genre are constructed around a theoretical conception of the idea of genre, such a proposition can only be formulated if one makes genre one of the concrete aesthetic and sociocultural configurations that appear and function in a given field of expression, in particular periods and contexts. The proposition loses its meaning with essentialist approaches, and still more so with transhistorical approaches that view genres as giving expression to universal archetypes – an assumption that this book has deliberately not repeated.[4] There is even an outright negation of history (forms, ideas, societies) in this latter approach, since cinematic narratives are supposed merely to reiterate ancient myths in particular genres, elevating them (in a way that is ideologically suspect) to the status of eternal, transcendental truths.[5]

The Birth of a Cinematic Genre

In order to turn a genre into a concrete object, the date of its appearance is ignored even more frequently than its evolution – even though this date is a point of "fact." This is unfortunate, given that there is indeed a time when the generic categories of "western," "detective film," and "musical" did not exist, and a period when spectators, critics, and producers made explicit use of them. Both factors need to be taken into account. On one hand, certain theorists attempt to identify a filmic point of departure for a genre that has neither an empirical nor a scientific justification, by regarding one particular work as the quasi-mythic origin of the genre, situated in a kind of "prehistory": Méliès' *Le Voyage dans la lune* (*Voyage to the Moon*, 1902) is the first science-fiction film, Porter's *The Great Train Robbery* (1903) is the first western, Lewis's *Blood Feast* (1963) is the first gore film, etc. On the other hand, with cinematic genres that partially borrow their content, their aesthetic, or their narrative schema from non-cinematic genres, commentators turn cinema into a form that perpetuates popular literature or theater arts through different means. The cinematic quality and specificity of a genre are not taken into consideration, since the question of its origin is displaced on to another terrain. The question, then, remains: why and how did one pass from the detective novel to the detective film, from the written science-fiction narrative to the science-fiction film, and from the Broadway stage-play to the Hollywood musical? A totalizing explanation of why one popular form of mass culture should pass from one medium to another, even though it could not be advanced for all genres, might supply certain elements of the answer, but it would not be able to explain why cinema seizes upon this material at a given moment, nor why the borrowing often results in an alteration or reformulation of the form.

A post-dated birth certificate

A cinematic genre only appears when it is named and designated as such, since its existence is tied to an awareness of it that is agreed upon and shared by a community. Thus, the first occurrence of a genre is not to be sought, retrospectively, in films that correspond to a category established *a posteriori*, but in the discourse held about the films. This fact is well known in the case of *film noir*, as we have already seen in tracing the origins of its generic appellation (cf. chapter 4, pp. 111–113), given that it was the creation of critics, but the same principle can be extended to all genres. Accordingly, the Hollywood musical appeared neither with *The Jazz Singer* (Crossland, 1927), nor with *Broadway Melody* (Beaumont, 1929) but from the beginning of 1931, when the term "musical" was used to designate retroactively films with diegetic music produced between 1928 and 1930. As Rick Altman has shown through his analysis of reviews from this period, the term arose from a perception of the faults shared by musical films, in a period when these productions were in decline, and progressively replaced former designations (1999, pp. 34–36). Similarly, even though the first significant uses of the term "western" date from 1910, it was not until the 1920s that it was regularly and widely used to characterize films about the West. The western, then, did not appear in 1903 with *The Great Train Robbery* or with Indian films about noble savages made during the first fifteen years of the twentieth century, but with the emergence of a historically attested awareness of the category. As Jean-Louis Leutrat indicates, the history of the genre commenced when "a 'discursive practice' specific to the cinematic western was consistently applied":

It is not enough to study the transformations of the western as a putative "natural object." Such an object simply does not exist.

> For the history of a natural object, one must substitute the history of the attempts at objectification that have constructed this domain – in which connections, encounters, alliances, power-games, and strategies have, at a given moment, formed something that has on occasions been able to function almost directly as evidence. (1985, p. 17)

As we have seen in the two preceding chapters, it is not possible for a genre to reside entirely in textual structures governed by a group of similar conventions. It exists only because it is also an interpretive category that can only be born when generic readings of films became established as a fact of reception. A genre can, then, have several birth certificates, registering different dates from one audience to another, or from one country to another, and eventually existing in certain contexts of reception, and not in others.

Thus the term *peplum* (classical epic) appeared in France during the 1960s, used by Parisian cinephiles who were regulars at the Cinéma Mac Mahon, near La Place de l'Étoile. It was then used by critics writing for *Cahiers du cinéma* and *Positif*, before being taken up by the general public to designate historical films on topics set in ancient times (biblical, Egyptian, Greek, Roman, or more imaginary), in which some or all of the characters sport a short tunic, the indubitable sign that they belong to the ancient world. Awareness of this genre, which revolves principally around Italian and American films, surfaces, then, well after the big productions of Italian silent cinema on such topics, such as *Quo Vadis?* (Guazzoni, 1912) or *Cabiria* (Pastrone, 1914), and the Hollywood historical epics of the 1920s, such as *The Ten Commandments* (De Mille, 1923) or *Ben Hur* (Niblo, 1925). This type of film suffered a relative decline at the beginning of the talking era, continued subsequently through the production in Mussolini's Italy of films on ancient subjects with a clearly ideological purpose – to celebrate the glorious past of the Roman Empire, as in *Scipione l'Africano* (*Scipio the African*) (Gallone,

1937). However, movies about the ancient world resurfaced *en masse* on Hollywood screens at the end of the 1940s, and later in Italy, following the success of *Labours of Hercules* (Francisci, 1957). In order for the *peplum* genre to be born, it was necessary, therefore, for big-budget American productions to reach French screens, as well as Italian films set in the ancient world in which high production values give way to an obvious and sometimes inventive lack of resources. It was just as necessary for a resurgence of cinephilia to occur – not entirely devoid of a rather affected taste for the trashy – as the prelude to critical interest in these films during the 1960s. The term *peplum*, at first reserved for Italian films, later became applied to all films set in the ancient world; however, this term, which encompassed films that were similar in subject, but widely different in their nationality, their budget, and their ideology, did not enter into either the practice or awareness of American filmmakers. Producers and critics beyond the Atlantic used the term "epic" in the 1950s and 1960s, replaced today by the still more general notion of the "blockbuster," to refer to historical films set in ancient (and non-ancient) times that elevate spectacle. The limits of the genre, then, are not all identical, since *The Birth of a Nation* (Griffith, 1915) coexists in this genre with the two versions of *The Ten Commandments* (De Mille, 1923 and 1956), *Spartacus* (Kubrick, 1960), and *Gladiator* (Scott, 2000). While the *peplum* genre was born in France during the 1960s (based on the grouping of both contemporary and older films, the vast majority of which were imported from Italy or the United States), its birth in America is yet to come.

Finally, many studies devoted to Hollywood genres insist on the necessity of adopting a "substantivized" generic label before awareness of a genre can come into being. The simple addition of a qualifying adjective to a generic noun that already exists takes place as a simple secondary determination, specifying a place, a tonality, or an atmosphere. The expressions "western melodrama," "western drama," "western comedy," "western romance," in which "western" is an epithet, make localization in the West a common point of reference between films that are identified as belonging to different genres. They confirm a tendency of film production to retell the story of the West. It was, however, only when the adjective unseated the different nouns to which it is attached that awareness of the western as a genre emerged. From this perspective, an adjective, even when recurrently placed alongside a generic designation, never constitutes a generic category in its own right. Even though romantic comedies, romantic dramas, romantic biopics, etc., exist, there is no "romantic" genre. The precision imparted by the adjective or the qualifying expression undoubtedly allows it to determine a sub-genre: for example, the comedy "of manners," "satiric" comedies, "action" comedies, and "romantic" comedies are sub-categories of the genre of comedy. Similarly, in the case of genres (re)defined by critics, the abandonment of the inverted commas that enclose a new designation also signals the consolidation of a genre. As Rick Altman shows through analyzing the different occurrences of the term "woman's film" in two publications by Mary Ann Doane, one written in 1984 and the other in 1987, *The Desire to Desire: The Woman's Film of the 1940s*, hesitations about designating the woman's film as a genre were reflected in a fluctuating use of inverted commas, sometimes used to enclose the term, and left off at other times (Altman 1999, pp. 73–76).

While this model for the formation of generic categories through "substantivization" is relevant in the context of Hollywood production and reception, it is more questionable when one leaves the American context of reception, or when one looks at a particular country's awareness of foreign genres. To take two genres that have long been recognized in France, but which have rarely been exemplified in French cinema: while the "western" has passed from American English into French, "musicals" remain *des comédies musicales* (musical comedies) in French. It is just as difficult, then, to know what to make of double generic appellations, such as "dramatic comedy." Is the term a portmanteau word that covers a mixture of genres? Does it express a resistance in French cinema and French cinematic vocabulary to the idea of specific generic structures? Is it a French variant of the melodramatic form? Or is it a specific genre, long-established in

French cinema, descended from adaptations of serious works from the "theater of the boulevard," such as Henry Bernstein's *Mélo*, which was adapted for the screen by Czinner in 1932 (*The Dreamy Mouth*), and remade by Resnais in 1986?[6]

Cultural interactions and cinematic recreation

The naming and awareness of genres therefore emerge *a posteriori* in conditions that are always specific, but the precondition for this emergence is the production of a sufficient quantity of films using the same formula for a genre to be identifiable. While it is difficult to assign an origin to a cinematic genre, only a combination of reasons can explain why such a series of films come to be made and produced successfully in the first place. The elaboration of a filmic formula of this kind (destined to become a genre because of its repetitions) takes place both because of the preexistence of a body of established cultural and cinematic conventions that the formula adapts through a process of alteration and *recreation*, and also because of historical changes that are also cultural and cinematographic. Conventions ensure that these new films are comprehensible by inscribing them in an ongoing tradition of known forms and distinguishing features, while the conjuncture of new historical circumstances is the source of a rupture that gives them their particularity.

Films noirs, for example, were inspired by the novelistic model of "hard-boiled fictions" popularized in crime literature by the likes of Raymond Chandler, Dashiell Hammett, James A. Cain, or Eric Ambler. Similarly, *film noir* follows in the tradition of the crime film (to which the pre-World War II gangster film belongs) while significantly modifying this tradition. In place of the "G Man," the FBI agent working for the government, *film noir* substituted the figure of the private eye, or solitary amateur investigator, for which Sam Spade played by Bogart in *The Maltese Falcon* (Huston, 1941) provides the archetype. Individualistic characters – alienated from society, caught up in a mysterious plot, and victims of a destiny that is expressed through the frequent use of the flash-back and the voice-off – replace the two groups of the organized crime mob and police institutions. In addition, the use of an alienated main character outside society is a semantic and syntactic trait imitated from both the gangster film and the social film of the 1930s. While gangster movies like *The Public Enemy* (Wellman, 1931) or *Scarface* (Hawks, 1932) ambiguously celebrate the anti-social, tragic figure of a legendary criminal who is the product and symptom of unemployment, prohibition, and a particular kind of social violence, social films, such as *I am a Fugitive from a Chain Gang* (LeRoy, 1932), *You Only Live Once* (Lang, 1937), or *They Made Me a Criminal* (Berkeley, 1939) frequently tell the story of an individual, a victim, who has only been made blameworthy or turned into a criminal by society.[7] Films in the *noir* style picked up this social isolation that was mainly characteristic of masculine heroes in genres of the 1930s, and generalized it to a feminine character by taking a woman out of her family setting in order to turn her into a *femme fatale*. Moreover, this isolation is not presented as the result of a social dynamic, but rather as a kind of natural given. The influence of gothic plots inspired from English models, and a Germanic visual style already naturalized in American cinema (particularly in "fantastic" films) also extended into *film noir*, especially in films like *Laura* (Preminger, 1944), *The Woman in the Window* (Lang, 1944), *Gaslight* (Cukor, 1944), and *Dragonwyck* (Mankiewicz, 1946). The genre only came into being when there was a crossing and modification of existing genres and styles, to which changes wrought by the war and its aftermath imparted a form.

The appearance of *film noir* in the 1940s expresses a pessimism and a feeling of powerlessness that coincides with an erosion of the ideology of national unity that characterized the war period. Just as the emergence of the character of the *femme fatale* reflects a crisis of masculinity, the absence of "normal" family relationships, which condemns the heroes to the experience of solitude and frustration, projects unease generated by changes to the status and role of women (a consequence, for example, of their mass recruitment into war industries). As Sylvia Harvey says, "the

147

feelings of loss and alienation expressed through the characters of *film noir* can be viewed as a consequence of both postwar depression, and also the reorganization of the American economy" (1993, p. 194). In addition, the atmosphere of *film noir* embraces, to cite the analysis by George Lipsitz, "the internal logic of social actions that are diametrically opposed: the general strike and the cold war":

> By placing the emphasis on an aspiration towards a life of community, on fear of isolation, on the necessity of striving for an irreproachable life, and on hostility towards those in authority, the *film noir* reproduces the motivations of wild-cat strikes and mass demonstrations. Even the paranoid expectation of social disapprobation that marks this genre is an echo of a new qualm of conscience arising from awareness that individual aspirations are likely to be judged as illicit when viewed against the standard of traditional norms. (1993, p. 171)

A revolt against legality, similar to that which characterized the wild-cat strikes of unprecedented magnitude that occurred in 1945 and 1946, is found in heroes who break the law in *film noir*, in which such revolt is presented as a norm of conduct for society as a whole. But at the same time, the feeling of fatalism and persecution that is presented in this genre reflects a feeling of guilt, and validates a vision of the world in which Americans are made the unhappy victims of external forces, or of internal betrayals – thus reflecting the conservative ideology of the Cold War. *Films noirs*, then, expressed both popular confusion in the face of an America that has not kept its promises, and also the Cold War paranoia that gripped the government and was passed on to Hollywood. They therefore crystallize actual contradictory anxieties, using older forms that they subject to modification.

The birth of a cinematic genre is always the outcome of a combination of factors, being the result of a process in which several cinematic genres and several cultural forms meet. However, there also needs to be a particular conjunction of historical circumstances for an identifiable filmic formula to become established.

The industrial conditions relating to cinema also enter into this conjunction. Thus, filmed westerns continue a mythology of the West that was shaped at the end of the nineteenth century and the beginning of the twentieth through vehicles other than cinema. Wild west shows established the stereotypes of the Plains Indian (with his feather headdress) and the adroit cowboy, as well as scenes showing attacks on the settler cabin, or on the pioneer wagon train. Illustrators, photographers, and painters of the West offered images of the landscape that were romantic and mysterious, or, following the example of Frederic Remington and Charles M. Russell, focused on the spectacular aspects of local scenes. "Pulps" (illustrated magazines involving series that aimed explicitly to make use of cinematic generic distinctions in the 1920s, and to provide an important stock of plots for films) popularized melodramatic episodes set in the West through their images and texts. Similarly, the stories in a significant number of "dime novels" (cheap novels with a large print-run), contrived around a variable repertoire of stock themes, helped to transform Buffalo Bill and the Dalton brothers into legends. Following Frederick Jackson Turner's book, *The Significance of the Frontier in American History*, written in 1893 after the taming of the West, the idea finally developed that the frontier, progressively pushed further westwards, had advanced democracy and shaped the character of the American people by liberating the pioneers from their European origins. During the first fifteen years of cinema, this myth of the West was often repeated in genres as varied as the journey film, the crime film, the melodrama, or the "slapstick comedy" that assumed a "western" color for the occasion.[8] But films which took place in the West became films about the West at the beginning of the second decade of the twentieth century when they began regularly to structure their stories around an opposition between "wilderness" and "civilization," and to organize their actions according to a melodramatic scheme in which Indians became the aggressors (even though burlesque forms still continued until the 1920s). During a period in which the arrival of new waves of immigrants was causing unease, the emergence of a national identity, including that embodied in cinematic

149

representations, found an American genre in films about the West that had a powerful potential to symbolize this identity.

Finally, changes that occurred within the American film industry were also essential factors in the emergence of this new genre. Cinematic firms progressively relocated to the west coast where they found an abundance of natural settings for westerns and, given that it is more difficult to shoot westerns in other countries, Europe in particular, western films seemed to provide a good strategy for conquering foreign markets as well as American ones. The massive production of films in this genre could, then, be justified entirely from an economic point of view. Once it had become synthesized and "lexicalized" by cinema, the western supplanted other categories of cinematic production, such as films about the Civil War, dramas set in the Far North, animal films, Indian films, and the western melodrama, which subsequently disappeared totally from the Hollywood repertoire during the 1920s.

The notion of genrification

A question arises as to whether it is possible to propound a general model of the formation of cinematic genres (capable of being articulated in terms of a theory of generic logic), rather than simply identifying particular historical occurrences that explain the genesis, emergence, and naming of a genre. With respect to this question, Rick Altman suggests that one should think about the birth of genres as a perpetual process of "genrification." By this neologism, he means "a constant dialectic between the consolidation and dissemination of categories" – a dialectic that governs the history of types and terminology, and which is closely tied to the capitalist need (characteristic of mass culture) to differentiate products (Altman 1995, p. 26) (cf. chapter 3, pp. 64–71). A twofold principle of expansion followed by consolidation thus governs an unending process in the production of genres, in which Altman (1995, p. 20) identifies four distinct stages:

- By imitating their own successful films, studios seek to initiate a cycle of films that will be *a priori* marketable, and which will be associated with their own label. To achieve this, they can add new elements to an existing genre, and by so doing partially renew its semantic and syntactic features. In addition, they often add a descriptive adjective to the prevailing generic term that highlights the distinctive nature of films in the cycle.

- If the cycle is successful, and other studios become equally keen to combine the ingredients of the same recipe, the cycle becomes a genre.

- The designation of the cycle, which was up until then conveyed by the adjective, is turned into a substantive, and can even become the name of the new genre.

- Once a genre has been taken up and shared by a number of studios, or when it has become saturated in some kind of way, it is more profitable for them to abandon it, or to use the genre as the basis for the creation of a new cycle, involving a new process of genrification.

Not all cycles become genres, and certain new genres consolidate themselves more quickly than others. As is shown by the cases of the western and the musical, genrification operates more easily and rapidly when the adjective that characterizes a cycle can be attached to a large number of existing generic categories. Moreover, this process of genrification explains why critics hesitate to regard certain series of films that were only made during a finite period as genres in their own right. We see this, for example, in the case of the disaster film of the 1970s, or of the action comedy at the end of the 1980s and 1990s – although this latter form, even though it is regularly shown on screens (from the various editions of *Rush Hour* (Ratner, 1998) to the majority of films recently produced (but not made) by Luc Besson), has possibly not yet completed the process of genrification.

Finally, the cycle/genre process, because of its dynamic nature, allows us to avoid certain confusions between *sub-genres* that are evident in the course of a genre's history. These confusions occur when an expansion or temporary diversification of the genre gives rise to a particular definition of the generic formula and cycles that becomes very important at a given time. That is why, for example, thrillers that put a female heroine on the screen at the beginning of the 1990s in an attempt to attract a female audience to the genre, as do *Single White Female* (Schroeder, 1991) and *Dead Again* (Branagh, 1991), do not actually comprise a subgenre, but rather a cycle, adding a dose of romanticism and an (ambiguous) dash of feminism to the thriller.

Genrification outside of Hollywood

This model for the creation of genres applies fairly well to Hollywood cinema – a cinema whose structuring logic involves studios and competition between companies, with the latter occurring in the cultural space of an autonomous filmmaking industry that is strong enough to absorb external influences (coming from other media, or other cinematic enterprises). Outside of this particular context the model needs to be reconceived, as in the case of cinema industries that are not autonomous – for example, French cinema during the 1950s, which was acutely aware of the need to maintain cultural identity while responding to the dominance and influence of American cinema. In this context, which differs from that of the American studios, the process of genrification also operates through expansion, but it grafts new defining characteristics and traits from other countries), or traits that are themselves derived from a blending of national cultural elements with American elements, on to existing genres (often national ones). The *série noire* genre, popular in France until the 1960s, is a good example.[9]

Before it entered French cinema (which was very inclined towards adaptations), this process of genrification began with the detective novel. The *Série noire* collection edited by Duhamel at Gallimard, which in the aftermath of the war published Anglophone authors (English, in the first instance, with Peter Cheney and James Hadley Chase, and then Americans, with

Raymond Chandler, James M. Cain, and Horace MacCoy), enjoyed a phenomenal success at the same time as American *film noir* arrived on French screens, and references to *film noir* as a genre were beginning to surface in French film criticism. This success prompted rival editors to seek to emulate it – in particular, with volumes in the *Fleuve noir* series, which recruited French authors to counter the Anglo-American offensive in the crime fiction genre:[10] authors such as Albert Simonin, Auguste Le Breton, San Antonio, and Michel Audiard, who introduced Parisian repartee word games and slang into the Anglo-American model. According to Pierre Billard, *Mission à Tanger* (*Mission in Tangier*) (1949), *Méfiez-vous des blondes* (*Beware of Blondes*) (1950), and *Massacre en dentelles* (*Massacre in Lace*) (1951), a police trilogy recounting the adventures of a journalist and his faithful photographer, directed by Hunebelle, with screenplay and dialogue by Audiard, made the connection between *série noire* literature and *série noire* cinema (Billard 1995, p. 548). The establishment of *série noire* cinema was assisted by Eddie Constantine, who played Lemmy Caution in *La Môme vert-de-gris* (*Poison Ivy*) (Borderie, 1953), the first installment of a series of movies dealing with the adventures of the FBI agent. This character, both weary and laconic, an American agent and solitary adventurer inspired by Peter Cheney's hero, imparts a parodic style that would characterize many *série noire* films, making the genre palatable to French audiences:

> The ambiguity of the character . . . expresses well the ambiguity of the French relationship with American cinema (a mixture of fascination and repulsion, of envy and rejection). At their best, *série noire* films are fake American films concocted with both the tenderness and derision aroused in the French filmmaker by American cinema. (Billard 1995, p. 550)

Following the adventures of Lemmy Caution, and parallel to them, the *série noire* film invested in the spy film. *Le Gorille vous salue bien* (*The Gorilla Greets You*) (1958), directed by Borderie, initiated a series of "Gorilla films" in which Lino Ventura would be

153

replaced in the title role by Roger Hanin. Hanin appears as an agent of the French Directorate of Territorial Security in *Le Tigre aime la chair fraîche* (*The Tiger Likes Fresh Meat*) (1964) and *Le Tigre se parfume à la dynamite* (*An Orchid for the Tiger*) (1965) by Chabrol. Apart from more traditional detective stories (such as the Maigret series with Gabin), the *série noire* also modified the crime film that, following *Touchez pas au grisbi* (*Grisbi*) (Becker, 1954), tended to focus on world-weary, aging professionals. The *série noire* film, by modifying the crime genre and the spy genre, thus initiated a new cycle. Nevertheless, there is no certainty that the process of genrification will be brought to fruition, even if films like *Classe tout risque* (*The Big Risk*) (Sautet, 1960) and *Le Deuxième souffle* (*Second Breath*) (Melville, 1966) attest to its persistence. Very early, in fact, the *série noire* cycle became marked by a tendency towards self-mockery and parody, culminating during the 1960s in Lautner and the "cult" adventures of the *Monocle noir* (*The Black Monocle*) (1961 to 1964), the *Tontons flingueurs* (*Crooks in Clover*) (1963), and the *Barbouzes* (*The Great Spy Chase*) (1964).

The genrification model (which postulates an expansion of a genre into a cycle and its disappearance with the consolidation of this cycle into a new genre) also lends itself to a reevaluation of postwar Japanese cinema, as is demonstrated by the *kaïju-eiga* or "monster films," which appeared in the wake of Inoshiro Honda's *Godzilla* (1954). These films cannot be considered as expansions of a supposed Japanese fantastic cinema, embodied in Japanese productions of the ghost film, *bake-mono* or *kwaïdan*, the origins of which reside with a Chinese story-form that was naturalized in Japan by kabuki theater. In fact, in a system of genres structured by a fundamental opposition between period films on subjects prior to the Meiji-era (*jïdaï-geki*) and films on contemporary subjects (*gendaï-geki*), the *kaïju-eiga* are films on a contemporary subject – they present monsters, often born or revived through atomic science, that threaten modern urban Japan. In contrast, the *bake-mono* – a very popular genre on the screen during the 1940s and 1950s, including such films as *Ugetsu monogatari* (*Tales of a Pale and Mysterious Moon After the Rain*)

(Mizoguchi, 1953) – are period films. Furthermore, while the *bake-mono* are domestic dramas (in which, for example, the spirit of a murdered spouse returns at night to avenge herself on those responsible for her death), the *kaïju-eiga* are national dramas, in which monsters endanger a whole country (Tessier 1990, pp. 111–121).[11] In actuality, the monster film was born out of the trauma of the nuclear explosions at Hiroshima and Nagasaki, and the acculturation of two American genres. The first genre consists of American fantasy films about monsters made in the 1930s, from which Honda's films were directly inspired – he would give new life to this genre in *King Kong Escapes* (*Kingukongu no gyakushu*) (Honda, 1967), in which the great ape, in a struggle for possession of a radioactive Element X, confronts Mechani-kong, a robot built in his image by the evil doctor Wu. The second genre is the American science-fiction film of the 1950s, imbued with Cold War paranoia and the threat of the atom bomb.

Hybridization and Mutation of Genres

The history of an established genre is marked by rises and falls in popularity, evident both in the size of the audience these films attract, and also in the number of films produced. Moreover, the semantic-syntactic balance that gives the genre its identity is constantly being modified as a result of economic and cultural changes that affect society, audiences, and the mode of production. This equilibrium also changes on account of the innovations that directors apply to the conventions of a genre which can, if taken up by others, create a new balance. Finally, it is permanently subjected to a process of genrification, which, even if it does not eventuate in the emergence of a new genre, encourages the mixing and hybridization of genres. "The history of a genre cannot be a seamless movement that makes an intention, an end-product, and an identity appear simultaneously" (Leutrat and Liandrat-Guigues 1990, p. 133).

155

Alliances and ruptures

These two terms, proposed by Jean-Louis Leutrat with respect to the western in his book *L'Alliance brisée* (1985), allow the history of a genre to be described in terms of successive combinations that temporarily fix the elements that compose it and then recede as they give way to new compositions. Thus, Leutrat (who downplays melodramatic elements as well as plots) sees the western as being characterized by two main contradictory alliances right up until the 1920s: with the historical film on one hand, and with the burlesque on the other. The alliance with burlesque is evident in the regular use of secondary characters, whose clumsiness or buffoonery is designed to cause laughter, and by recurrent comic situations. But the affiliation between this genre and the slapstick is particularly evident in the rhythm of the narrative and the physical movements of the actors, whose bodies "guide the fiction, imposing a shape on it, and not the other way round" (Leutrat 1985, p. 134). From action scenes and stunts (that imitate elements from circuses and the rodeo) to burlesque episodes, acrobatics and gesticulations are given pride of place at the expense of any psychological depth. The acting style of Tom Mix, the star of almost 200 films about the West in the 1910s and the 1920s, is reminiscent of that of Buster Keaton and Harold Lloyd in its tumultuousness and physical exploits.

This alliance with the burlesque weakens and finally fades at the end of the 1920s. Psychological depth, acquired by the admission of History into the genre when it clearly became the story of the origins of the American nation, was increased by the advent of speaking pictures and the dominance of a "natural" style of acting (displayed by Gary Cooper, for example). This development eventually pushed out of the western the setting and comic elements that it had shared with burlesque. Rhythm, the spectacle of agile bodies, movement, and action surrendered their primacy to a new focus on the legend of the beginnings of America, and to human interest. Following the example of the itinerant westerner in *Straight Shooting* (Ford, 1917), who discovers both the cruelty of the rich landowner for whom he is preparing to work, and also love in the person of the daughter of the poor farmer, the heroes played by Harry Carey from the 1910s onward aroused empathic identification, compassion, or fear, which became substituted for the spectacle of physical feats.

The temporary alliances that tie one cinematic genre to another or to other forms of cultural expression encourage, and explain, the mixing of genres. It is not surprising that such alliances tend to be entered into with a form that is dominant in a given era, or with a genre whose ideological contents propose or impose responses to problems that are inherent in the particular conjunction of circumstances in the period under consideration. We have already seen (cf. chapter 4) how the context of national unity and an appeal to traditional communal values during World War II encouraged an alliance between the musical and the western. Similarly, during the 1940s and at the beginning of the 1950s, *film noir* influenced many other genres, including melodrama. The fatalistic atmosphere of *film noir*, oppressive settings, and strongly contrasting lighting accentuated the tendency of Hollywood melodramas to turn mundane actions into expressive symbols, and to displace and condense emotional states in the elements of the setting. In addition, the criminal framework of *film noir* often combined with melodramatic motifs during this period, which had the effect of rendering distinctions between the two genres obsolete in films such as *Leave Her to Heaven* (Stahl, 1945) or *Mildred Pierce* (Curtiz, 1945) (adapted from a novel by James M. Cain).[12] In the latter, the police inquiry motivates the very form of the narration: three stories about Mildred told in flashback. In them, she explains the circumstances surrounding the murder of Monte Beragon, her associate and second husband, and recounts the story of her life, of her professional rise up until her fall, involving a setback that is simultaneously professional, erotic, and maternal. The film presents an arresting visual contrast between the uniform lighting of the long sequences narrated by Mildred the character-narrator, and the strongly contrastive lighting that marks the scenes in the present, from the initial murder of Beragon to the lies Mildred tells to the police investigator. The discourse of the female character, centering on her maternal love, her desire to succeed professionally, and her double betrayal by her daughter and her male associates – characteristic themes of the female melodrama – is thus literally captured, as Pam Cook (1978) notes, by the visual style and the masculine discourse of the *film noir*. This subordination of a feminine discourse to a masculine one within the film reflects, moreover, the history of the film's screenplay.

The first versions, faithful to the rules of the 1930s' woman's film, were written by a woman, Catherine Turney. But the successive rewritings by male screenwriters, which would turn *Mildred Pierce* into a *film noir*, modified them to such an extent that Turney chose to remove her name from the credits (Williams 1993, pp. 115). For Pam Cook, the first scene (the murder of Beragon), as is typical of *film noir*, establishes an atmosphere of suspicions that are reiterated in the later sequences in the present, forcing the viewer to align himself or herself with the point of view of the male detective's investigation, rather than with the story told by Mildred. The beginning of the film shows the reflection of Monte's bullet-ridden body in a mirror, then a head shot of his agonized face as he utters the name of Mildred. Instead of a reverse shot showing the person who fired the gun, this opening shot is followed by a shot of the desperate Mildred who is walking on a pier. The viewer eventually learns from what follows that a long time separates the two events, and that Mildred is not guilty, but this initial dissimulation, by placing the heroine under suspicion, throws a veil of doubt over Mildred's accounts. The discourse of feminine melodrama is muddled here by its subordination to *film noir*, and Mildred Pierce, in the manner of many other heroines of films in which two genres are mixed, can be considered as either a strong woman or an alienated one, as a victim figure or a guilty one. This interpretive openness reflects both the misogynistic hesitations of Hollywood cinema, and the ambiguous relation between good and evil that is intrinsic to *film noir*. Moreover, this double language seems to be characteristic of gothic films in the 1940s and 1950s, which Noël Burch considers to be the exact feminine counterpart of the masculine *noir* genre; indeed, there is general agreement that these gothic films combine melodrama and *film noir*. Such films about paranoiac women who suspect – justifiably as in *Gaslight* (Cukor, 1944), *Dragonwyck* (Mankiewicz, 1946), or *Secret Beyond the Door* (Lang, 1948), or unjustifiably as in *Rebecca* (Hitchcock, 1940) or *Suspicion* (Hitchcock, 1941) – that their husbands wish to kill them, leave intact questions about the intentions of the husband and the masochistic inclinations of the woman. When films show the fears of a woman character to be justified, they maintain a suspicion that she brings her tragic fate upon herself because of her own desires. When she is mistaken in her suspicion, the abrupt happy ending still leaves a doubt about the actual innocence of the husband, and about the woman's somewhat masochistic acceptance of this belated revelation (Burch 2000, pp. 120–121).

Reversals and successes

In the course of their history, genres experience good times as well as periods that are less prosperous. These variations in their popularity can be explained both by the degree of sociocultural agreement between their themes, values, and imagery and the real-life preoccupations of the audience, and also by the ideological profit that the cinema industry or those in political power can draw from their stories. Thus, the success of science-fiction films during the 1950s owes much to the way they reflected fears about the possibility of a nuclear conflict that were diffused through the population, and also the ideological suppositions of the Cold War, in which "the Other" was perceived as concealing an enemy that was as disturbing as it was powerful. During the Occupation, the vogue for melodramas in France (comprising nearly 90 of the 200 films produced during this period) gave pride of place to female characters and reversed, as Noël Burch and Geneviève Sellier have demonstrated, the relationship between male and female characters and actors established in French cinema during the 1930s:

159

> Prewar cinema especially privileged masculine leading roles, while the cinema of the Occupation, contrary to prevailing trends and standards, far more frequently placed women in positions of authority. This is a paradox if one thinks of the formidable offensive launched by Vichyist ideology against any manifestations of feminine independence . . . Thus, the cinema of the Occupation witnessed an idealization of female characters that relates directly to an image-making intent. From Gaby Morlay to Madeleine Sologne, women were supposed to convey an imaginary national and moral identity that had been severely wounded by the humiliation and defeat of the German occupation and two million prisoners of war deported to enforced labor (STO).[13] (1996, p. 101)

Melodrama, in the course of paying its debts to prewar poetic realism, bears the mark of this defeat and expresses patriarchy's failure, causing new female figures to be brought into prominence. Some of these dramas and melodramas present a different kind of female desire as the main stake of their story, a desire that is no longer the frivolous, seductive desire of the boulevard, nor the dangerous desire of the naturalist tradition. This new kind of desire can be found, for example, in *Lumière d'été* (*Light of Summer*) (1942) or *Le ciel est à vous* (*The Sky is Yours*) (1943) by Jean Grémillon. They explore, in particular, conflicts between duty and desire. However, a large number of melodramas made during this period are contrived as the unofficial instrument of Pétainist propaganda. In these films, women are "militant," mothers of families, or else pure, chaste, and humble young women with angelic faces who place themselves in the service of a program of moral regeneration. Actresses such as Gaby Morlay, who abandoned the light-hearted register of the boulevard during the Occupation (which had been her speciality before the war), or Viviane Romance (who cast off roles as a tart to reincarnate herself as the suffering heroine), turn their characters into inspirational maternal figures that serve an emblematic function within the melodrama. Even Guitry temporarily put to one side the ribald, libertine register of the boulevard and his persona of the all-powerful seducer in order to enact the story of a mature sculptor, in *Donne-moi tes yeux* (*My Last Mistress*) (1943), who breaks off his relationship with his model, whom he loves, because he is becoming blind. The young woman, upon discovering the true reason for his action, finally becomes his wife and his guide. The theme of blindness, and the tone and treatment of the relations between the couple, inscribe this film in the same melodramatic vein as *L'Ange de la nuit* (*Angel of the Night*) (Berthomieu, 1942) and *Vénus aveugle* (*Blind Venus*) (Gance, 1940). In *Le Voile bleu* (*The Blue Veil*) (Stelli, 1942), often considered the cinematic quintessence of Vichyssois melodrama, Gaby Morlay plays Louise Jarraud, a woman who, having lost her husband in World War I in 1914 and her own son at birth, decides to devote her live to caring for the children of others. In this film dedicated "to all those women who sacrifice their lives to children," she raises children who are neglected by parents distracted from their educative mission by their egoism, the pursuit of their artistic career, and their taste for pleasure and money. This universal mother is a true incarnation of duty and the guardian of Marshal Pétain's moral values, who, through her unfailing sweetness and gentleness, is meant to remind people of their faults, while implicitly denouncing the depravity and moral laxity of the Third Republic (which had only led to defeat!). Having grown old, without resources, she is cared for in a hospital by Gérard, one of the children she has raised who has become a doctor. In turn, he entrusts to her the education of his own children. Louise Jarraud (the feminine cinematic counterpart to the Marshal himself, who, also being childless, was concerned to extend his universal paternity over the whole French population) is the product of an ideological environment in which "cinema, mindful of the need to seduce while instructing, chooses the register of melodrama, which privileges feeling through the intervention of the feminine, in contrast to political discourse, which uses patriarchal admonition" (Burch and Sellier 1996, p. 100).

The success of a genre is not only measured by the number of spectators, or by the number of films produced; it is also seen in the mode of production and the distribution circuit of its films. The hierarchy of genres (which results from a combination of their cultural legitimacy and their commercial profitability) is a moving matrix in which the successes and setbacks of different genres can be read. For example, the gore film, at first limited to low-budget productions, benefited from the easing of censorship regimes, from the desire of producers to reach a young audience, from the commercial success of some of its films, from the showing of violence in auteur films, and the advent of a fantasy cinema based on special effects, becoming in the 1980s "a second kind of horror film" – as evident in *The Shining* (Kubrick, 1980) or in the films of Cronenberg and Carpenter (Rouyer 1997, p. 85). In the course of attracting commercial interest and gaining its pedigree, this genre was so successfully exploited by big Hollywood productions that it lost its specificity in the 1990s to become a "gore effect" that is recurrently found in action films of all sorts (war films, science-fiction films, thrillers, etc.).

For a long time, until fairly recently, there was a multiplicity of different theater types, from palaces in city centers to small halls in the suburbs. The different types tended to opt for different types of programs, with prestige films and exclusive releases being shown in the one, and low-budget films or, towards the end, release prints and low-cost foreign imports in the other. This variety allowed genres that were not in favor to survive in Western countries. Such survival seems very improbable today, at a time when the multiplication of copies is accompanied by a reduction in the number of offerings shown on screens. Similarly, the existence of the double-program in the United States during the classical era could allow a genre to survive in the B series. The western, for example, encountered an impediment at the end of the 1920s: it did not seem possible, for technical reasons, to shoot movies with sound outside a studio, which is a nuisance for a genre that is characterized by natural movement and setting. These difficulties did not prevent numerous westerns from being made during the 1930s, when the genre recentered itself in the B series, with songs being used to enrich the plot, giving birth to a cinematic line of "singing cowboys." Compensating for a lack of other resources, such songs also allowed these films to tap the more rural and semi-urban audiences of small theaters, and to kindle greater interest among members of the female audience. There are not many category-A westerns during this period, despite several big-spectacle productions shot in 70 mm, such as *The Big Trail* (Walsh, 1930) and *Billy the Kid* (Vidor, 1930). One has to wait until 1939 for prestige westerns to return in force – and the transition of John Wayne from B-series to A-series movies with *Stagecoach*, after ten years of good, loyal service in low-budget westerns at the small firm Republic.

Eclipses and resurgences

The history of a genre also has its natural lifespan. The burlesque disappeared at the beginning of the 1930s, the western, temporarily revitalized by the supply of Italian productions, languished in the 1960s and disappeared in the following decade, which also marked the end of the musical. But this demise should not be explained solely in terms of the all-powerful logic of generic evolution, which views a genre as becoming weakened through the reuse of its own characteristic mannerisms. Such demises are also caused by sociocultural, technological, and economic changes. Sociological shifts in audiences, the disappearance of the B series, the decline of Hollywood studios, and competition with other cultural industries such as television, for instance, help to explain the weakening of Hollywood genres in the 1960s. It is a similar story with the French detective film – a very successful genre for which male stars had a predilection during the 1970s and 1980s – that has almost disappeared from the big screen today, to the benefit of television series. The traditional canons of the genre (in which the police investigator always ends up discovering the truth and reestablishing order within a social group whose "milieu" is structured into a micro-society confined to precise locations) has been extended beyond cinema into series that have a patrimonial flavor, such as the different television versions of the *Investigations of Inspector Maigret* (a hero created by Simenon). On the other hand, the return of cop figures in television programs, as well as legal magistrates exposed to the political order (as in *Le Juge* (*The Judge*), Levebvre, 1984) and vengeful heroes (as in *Liste noire* (*Black List*), Bonnot, 1983), allows the recuperation of the police genre through the medium of television, in which successful crime series (*Navarro, Julie Lescaut*) function as shared fictions reflecting everyday life. The characters in these television series express violent tensions between the political order and the social order, with sympathy being accorded to the policeman on the street, who is not only more in touch with society, but also more "human" (Philippe 1996).

One can therefore consider certain genres as dead genres. That does not mean that westerns or burlesque comedies will no longer be produced sporadically, nor that these generic categories will no longer be used. The interest of cinephiles, the projection of films in screen archives or in art-film theaters that show repeats, and the circulation of older films through television, video, and DVD copies in an attempt to reach a wider audience, can all prolong their existence in terms of categories of reception. Is such an eclipse of a genre permanent, or only temporary? In contrast to critics who like to prophesy the return of a genre after having come out from watching a musical or a western shown on contemporary screens, I do not believe that any dead genre can have a return in the strict sense. Unlike the phoenix that is reborn from its ashes, a cinematic genre cannot revive itself in the same form in a different context of production and reception. That is why it seems preferable to speak of a *resurgence*, drawing an analogy with rivers that have gone underground. When such rivers resurface, having had the composition of their water changed by the subterranean geological environment through which they have passed, the configuration of the new terrain where they now flow forces them into a very different riverbed. When a genre resurfaces, which sometimes happens, it does so with a new balance of semantic and syntactic traits, and in a new interpretive context. Finally, we should note that the factors that cause a genre to resurface after an eclipse are the same ones that cause genres to have a very long life. The same is true of all genres that have fairly fluid boundaries, such as drama or comedy, that persist through the history of cinema, or reappear in dictionaries of generic designations in use in different countries, or in different eras.

The resurgence of the women's film of the 1970s, with *Alice Doesn't Live Here Anymore* (Scorsese, 1974), *Three Women* (Altman, 1977), *Looking for Mr. Goodbar* (Brooks, 1977), *Julia* (Zinnemann, 1978), *Remember My Name* (Rudolph, 1978), *Girl Friends* (Weill, 1978), and *An Unmarried Woman* (Mazursky, 1978), are inscribed in a context that is very different from that of the 1930s and 1940s, marked in particular by women's liberation and the feminist movement. While feminism is not the direct cause of these new women's films, these films touch upon the issue of feminism by organizing their story around the discovery of self or the gaining of independence by a woman. Their ambiguous endings reveal the desire of Hollywood to address these films (at a time when the differences between intended audiences seemed to be very clearly marked) to modern women who are more or less aware of feminism, while nevertheless retaining a more heterogeneous audience who would be alienated by a clear alignment either for or against a hotly debated feminist ideology (Kuhn 1993). According to Charlotte Brunsdon (1993), these new women's films adhere to a discourse that is fairly close to that of modern women's magazines during the period, such as *Cosmopolitan*, that offer an image of femininity characterized by the contradictions between older stereotypes and a project of emancipation and personal and social self-realization. Their female readers would be the type of viewers who watched these films in the 1970s.

To socioeconomic changes must also be added technological changes as forces that modify the formula of a genre after its resurgence. Science-fiction, a genre undoubtedly less threatened by the decline of studios because of its habit of developing through cycles, reappeared in force at the end of the 1970s following *Star Wars* (Lucas, 1977). But the mythology of the frontier (the conquest of space), paranoid anxieties about invasion, and mad or dishonest scientists are relegated to a secondary level by an aesthetic of special effects. This displaces the question of the distinction (or confusion) between human beings and scientific artifacts

165

– which is at the heart of the science-fiction genre – from "real" bodies to images of bodies, as is clearly evident in Cronenberg's films or *The Matrix* (Wachovski brothers, 1999). Moreover, the "pyrotechnical" use of special effects and synthesized images turns the diegetic world of science-fiction into spaces of play, in which the succession of sequences often obeys a paratactic logic (Jullier 1997). The transfer of the video-games industry into the cinema industry (in both senses of the word) is also manifest in this new generic form. It is not, then, the use of new semantic material – biotechnology, for example – that has been instrumental in modifying the formula of the genre, but syntactical changes. A linear narrative in which episodes are linked together has been replaced by a principle of juxtaposition, evident both in the co-presence of creatures or various kinds of objects in the field within the frame, and also in a succession of action scenes.

The history of cinematic genres is, as we have seen throughout this chapter, a complex phenomenon requiring us to take into account and *articulate* the interrelations between several different dimensions. Retracing the history of a genre, then, involves examining a generic category and a group of films sharing a similar organization of semantic and syntactic traits in order to establish their correlations with social, cultural, and cinematic history, and their relationships with other genres. To sum up, there are seven complementary and interrelated aspects that should be considered:

1   The history of the generic process itself.
2   The interactions between the genre under consideration and other genres.
3   The relationships and interchanges between genres and non-cinematic cultural productions.
4   Cultural transfers between one form of cinema (national, for example) and another.
5   The evolution of the conditions of film production.
6   The history of reception and changing audiences.
7   Non-cinematic history, in its different social, cultural, political, ideological dimensions, etc.

Notes

1 See, in particular, Hegel's comments on genre in Section III, Volume II.

2 For a detailed account of *L'Évolution des genres dans l'histoire de la littérature* (Ferdinand Brunetière (1890) vol. 1, Paris, Hachette), see, in particular, Jean-Marie Schaeffer (1989) *Qu'est-ce qu'un genre littéraire?*, Paris, Seuil, pp. 47–63.

3 Referring no longer to single genres, but to the totality of cinematic art, this idea is found, for example, in Rohmer, who picks up the organicist schema according to which art is an autonomous organism endowed with its own life, an infancy, a maturity, then a senescence. On this subject, see Jacques Aumont (2002) *Les Théories des cinéastes*, Paris, Nathan, pp. 120–123.

4 See, for example, Stuart Kaminsky (1974) *American Film Genres: Approaches to a Critical Theory of Popular Film*, Dayton, Pflaum.

5 On this subject, see Jung's works on myth, and those of Mircea Éliade, whose writings are steeped in a "universal syncretism."

6 On this subject, see, for example, Geneviève Sellier (1999) "Henry Bernstein et le cinéma français des années 30," in *CinémAction*, 93, pp. 82–88.

7 See, for example, Jean-Loup Bourget (1983) *Le Cinéma Américain (1895–1980): de Griffith à Cimino*, Paris, Presses Universitaires de France, pp. 76–78.

8 Also contributing to the origins of the genre were songs about the West, circuses, theatrical adaptations of the dime novels, rodeos, etc. For a detailed history of the origins of the genre, see Jean-Louis Leutrat (1987) *Le Western: archéologie d'un genre*, Lyon, Presses Universitaires de Lyon; and Larry Langman (1992) *A Guide to Silent Westerns*, Westport, Greenwood Press.

9 For a summary in English on the *série noire* and French detective films in the 1950s and 1960s, see Ginette Vincendeau (2003) *Jean-Pierre Melville. An American in Paris*, London, BFI, pp. 99–174.

10 Duhamel's series also recruited French authors during the 1950s, but had most of them sign their contracts under an American pseudonym.

11 See also Donald Richie (2001) *A Hundred Years of Japanese Film: A Concise History, with a Selective Guide to Videos and DVDs*, Tokyo, Kodansha International.

12 For a general treatment of the contamination of the melodrama by
    film noir, see Jean-Loup Bourget (1985) *Le Mélodrame hollywoodien*,
    Paris, Stock, pp. 257–265.
13 *Service du Travail Obligatoire* (STO) was the forced relocation of
    thousands of French workers to Germany during the occupation
    of France to assist in the German war effort.

Chapter 6
Genres in Context

A genre, individually considered, is molded and changed by history as well as by intermingling with and distinguishing itself from other cultural forms, including other film genres. The social, cultural, and cinematographic environment is a fundamental force in the genre's appearance and evolution, which means that we need to give further consideration to the cultural influences on genre. An examination of lists of genre categories and the pronounced heterogeneity they display (which we observed in the first chapter of this book) seems to suggest that there are two kinds of film genres: local genres determined by, and named after, a period or a location, and transhistorical and transnational genres. In the case of the latter category, even if the same name is used (such as "melodrama" or "comedy") to characterize films belonging to different periods or different cinematic traditions (thereby demonstrating the appearance of universality), in actual fact this masks national, historical, and cultural differences that are fundamental to the understanding of different generic formulas, which always eventuate in specific contexts. On the other hand, we must consider not only the historicity of a specific genre (as we did in the preceding chapter), but also the history of the systems, the cartographies or the generic groupings in which each genre is produced, understood, and received. Examining these generic logical systems enables us to minimize a tendency inherent in monographs devoted to a particular genre: they usually present a strong centripetal impression, because the genre under consideration occupies, so to speak, the center of a canvas on which the extremely varied strands of influence (contemporary or historical, cinematic or cultural) come together, unite, and disintegrate.

Cultural Identity and the Circulation of Genres

The social and cultural function of a genre and the organization of the semantic and syntactic features that give it its form are intrinsically linked, and do not constitute a stable given. This is why, in tending to view genres that cross the history of cinema, or appear in most lists of generic categories as archetypal forms to which specific film production and reception contexts would simply lend local color, transcultural and transhistorical analyses often confuse genre as a category with genre as a group of films. Thus, even though there is a generic category "comedy," used in different countries or diverse periods, it includes other categories (with which it is at times coterminous in generic repertories) that are less widely accepted, and which are specific to a cultural or historical period (such as screwball comedy, comedy of manners, slapstick comedy, black comedy). Moreover, "comedy" suggests more the tone of the films that it designates (they are supposed to generate laughter) than the recurrent semantic and syntactic features that make a group of films a genre, or an explanation of the social or cultural signification of the genre.

Transnational genres and local genres:
a misleading dichotomy

It is easier to recognize the cultural identity of generic categories that have a restricted usage, or of genres that designate a set of films clearly defined in terms of geography and history, than it is to understand the cultural and aesthetic differences intrinsic to the larger generic categories.

Thus, no one would dispute the impact of the political context on the appearance of the *levita* genre (or "redingote cinema") in Spanish cinema during the Franco era, a genre based on literary adaptation that privileges historical legacy and restoration in order to activate conflicts and intrigue that always culminate in a moral and edifying conclusion.

In the same vein, the *vaudevilles militaires* (literally, "military vaudevilles") seem to constitute a genre typical of French cinema (in which the number of examples is manifestly higher that in other cinemas). Especially common in the 1930s, with films like *Les Gaietés de l'escadron* (*Fun in Barracks*) (Tourneur, 1932) or *Les Dégourdis de la 11ème* (*The Smart Guys of the Eleventh Company*) (Christian-Jaque, 1937), they deal with comic events of a life in barracks that lacks achievements or greatness, with conscripts vying to outdo each other in laziness, resourcefulness, and cunning in an attempt to escape the dump and avoid maneuvers, or to get round the vigilance of a visiting general. Underneath their inglorious appearance and their less-than-flattering portrayals, these films nevertheless provide a cinematic image of "regimental memories." In France, military service, which was compulsory for all men up until 1997, historically played a very important role in the consolidation of national identity and the construction of the French Republic at the end of the nineteenth century, given that *all* male citizens, irrespective of class, were obliged to undergo national military service, often in distant places, and could be mobilized in the event of conflict. But regimental memories were also a recurrent topic in ordinary male conversations. Men who had completed their military service (particularly if they had not been involved in colonial or global conflicts, on account of the generation to which they belonged) would recount episodes from their military life, often in a jocular tone: fatigue duties, avoidance tactics, their relationships with commissioned officers, friendships they had formed during this time, etc. By popularizing and elevating the spirit of male camaraderie, most of the *vaudevilles militaires* also participate in the national ideology supporting conscription, in a comic vein, as is especially evident in two cycles from the 1970s, one launched by *Les Bidasses en folie* (*Rookies Run Amok*) (Zidi, 1971), and the other by *Mais où est donc passée la 7ème compagnie?* (*Now Where did the Seventh Company Get to?*) (Lamoureux, 1973), in which reluctant conscripts and regular soldiers who are rather cowardly reveal an unexpected courage.

Specific to German and Austrian cinema, the *Heimatfilme*, inspired from reactionary regionalist novels in the 1920s, often take the form of an educational documentary on the unique character of Germany. They were produced as much under the Weimar Republic as under Nazism, and became the most popular genre in these national cinemas during the 1950s. This is evident in the immense success of *Schwarzwaldmädel* (*The Black Forest Girl*) (Deppe, 1950) that attracted more than 16 million German viewers. In this era, although often set in such mythical settings as the banks of the Danube or the Alps of the Black Forest in Germany, films do not make any explicit reference to any specific geographical places, nor the idea of nation or homeland (*Vaterland*). Instead, they evoke the idea of a space filled with sweetness and harmony, in which people feel "at home with themselves" (*heimlich sein*). As Pierre Sorlin argues in his analysis, the *Heimatfilme* present a utopia, a timeless dream, a simple and reassuring response to Germans who were asking themselves "Where is Germany?" in the aftermath of Nazism, defeat, occupation, and partition: "it is there in the place where you feel at home with yourself, in the *Heimat* [homeland]" (2000, p. 42).

In Germany, the consequences of Nazism had led to a strong questioning of pan-Germanism and Prussian militarism. The *Heimatfilme* authorized the reconstruction of an ideal past, liberated from all kinds of militarism, and displaced into the western or southern provinces of the country (Sorlin 2000, p. 44). Strongly reactionary, the *Heimatfilme* thus emphasized peaceful and quasi-timeless local communities in which the social group and its traditions transmit authentic marital and family values capable of resolving all conflicts. Eventually, all those who have been tempted by the sirens of modernity and independence end up partaking of these values in a kind of communion. That is why in the 1960s a new form arose that challenged the *Heimatfilme*, denouncing the idyllic vision and suppression of memory promoted by the genre in order to underline the "daily fascism" exercised by the community. *Jagdzenen aus Niederbayern* (*Hunting Scenes From Bavaria*) (Fleischmann, 1969), for example, tells how at the time of the annual harvest festival, villagers persecute marginal figures: a simple soul, a disabled person, a prostitute, a widow in too much hardship to remarry, and a homosexual who is beaten up following an actual manhunt. This kind of rereading of the genre was pursued during the 1980s with *Heimat* (*Homeland: A German Chronicle*) (Reitz, 1981–4), a very long film, initially made for television and shown in cinemas in several parts, recounting the life of a German family from 1919 to 1982 from a Marxist perspective.

French *vaudeville militaire*, *levita* cinema, and the *Heimatfilme* are genres that have known both success and notoriety in their own national contexts. Their strong national, ideological, and cultural roots, however, have meant that they have enjoyed only very limited distribution and almost no recognition as genres outside the borders of their own countries except by specialists. While the cultural identity of local genres is evident, it is often hidden in the genres that are present in several repertories of generic categories, as well as those in several other cinemas. However, these local genres cannot be thought of as transnational prototypes tied to archetypal cognitive, expressive, and emotional schemata. In fact, categories such as melodrama, comedy, and adventure films derive from very general cultural schemes that are common to Western culture, which means that only ethnocentrism would lead one to invoke them as interpretive frameworks for understanding Indian or Japanese cinema, for example (unless only films directly inspired from Western melodramatic models are to be considered melodramas in those countries). Moreover, certain of these categories recombine very different phenomena within fairly fluid boundaries – the adventure film, for example, can be a colonial film, a war film, a sword and cape film, a pirate film, etc. – meaning that they receive very distinctive embodiments in different national cinemas.

Remakes provide an excellent touchstone for judging the determining importance of historical and cultural traits in the appearance of a genre. For example, an analysis of Hollywood remakes of French comedies in the 1980s and 1990s that were made shortly after the French version reveals the importance of ideological and aesthetic cultural identity in the comedies of both French and Hollywood cinemas (Moine 2002). *Three Men and a Baby* (Nimoy, 1988) and *True Lies* (Cameron, 1994), which share a similar comic register, based respectively on *Trois Hommes et un couffin* (*Three Men and a Cradle*) (Serreau, 1985) and *La Totale!* (Zidi, 1991). But the spirit of the boulevard and the comedy of manners that impregnates the story of the discovery by three confirmed bachelors of the joys and difficulties of a "mothering" fatherhood, or the story of the lies and habits of the couple in *La Totale!*, tend to be replaced in the American remakes by the rhythm and events of action comedy. Thus, the importance and treatment of the drug story in Coline Serreau's film differ radically from those in the film by Leonard Nimoy. In both cases, the heroes are certainly confronted with a double delivery that troubles them in different ways – that of a baby by its mother, and that of a packet of heroin – which triggers a certain number of *quid pro quos*. But the drug business remains a secondary plot that is intimately linked with the baby in *Trois Hommes et un couffin*. In order to get rid of the heroin and to evade the inquiries of the police and reprisals by the drug dealers, Michel dupes a young inspector and dumps the drugs in a dustbin in Monceau park. He has used two nappies to swaddle the little girl, and when he stops at a park bench to change the infant, he throws away both the wet nappy and the nappy in which the drugs are hidden in a single action, meaning that the drug dealer has only to pick it up. In contrast, the three friends in *Three Men and a Baby* join forces with the police to trick the drug dealers and put them in prison, and this active collaboration dominates the whole second half of the film. Similarly, the epilogue of *Trois Hommes et un couffin* shows men who are depressed because they are unable to bear the emptiness left when the baby has been taken back by its mother. Fortunately, the young woman comes back with a renewed request for help, giving them a pretext for enthusiastically agreeing to look after the baby once more. The film ends with the first steps of the little girl. The ending of *Three Men and a Baby* reaches a dead end with the absence of the baby, who has also been taken by her mother, and the "lack" that the three men feel. No sooner have they separated from the baby than they rush to the airport to prevent the mother and the girl from boarding the aircraft. The film ends with the image of a foursome (the three men and the young woman) who are pushing a pram together. Not only does this ending provide a solution (an expanded family), instead of leaving everything open as is implied in the shot of a growing child, but it favors fast-moving action at the expense of reflection. In the French version, the idleness of the three men, their moroseness, their slips, allow a male desire for children to be glimpsed without being made explicit. This divergence between the French version (which cultivates ambiguity, allusion, and psychological depth) and the American version (which privileges action by not hesitating to make the story more spectacular) defines two different ways of making comedies and, in addition to this, undoubtedly, two different ways of telling stories, and two different functions of cinema (Ginette Vincendeau 1997).

The genre of melodrama, or melodramatic genres?

An examination of collections of films from a variety of cinematic horizons – grouped under the label "melodrama" in France – clearly illustrates the insufficiency of a single generic term and its limited ability to explain and account for the codification and meaning of melodramas produced in different contexts. We should note, moreover, that the abundance of formulas for cinematic melodramas should be seen in relation to the different forms of melodrama to which the nineteenth century gave birth in Europe and America before the advent, and outside, of cinema.

175

The cultural polysemy of cinematic genres should be seen, to some extent, as related to that of literary, theatrical, and operatic genres. Given that the history and forms of melodrama could fill a whole book by themselves, I will limit the present discussion to a comparison of two contemporary national expressions of melodrama: the Hollywood melodrama and the Italian melodrama of the 1950s, as an example. This comparison will show clearly that cultural influences strongly determine each of the two generic formulas.

From the outset, as Jean-Loup Bourget demonstrates, Hollywood melodramas owed a great deal to the Victorian novel, in contrast to French and Italian cinematic melodramas that situated themselves more directly in the tradition of theatrical melodrama: "English [critics] tend, moreover, to reserve the appellation of '(crime) melodrama,' '(war) melodrama,' etc., for action films characterized by their plot and events, and to prefer the sentimental term 'romantic drama' as a designation for the genre" (1985, p. 12). For Bourget, the Hollywood melodrama (that is, the "romantic drama") is defined as a film that displays the three following characteristics: a character who is a victim (often female), a recourse to providential or catastrophic events deriving from a realistic causality, and a treatment that emphasizes the pathos of the situations depicted and/or the violence of events. In accordance with this program, genre films produced in Hollywood during the 1950s are often "flamboyant melodramas," in which color, music, and the large screen are combined to constitute a sumptuous form. Clichéd situations (such as terrible accidents, often having an expiatory function, infirmities that inscribe their status as victims in the bodies of the protagonists, rivalries between brothers who are enemies, and hidden secrets that provide an obstacle to happiness) perpetuate the themes of this genre in Hollywood (Bourget 1985, pp. 32–63). *Magnificent Obsession* (Sirk, 1953) thus opens with a speedboat accident, the victim of which is Bob Merrick, a rich, selfish playboy. He is saved with the help of a cardiac machine, but his rescue is achieved at the cost of the life of Doctor Phillips, an eminent surgeon who dies at the same moment because the equipment is not available to be used on him. Indirectly responsible for the death of the doctor to whom he owes his life, Bob subsequently causes the blindness of Helen, the wife of the former. Having fallen in love with her, and keen to do everything in his power to help her, he precipitates the accident that renders her blind through his persistence – she is knocked over by a car when she tries to escape from his excessive solicitousness. In *An Affair to Remember* (McCarey, 1957), Terry is unable to turn up at the rendezvous that she and Nickie had arranged at the top of the Empire State Building six months after the cruise on which they met (the time needed to be sure of their love and to set each of their lives in order). She is knocked over by a car and becomes paralyzed, without Nickie being aware of it. Cal, the "bad son" played by James Dean in *East of Eden* (Kazan, 1954), who believes he is wicked and is persuaded that his father does not love him, learns that his father has hidden the truth of their mother's disappearance from his two sons. She was not a saintly woman whom death snatched away from the family, but ran a brothel in Monterrey. Obsessed with this secret (which he ends up revealing), he increasingly comes into conflict with his father and his brother Aaron, and grows closer to Abra, the fiancée of the latter. The father, having been knocked down during an argument, finally realizes his mistake, and Cal, who has supplanted Aaron in the heart of Abra, marries the young woman and assumes control of his father's farm while Aaron leaves to fight on the French front. As the title of the film suggests and the sheriff explains, "Cain shall withdraw from the presence of Yahweh and will dwell in the land of Nod, in the east of Eden." Pairs of brothers, real or symbolic, sometimes enemies, with one being good and the other bad, the one a true son and the other a wicked son or a bastard, are also found in the form of Frank, the prominent father of a family, and Dave, a bohemian writer who gambles and drinks, in *Some Came Running* (Minnelli, 1958); in Kyle and Mitch, the two male protagonists in *Written On the Wind* (Sirk, 1955); and in Theron, the legitimate son who refuses to admit paternity of the child he has conceived with his girlfriend Libby (thus replicating the fault of his father); and Rafe, the illegitimate son who marries Libby to protect the child from the life of shame that he has known, in *Home From the Hill* (Minnelli, 1959).

But, even more than clichéd situations, it is a stylistic criterion, color, that determines the affiliation of a Hollywood film with melodrama in the 1950s, being joined with music to serve a common expressive function. In the context of a competition with television that prompted Hollywood to use color ever more frequently on the big screen at a time when color was still a novelty, color "accentuated the spectacular, and therefore melodramatic, aspects of films, while black and white underlined its seriousness, and often its literary affiliations, by reinforcing the somber atmosphere of drama" (Bourget 1985, p. 265). Film drama, for which directors often choose interiorization – even when they are adapting works by authors of melodrama, as Mankiewicz did with *Suddenly Last Summer* (1959), after Tennessee Williams – seems to distinguish itself from melodrama by the use of black and white. In addition, color in melodrama, just as in the musical, is used to create unrealistic effects. The color palette of *Written On the Wind*, for instance, is fundamentally expressive and symbolic, with red and bright pink strikingly serving to characterize the Hadley brother and sister, two characters consumed by a devastating passion. Kyle wears a scarlet dressing gown, and everything about Marylee is red, from her clothes to her fingernails, including her car and telephone. This use of color and the big screen became the signature of a kind of melodrama in which violence, inherited from the 1940s influence of *film noir*, is thereafter primarily encoded at a visual and formal level. Thus *Party Girl* (Ray, 1958), whose screenplay indisputably bears the mark and spirit of *film noir*, displaced the criminal plot into the mode of melodrama by practically using only vivid yellow and red colors to accentuate conflicts and passions. This flamboyance accompanied, as if by way of compensation, a waning of sentimentality and of the presence of ambiguous female victim characters typical of the 1930s and 1940s. The period – marked by "a re-partition and separation of the roles of providers and reproducers according to their sex, imposed both by rhetoric and the economy" – tends to make mothers responsible for the ills of American society, and women the guardians of the domestic sphere (Walker 1993, p. 222). Even though in reality a greater number of women worked after the war than before it, the dominant ideological discourse, by extolling the ideal cultural role of women as that of wife and mother, separated the examination of gendered roles from that of social problems. In this context, Hollywood cinema privileged family melodramas at the expense of female melodramas and women's films centered upon the character of a woman. One still finds them, however, in films of different genres dealing with psychoanalysis and femininity, such as *Whirlpool* (Preminger, 1949) or *The Three Faces of Eve* (Johnson, 1957) (Walker 1993). Finally, even though certain films, usually remakes – such as *An Affair to Remember* (McCarey's color remake of *Love Affair*, his 1939 film) – preserve the attributes of the erotic melodrama, the spectacular effects of color are substituted for those of deep emotions.

Italian melodramas of the 1950s, although they form a far less homogeneous group than Hollywood melodramas of the same period, share a common aim – to pay homage to Italian identity through two forms: filmed operas, and popular sentimental dramas that show the influence of theatrical arts. Filmed operas, nostalgically celebrating national greatness and unity, allowed for the revival, after the period of Mussolini's rule, of an acceptable patriotism and a relegitimation of the concept of nationhood. They elicited a profound response because the lyrical tradition was deeply rooted throughout the peninsula, being close to the hearts of different groups in the population, and because opera, even before the unification of Italy, was already a national art form. Moreover, the destruction of many lyric theaters in the provinces was conducive to an expansion on screens of a genre that seemed capable of competing with Hollywood in its spectacular nature, and with its Italian stars whose fame appeared to offer a national counterbalance to the halo surrounding American stars (Giacomini 2000, pp. 217–218). After the war, Gallone thus successfully exploited the tumultuous passions of the lyric repertoire across a dozen films, from *Rigoletto* in 1947 to *La Tosca* in 1956, including *Casta Diva* (1955) and *La Traviata* (1947), which departed from the libretto by showing a meeting

179

in the final sequence between Verdi and Alexandre Dumas over the tomb of Marie Duplessis. In an altogether different style, *Senso* (*Livia*) (Visconti, 1954) begins the story of the love of the Countess Serpieri for the Austrian lieutenant Franz Malher (as passionate as it is unhappy) by showing a scene being enacted at La Fenice in Venice from Act III of *Il Trovatore*. The twin threads of patriotic and erotic passion, which are woven through the melodramatic weft of the film, begin to unroll during this performance: a multitude of tricolored leaflets descends at the end from the chorus of soldiers on to the parterre occupied by Austrian officers; the Countess and Franz make their acquaintance by exchanging several comments on the opera, a melodrama (which the Countess says she only likes when it is staged), while the diva is singing the aria *D'amor sull'ali rosee / vene, sospir dolente*. As Stefano Socci remarks, "the heart of *Senso* is in fact a prism formed of mirrors reflecting spaces as much as melodrama: the theater, a select place, but also the scene of life and reality, with loves, wars, sacrifices, tears, griefs, passions, betrayals" (1993, p. 116).

The lyric vein of melodrama, important during the first half of the decade, slowly dried up at the end of the 1950s when the distancing of the war and the improvement in the standard of living led directors and the audience to turn towards the representation of familiar problems and ordinary people. François Giacomini compares this decline to the end of the early style of neo-realism, which, moreover, had not neglected melodrama, as, for example, in Visconti's *Bellissima* (1951) or Antonioni's *La signora senza camelie* (*Camille Without Camelias*) (1957), in which women from the lower classes cling to the illusory dream of a distinguished career in the movies: "with different narrative and artistic schemes," the two filmic forms "often convey adjacent ideas: pessimism about human nature, an exaltation of superior values viewed through the lenses of individual destinies, and the absence of a happy ending" (Giacomini 2000, p. 218).

After the war, sentimental melodramas very successfully exploited the local Neapolitan dialectical tradition of the *scenaggiata*, "a spectacle conceived for the stage or screen (taking the words and melodies of popular songs as its point of departure) that dramatizes melodramatic characters and situations from the *malavita* . . . lost women and Madonnas of the roses" (Schifano 1995, p. 21). Roberto Amoroso, who specializes in this formula, sees the *scenaggiata* as being relaunched with *Malaspina* (Fizzarotti and Amoroso, 1947). The plot, revolving around passions, love betrayals, and crimes of honor, takes place in contemporary Naples, and dialogues in Neapolitan dialect (scarcely recognizable as Italian) are layered over, and sometimes mingle with, the words of the title song played outside the field of the shot. This genre saw its moment of glory in the 1950s with films that were produced in Rome (by Titanus Studios, for example) and generally shot in the South of Italy. Such films were often embellished with songs in dialect – often "Italianized," however, so as to appeal to a larger audience. These melodramas like to tell the stories of families trying to maintain their cohesion, in which passion, either guilty or redemptive, but often theatricalized, is preferably embodied in the female characters. The heroine – pure and weak, guilty of a former "sin" (a term recurrently used in the films) that is always present, or a resolute adventuress, following the example of her cousins in Hispanic melodramas, such as *Susana demonio y carne* (*The Devil and the Flesh*) (Buñuel, 1950) – presents a threat on account of her sensual nature and her erotic power. It is not uncommon in the screenplays to find that the woman's infidelity, real or imagined, and the murder of a rival by a friend or a jealous lover threaten the couple or a family before a final development can end up reuniting the household anew, as in *Catene* (*Chains*) (Matarazzo, 1950). This film began the career of a mythical melodramatic couple formed by Yvonne Sanson and Amadeo Nazarri, formerly a young lead in the 1930s who later took on roles as a father or older brother, and launched the strain, in its Italianized form, of the Neapolitan melodrama. The same Matarazzo would enjoy a colossal success in Italy with 16 other films of this type during the decade, such as *Tormento* (*Torment*) (1951), the story of a woman whose misery and the condemnation of her husband (unjustly convicted through a judicial error) force her to abandon her child to her horrible mother-in-law, or *La Nave delle donne*

181

maledette (*The Ship of Condemned Women*) (1954), which begins with a crime and false evidence: a young woman from a good family, guilty of infanticide, asks her poor cousin to confess to the crime that she has committed. Beyond popular cinema, the South of Italy, its settings, and its melodies, seem to be the chosen ground for melodrama, even in its neo-realist incarnations. The Neapolitan heroine of *Un Marito per Anna Zaccheo* (*A Husband for Anna*) (De Santis, 1953) is seduced by a married man, resists an old *camorrista*, before succumbing to an ill-fated passion for a sailor from Ravenna, a man from the North whose inability to understand the passions of the South is manifest when a scene from a *scenaggiata* makes him burst into laughter while the rest of the audience is in tears. Famous Neapolitan tunes accompany the story of an English couple undergoing a crisis in *Viaggio in Italia* (*Journey to Italy*) (Rossellini, 1953). The exhumation in Pompeii of the bodies of two lovers buried by the ashes from Vesuvius, and a traditional procession celebrating the Virgin Mary (which interrupts their journey, separating them momentarily in the crowd of worshippers) are the agents of their reconciliation.

As one can see, even though American and Italian melodramas have in common an intense action that articulates events and developments involving stereotypical characters, numerous traits distinguish them. The typology of characters and the nature of the clichéd situations are not the same in the two cinemas during the 1950s. Italian melodrama bears witness – in its alliances with opera and history, as well as with the Neapolitan tradition – to a national or regional cultural identity. While the music in these movies accentuates the pathos of events and fills out the emotional ambiance of the plot situations, as it does in Hollywood movies, its expressive function is doubled by a strong identificatory connotation and the meaning of the passages that are sung – most obviously in the filmed operas, but also in the melodramas produced in Naples, and in certain melodramas from the South. These songs are more numerous that in American films, in which they usually appear only in the form of title songs while the opening or final credits are rolling, only rarely finding their way to the interior of the film (as in *An Affair to Remember*). Finally, the use of color, a determining factor in the semantic aspect of Hollywood melodrama during this period, is almost absent from Italian melodrama. In a Europe still accustomed to black and white, Mattarazzo's attempts to use color ended in failure (Sorlin 2000, p. 39).

To employ the same generic label to designate phenomena occurring in very different contexts, therefore, is to use it to substitute one form or mode that is culturally dominant in a given cultural era for the actual genre. Bearing this in mind, Linda Williams proposes to distinguish "melodrama" as a genre from "melodrama" as a mode in American cinema. The first characterizes "women's films," family melodramas, and certain biographical films; the second includes the preceding genres, but is especially, for Williams, the basic register of American popular cinema itself, involving stories that lead us to experience compassion for the characters (innocent victims of forces beyond their control) through sensational scenes to paroxysmal moments in which the moral virtue of the characters is revealed. These moments, which spectacularize and amplify a "feminine" pathos (as in the majority of films in the genre of "the melodrama") and a "masculine" action do not interrupt the narration, but progress and sustain it (Williams 1998). Moreover, Williams indicates that the prime function of the melodramatic mode is also to combine in the same film strongly emotional moments of action and pathos. Thus, traditional masculine genres, such as the war film, work in a melodramatic mode when they present both the spectacle of war actions and the tears of the hero, which has the effect of rendering the acts of the protagonists innocent by making them victims who elicit the sympathy of the viewer.

The *Rambo* series, often interpreted as emblematic of a conservative Reaganite America aiming to rehabilitate macho values via virile, muscled heroes in order to get rid of bad memories of Vietnam, belongs to the action film genre as much as to that of the war film. But it also exploits a melodramatic mode by shrouding John Rambo in a melodramatic aura of pathos as a victim who is only asking to rediscover a lost state of patriotic innocence in which "our country loves us as much as we love it." In *Rambo* (Kotchev, 1982), the former Vietnam war-hero, having returned to his country, becomes a lone guerilla in a small American town before collapsing at the end of the film into the arms of his former colonel, to whom he has agreed to surrender. The spectacle of the actions of the former green-beret is followed by the pathos and distress of a man who weeps at the loss of the war, of his friends, and of his innocence. As Linda Williams indicates, this series, like many war films devoted to Vietnam, "reconfigures victims and villains." It does not only turn exploits and actions into a spectacle, but also works through the *mise en scène* of these exploits "within a melodramatic mode struggling to 'solve' the overwhelming moral burden of having been the 'bad guys' in a lost war. The greater the historical burden of guilt, the more pathetically and the more actively the melodrama works to recognize and regain a lost innocence" (Williams 1998, p. 61).

The circulation of genres

The dichotomy between local genres and transhistorical or transnational genres can partly be resolved, then, if one sees in it the application of two different uses of the notion of "genre" – according to which it refers to a mode where this word designates a cultural formula that is ideologically and temporally specific, endowed with stable semantic and syntactic traits.

To that, one must add the processes of importation, integration, and acculturation of genres whose numbers increase as a cinema grows more dominant, with its models circulating in the international arena. Genre films, when they are exported, thus contribute to the construction of an international awareness of the genre, even if that does not mean that viewers everywhere respond to the films in the same way. On one hand, generic denominations can be accepted into national lexicons either without being translated – as with the "western" or the "thriller" – or through a translation – as with the *comédie musicale* (a term very distinct from *operette*) which adapts the American "musical" into the French lexicon.

It can also happen that the context of reception can reconstitute a generic category within different national boundaries, as occurred with the *peplum*, which in France included the string of Italian films on ancient subjects or films that were made in co-production with Italy, and only a small number of the Hollywood epics and grand-spectacle films. A generic category from a foreign country can also be adopted for the sake of redefining it with a new label to be used in local productions. Thus, as Ib Bondebjerg (2000) demonstrates, Danish critics used the term "musical" from the end of the 1950s to characterize not only Hollywood musical films, but also national productions that included songs, music, and dancing. Achieving a big popular success from the 1930s, numerous Danish musical films were designated for nearly thirty years as "operettas," following a European and Danish tradition, or through the appellation *lystpil*, a term that refers both to the tradition of German comedy (*lustspiel*), very influential on Danish cinema, and also the more Anglo-American tradition of the romantic comedy and the musical film. Their female stars, like Marguerite Viby (a pure product of the Danish music hall and a peerless star of the genre from the 1930s to the 1950s) and Lillian Ellis, were perceived as the embodiments of a Danish national identity that was opposed to Hollywood – which was then perceived either as a threatening form of alterity that served to define Danish style and identity by way of contrast, or as an ideal form of the Other that Danish cinema would never manage to equal. Thus, the film *Alle går rundt og forelsker sig* (*Everybody Falls in Love*) (Gregers, 1941) was called an "operetta" on its release, and one reads in the press that its star, Lillian Ellis, who plays the role of Mette Madsen, was still a dazzling young woman from Copenhagen, despite the years spent overseas: Danish cinema was going to offer her a chance that her earlier career in Hollywood had not offered her. Whether critics criticized this film (which still mixed Danish and American elements) as a pale imitation of American musicals, or praised it, they still identified it as an expression of Danish identity. The application of the term "musical" to designate Danish musical films, which emerged at the end of the 1950s, was the result of aesthetic changes inspired by Hollywood style (such as a better integration of the dance numbers with the narration). These films also partly originated from the situation of Danish cinema during the war:

> The Germans wanted their films to have primacy, but the Danes did not accept that. To the contrary, Danish cinema was revitalized by it and became more popular than ever. This also means that Danish producers and filmmakers launched themselves in new directions, trying to develop new forms out of other genres that had until then been largely the preserve American or European cinema. The advent of screwball comedies, the crime film, the *film noir*, the thriller, and the musical film were important during the 1940s, but they also established the foundations of forms to come in the 1960s. (Bondebjerg 2000, p. 200)

Also, when the term "musical" became established at the end of the 1950s as a term to describe "new" Danish musical films, it was used retroactively to describe all films that exploited the Hollywood syntax of this genre. *Alle går rundt og forelsker sig* was thereafter seen as the first Danish musical, shot in the modern style of the American backstage musicals. From this time onwards there was emphasis on visual references to, and musical borrowings from, the American genre.

The circulation of generic appellations is, then, also a circulation of forms that become modified as a result of the changing circumstances of their production. The case of the Italian westerns made in the 1960s illustrates this. This genre was adopted in Europe by the Spanish, the British, and above all by the Italians, who gave a second life to a genre that had fallen into disuse in the United States, where it had suffered a decline on the big screen. This was certainly not the first non-Hollywood incursion into a genre whose visual elements, semantics, and meaning were intimately tied to American history, its landscape, and its ideology, since the silent cinema in Europe had already produced westerns, such as the French short films of Jean Durand during the

1910s, often shot in the Camargue – for example, *Calino veut être cowboy* (*Calino Wants to Be a Cowboy*) (1911). Nevertheless, it was the first time that a significant number of westerns had been produced outside of Hollywood – with a resounding success, moreover – justifying the emergence of the "European western" as a genre. In crossing the Atlantic, the western underwent a metamorphosis. Shot in desert landscapes that could evoke the American deserts, the films displayed a clear preference for Mexican subjects, and the sounds of the names of many characters (e.g., Django, Spirito Santo, Trinita) bring a touch of Latinity to the adventures of the West. Sometimes described as "carnivalesque" because of the overturning of the codes and values of the American western that they perpetrate, and because they give pride of place to dirty or grotesque bodies, they replaced the often aged and worn-out westerners in the American films of the preceding decade with cynical heroes, of whom Clint Eastwood is the emblem, or else sadistic and cruel characters. In *C'era una volta il West* (*Once Upon a Time in the West*) (Leone, 1969), Henry Fonda, a star who eminently symbolized the deeds of the West, having played the noble Wyatt Earp in *My Darling Clementine* (Ford, 1946), becomes the cruel Frank who has hanged the brother of the man with a harmonica in particularly atrocious circumstances. The characters in Leone's "dollar" trilogy – *A Fistful of Dollars* (1964), *For a Few Dollars More* (1965), and *The Good, the Bad, and the Ugly* (1966) – are characters without faith or law, bounty-hunters or treasure-seekers without scruples or morality. The world of the Italian western is one of exaggeration. Violence is pushed to its height in *Il Grande silenzio* (*The Great Silence*) (Corbucci, 1968), in which Loco, the most bloodthirsty outlaw in Utah – acted by the disturbing Klaus Kinski – kills the sheriff who has arrested him, then the hero, Silence, before getting away with total impunity. At a formal level, everything thus works towards intensification: the emptiness of space, temporal dilation of scenes accentuated by an emotionally wrenching musical score, caricaturing exaggeration of realistic details, and the multiplication of facial close-up shots – elements that are condensed in the gunfight between Frank and the man with the harmonica at the end of *Once Upon a Time in the West*. The Italian western thus denies the myths of the western (law, civilization, the frontier), even though reference to the American model is visible: through the caricature of certain conventional motifs, the use of American actors, the playful exploitation (but one that is not without a certain fascination for Hollywood cinema) of American pseudonyms (Sergio Leone/ Bob Robertson), or the practice of parody. The long wait of the killers at the station in *Once Upon a Time in the West*, for example, is taken from *High Noon* (Zinnemann, 1952), but the presence of a fly that continually annoys Jack Elam introduces a disrespectful touch of humor into the allusion. In addition, in crossing the Atlantic the western changed sufficiently to provoke purists into refusing to accept it completely as part of the genre. They saw it as nothing more than a degradation of the western motivated by commercial interest, or baptized it with the pejorative term, "spaghetti western."

Generic Regimes

Genres, whether one thinks of them as categories of classification, production, or interpretation, are not self-contained entities, as is shown by their history, which is made up of interactions, reciprocal influences, and successive genrifications that result in a constant mixing of genres. They are defined in a differential manner and are organized into systems and hierarchies in which each finds its place, its form, and its boundaries through its relationship with other genres. The history of genres is therefore also that of *generic regimes* that each cinematic context establishes in a way that is always evolutionary.

The rationale of generic regimes

A generic regime is, above all, determined by the group of generic categories that comprise it, and by the relations they maintain between them. These relationships cannot be thought of in terms of coexistence and juxtaposition, since genres construct themselves, as we have seen, out of each other. A generic regime is not, therefore, the map of a headquarters in which clearly distinct spaces are divided up with definitive boundaries. Moreover, they offer a collection of genres that are not all to be viewed on the same level, since they are organized in a hierarchical fashion, and in several different ways.

On one hand, a hierarchy of genres exists, based on a distinctive criterion of critical, aesthetic, and ideological judgment. In French cinema of the 1950s, for example, melodrama, especially female melodrama, was a genre with a poor press, owing to a cultural refusal to speak about the relations between the sexes in moral and affective terms. This promoted a discourse on gender that "favored a masculine point of view involving seduction and conquest, translating into an eroticism that was restricted to language in the 1930s, but enlarged to include the image of the female body in the 1950s" (Burch and Sellier 1996, p. 248). Added to this cultural disparagement was the opprobrium cast over the genre by the ideology propagated in Pétainist cinema during the Occupation.

On the other hand, certain genres appear as dominant forms when judged by the quantity of films produced, their success, and their ability to disseminate and export certain of their traits into other contemporary genres. Thus, Steve Neale proposes a comprehensive diachronic scheme of generic regimes in American cinema that he organizes according to the prevalence of one or two genres in what he defines as successive "eras" of Hollywood cinema (1995, pp. 174–175). He argues from an evolutionist perspective inspired by the "struggle between genres" proposed by the Russian Formalists (cf. chapter 5, p. 133), in which dominant genres structure production, and transform the formulas of other genres before being replaced by others as a result of shifts in the audience and ideological, economic, and technological changes. For Neale, early American cinema, formed out of the conjunction of other artistic forms, such as photography, the magic lantern and other optical spectacles, and the vaudeville, was dominated by three genres which arise out of these forms: "views," the special-effects film, and the "slapstick" (that is, the comic burlesques characteristic of Mack Sennett's Keystone Studios). The formation of studios, the growth of audiences in the more suburban areas, an increase in the length of films, and then the arrival of speaking motion pictures progressively brought melodrama and comedy to the forefront. It is not surprising that the western entered into alliances first with the burlesque, and then with melodrama and, to a lesser extent, with the musical. After World War II, in a period marked by ideological crisis and then the weakening of the studio system, the drama and the epic (that is, grand spectacle) arranged a new landscape of genres by entering into the western, the war film, and the musical, before giving way to the science-fiction and horror elements that constituted a major aspect of the new "blockbusters."

To these hierarchical parameters that determine the logical system of generic regimes, one must add an identifying parameter that was very important for non-autonomous cinemas (especially European cinemas after World War II). Such cinemas are powerfully subject to the influence and penetration of other cinemas, meaning that their own generic regimes come into contact (through competition, retreat, resistance, enrichment, or acculturation) with other generic regimes – in particular, those of a dominant Hollywood cinema. This phenomenon had repercussions both at the level of production, and also at that of reception. Thus, French cinema of the 1950s (concerned to respond to American competition on its own terrain) oriented itself to some extent towards big productions – either national ones, like *Si Versailles m'était conté* (*Royal Affairs in Versailles*) by Guitry, or co-productions mounted with Italy or Spain – and showed a greater inclination to codify genres such as the crime film, the operetta, the historical film, and the literary adaptation. These last two genres often merged into a grand French patriotic spectacle spiced with a dash of eroticism and libertinism with the cape and sword film, which enjoyed its hour of glory right up to the beginning of the 1960s, even having its own undisputed star, Jean Marais, the hero of *Nez de cuir* (*Leathernose*) (Allégret, 1951), the *Comte de Monte-Cristo* (*The Count of Monte Cristo*) (Vernay, 1954), *Le Bossu* (*The Hunchback of Paris*) (Hunebelle, 1959), *Le Capitan* (*Captain Blood*) (Hunebelle, 1960), *Le Capitaine Fracasse* (*Captain Fracasse*) (Gaspard-Huit, 1961), *La Princesse de Clèves* (*Princess of Cleves*) (Delannoy, 1961), and *Le Masque de fer* (*The Iron Mask*) (Decoin, 1962). If one also takes reception into account, the issue becomes even more complicated. It then turns out that there was not only one generic regime in French cinema of the 1950s, but two: the first governing national production during this period, and a second one that shaped the reception of a broader spectrum of films in which genres belonging to the national cinema coexisted with the genres of imported films for which there were no national equivalents (for example, the western and the musical). Undoubtedly, one could go even further and speculate on the existence of several generic regimes that existed concomitantly (although this would need to be confirmed by an in-depth study of critical reception), which viewers drew upon and manipulated in identifying the genre of a film and situating it in a generic and cinematic context. In identical periods and geographical settings, the different agents of reception, the highbrow press, the popular press, and different types of audience do not organize themselves in the same way. Nor are the generic regimes of viewers organized according to the same logic, given that these agents of reception are differentiated from one another by the social and aesthetic experience of cinema underpinning them, their cinematic culture, their system of values, and the extent to which they accept or reject a national cinema as expressing a national identity. Just as genres, considered individually, are categories of interpretation (that is, possible ways of mediating between the world of spectators and the world of films), generic regimes are also frames and logics within which these interpretations can be realized.

It is therefore necessary, in order to understand a generic regime, to take into consideration the place that genres occupy in the organization of cinematic production and its reception, as well as the uses that they fulfill. Given that the function of genres is not always the same in all places, rather than questioning their existence in this or that context, it is better to determine the role that they play. That, in turn, requires us to abandon any attempt to give a universal signification to the notion of genre, and to locate its meaning and operative value in each particular context.

The Hollywood genre system

The Hollywood system of genres in the classical era is unquestionably the most widely known and studied generic regime. We have already noted the influence of genres and genre films in the studio system, as well as their importance at an ideological and economic level (cf. chapter 3). One can enlarge this study of the Hollywood system by suggesting (following the work of Jean-Pierre Esquenazi) that its genres are also "idioms" of Hollywood style – temporary and variable solutions found to ally a *spectacular style* (dominant in earlier times, based on the model of the popular live show) and a *narrative (romanesque) style*, perfected when cinema became involved with representing stories (Esquenazi 2001a, pp. 33–45, 92–95). Taking his inspiration from, and reproducing the findings of, Bordwell, Staiger, and Thompson (1985) on Hollywood style, Esquenazi, instead of considering that the spectacular style had disappeared after 1910, having given way to the novelistic form, proposes to define Hollywood style in terms of an *integration* of spectacular and narrative elements. The burlesque found in silent cinema after World War I, because of the appeal of heroic actions, the succession of numbers, gags, or acrobatics, and the use of a horizontal forward-placing of figures, confirms that the spectacular had not disappeared from film narrative at this time. Subsequently, the musical, which integrates narrative fragments and spectacular sung and danced fragments, attests to this basic duality of Hollywood style. Similarly with adventure films, in which combats and dangerous encounters provide highlights in the actions of a hero; with comedies that were sprinkled with burlesque moments (to a greater or lesser extent, depending upon the inclinations of the director); with *film noir*, in which the spectacle of a *femme fatale* is articulated in the story through a subjective continuity from the point of view of the male character; with melodrama, in which the spectacle of pathos, underlined by an expressive musical score, imparts a rhythm to the story; with the horror film and the fantastic film, in which scenes that provide explanations for phenomena, dispute their existence, or present discussions about decisions to be taken alternate with scenes showing attacks and invasions; with the war film, in which heroic actions or slaughters are depicted in the story of an individual, either an officer or a private, or of a small group of soldiers, etc.

Hollywood genres, therefore, can be apportioned between genres of two types: either genres that incline towards narrative (such as melodrama or comedy) but contain spectacular elements or moments, or else genres that are inherently spectacular (such as adventure films, action films, epics, etc.), but which nevertheless recount the stories of characters revealed through a point of view that may be subjective. The division of labor between different teams in the studios seems, moreover, to confirm this double dimension of genres. The song and dance numbers of musicals, for example, were handled by specialist teams. Hollywood studio genres, then, are at the confluence of a logical system that is not merely economic, commercial, and ideological, but also stylistic.

Generic regimes outside of Hollywood

Scholarly studies of the nature of genres, of which there are many focusing on classical Hollywood cinema, and some productive ones relating to Japanese cinema – two cinemas that are strongly structured into a system of genres – is still a relatively virgin field in the case of European cinema. As far as French cinema is concerned, this absence can be explained by the status of genres in cinematic production. To cite Pierre Billard, "French cinema is very interested in the cinema of genre, but it is not its genre"

(1995, p. 553). Nevertheless, a French genre cinema exists, and the films that belong to it, without being generically formatted, are generically marked. As we have seen, genres flourished during the 1950s, but the 1930s also attest to their presence – in dramatic comedies inspired by both serious and frivolous popular authors (Bernstein, Bataille, Feydeau, and Achard, but also Pagnol and Guitry, who moved from the stage to the screen), in filmed operettas, and in colonial films which, from *Le Grand Jeu* (*The Big Game*) (Feyder, 1933) to *La Bandera* (*Escape From Yesterday*) (Duvivier, 1935) and *Le Roman d'un Spahi* (*The Story of a Soldier*) (Grémillon, 1936), celebrated exotic adventures, and the spirit of sacrifice and heroic deeds of colonial army corps.[1] But the lack of a stable market and the absence of firm production structures explain why genres in French cinema tend not to solidify and become divided and diversified into a multitude of sub-genres, or else series.

The absence of analyses of generic regimes in French cinema and the relative poverty of studies of genre are explained not merely by the difficulty of discerning a phenomenon that is more unstable than the genre system of the Hollywood studios or that of Japanese cinema.[2] It also comes from a preoccupation with Hollywood cinema genres, and more particularly with those, such as the musical or the western, that are strongly codified and reasonably easy to identify. Hollywood-focused research, instead of encouraging a comparative type of research into the nature and organization of genres, restricts the field of study. When critics fail to find a structured system of genres like that of the studios, they too quickly deduce an absence or weakness of a generic regime, when, it fact, it may not be organized according to the same logical system. Finally, the understanding of French cinema propounded by critics and university scholars, who favor auteurs, schools, and movements at the expense of generic groupings, is another cause of this neglect. As Ginette Vincendeau remarks, for example, "the realism of Gabin's films is often a *melodramatic* realism, a fact that the label of 'poetic realism' used in the 1930s and 1940s has obscured" (Vincendeau and Gautier 1993, p. 120). Whatever the realist roots of these films, they present emotional conflicts in a melodramatic register, involving a passive protagonist who in this case is a male character-star. One can regard *Le Quai des brumes* (*Port of Shadows*) (1938) or *Le Jour se lève* (*Daybreak*) (1939) by Carné as representing a flowering of poetic realism, but they can also be analyzed – as can the later film *La Verité sur Bébé Donge* (*The Truth About Bebe Donge*) (Decoin, 1951), which incorporates elements of *film noir* – as different facets of the same genre, melodrama.

Research concerning the logical systems and meaning of generic regimes seems, however, more advanced in Italy, notably because of the strong presence of three well defined genres on national and foreign screens during the 1960s: the Italian western, the *peplum*, and the Italian comedy. To take only this period, it appears that these three dominant genres embodied a tension between a nationalistic pole and an international pole heavily influenced by Hollywood. As Jean Gili (1983) has shown, comedy was strongly rooted in a multifaceted Italian reality, and in national or local traditions of spectacle. This genre, which gained its autonomy in Italy at the end of the 1950s, nevertheless sustained longstanding links with melodrama (in which laughter was never far from despair). Under the determining influence of neo-realism, which relaunched comedy by subjecting the problems of society to a treatment involving humor, irony, and satire, these films denounced the dream of an economic miracle and mixed funniness with the blackest despair, from *I Soliti ignoti* (*Big Deal*) (Monicelli, 1958) to *Brutti, sporchi, e cattivi* (*Ugly, Dirty, and Bad*) (Scola, 1975), or to the gallery of amoral, cynical, and destructive "monsters" in *I Mostri* (*The Monsters*) (Risi, 1963) who reflect a crumbling society whose structure is depicted in the film by a series of sketches. The use of a familiar star system, which makes the same actors (Gassman, Tognazzi, Manfredi, Sordi, etc.) heirs to the *commedia dell'arte*, also helps to invest comedy with a very strong Italian identity.

The Italian western, by using and altering the conventions of the American genre, and by revealing a critical fascination for Hollywood cinema and mythology (see above, pp. 186–188), is situated at the opposite pole. The *peplum*, for its part, occupies an intermediate position. Because of its "ancient" subject matter, which partly attaches it to a national past, and the longstanding existence in Italian cinema of grand-spectacle films on Roman subjects, and recurrent heroes like Maciste (created by *Cabiria*, Pastrone, 1914), it has an Italian continuity. But in the 1950s it is more accurate to say that this genre returns to Italian cinema via the epics of Hollywood cinema, which were themselves earlier influenced (around 1915) by the grandiose settings and elaborate camera movements of Italian films. One of these movements, the "*Cabiria*" traveling shot, taken up by Griffith, even kept an onomastic trace of its Italian origins. In addition, certain grand-spectacle Hollywood films, like *Ben-Hur* (Wyler, 1959) or *Cleopatra* (Mankiewicz, 1963), were mostly shot in Italy, with a technical and artistic team composed partly of Italians. A series of convergences between the western and the *peplum* finally confused the identity of this latter genre. The same directors made westerns and *peplums* (Leone, for example, made *Il Colosso di Rodi* (*The Colossus of Rhodes*) in 1960), and the vision of ancient Rome, the interpretation and the *mise en scène* of national history, was sometimes constructed in terms of the model of the American western. The journey towards the West, the search for the promised land – the mythic, historical origins of the American nation so exalted in the preceding decades by Hollywood – thus furnished Italy with aesthetic frameworks and figures through which it could express its own history. This detour via an American cultural production takes the form of filmed cavalry charges accompanied by sound-effects, the inclusion of music numbers as in a western – *Le Legioni di Cleopatra* (*Legions of the Nile*) (Cottafavi, 1960) – or a long march to the site of Rome, with covered wagons and incidents along the way – *Romolo e Remo* (*Duel of the Titans*) (Corbucci, 1961). With all of this taking place, naturally, in a setting of deserts and canyons. Furthermore, historians of Italian cinema often view the *peplum* and the western as "seams" rather than genres, on the grounds that they are defined more by a search for commercial profit and by their content than by their formal conventions. In the context of Italian cinema of the 1960s, it is therefore not impossible to describe the logical system of a generic regime as a way of viewing the problematical identity of a cinema that is both national and international facing the American giant, and a way of representing an Italian cultural identity caught between regional, national, and international determinants.

The series and generic labels of early cinema

If one gives its present meaning to a genre, it is hardly surprising that it is not to be found in early cinema – which should remind us of its inescapable "extraneity."[3] Early cinema is foreign to the cinema that has followed it, just as it is for the contemporary viewer, who has interiorized the codes and conventions that Noël Burch calls the MIR (Mode of Institutional Representation), which was progressively established during the 1910s.

> The period corresponding to institutionalization had involved the putting in place of the necessary conventions and logical system required to understand animated images (designated as a cinematic language). It was also the site of the passage from a *mediating heterogeneity* (the integration of the film with a panoply of means of expression that are external to it) to a larger and larger heterogeneity that would manifest itself, among other ways, through the organization of a hierarchy that was material (the prioritization of the visual over sound) and codifying (the priority of narration over simple demonstration [*monstration*]). (Gaudreault and Simard 1995, p. 24)

To that should be added the variability of the different practices employed in the making and reception of early cinema, which did not constitute a homogeneous and stable collection. In this context, it is difficult to find stable figures and motifs that could allow one to divide up and locate groups of films that bring together shared thematic, formal, or ideological traits established during this period. Indeed, as Livio Belloï reminds us, one of the distinctive features of cinematic production resides in the fact that "it is configured according to a general dynamical system and dialectic that appear to reject any kinds of stability, in order to privilege, conversely, processes of violent changes, involving abrupt disruptions that are sometimes unexpected" (1998, p. 70). Furthermore, early cinema is characterized by an intense "circulation of signs," to adopt an expression used by Noël Burch, a practice of plagiarism and piracy made possible by the absence of any artistic property rights in cinema before 1908: "films could be copied for their matter, their *mise en scène*, or their script by any number of other filmmakers, whether compatriots or foreigners, without any possible retaliation" (Burch 1990, p. 189). The circulation of signs therefore led to borrowings, relationships, and resemblances that unified groups of films. This practice contributed to the creation of generic effects and of generic corpora that are in no way comparable to the production of genre films in classical cinema.

An empirical first step for discerning the generic regime of early cinema consists in examining "how those who were responsible for circulating filmic artifacts named them, and what we can learn from this act of naming" (Jost 1998, p. 100). An examination of the generic appellations in use reveals that people drew upon categories that were both fluid and fluctuating, which attests to a fairly weak sense of genre that was, in any case, neither shared nor widespread. The labels given by publishers in their catalogues primarily have a descriptive and commercial function that is aimed at influencing the choice of cinema managers wanting to compile a varied program. Pathé's catalogue, for example, proposes "series" from 1903 onwards, that is, headings under which films are mentioned. These number over a dozen by 1907, comprising open-air scenes, comic scenes, scenes with special effects (or of transformations), sports scenes and acrobatics, historical, political, and current affairs scenes, military scenes, saucy scenes of a risqué character, ballet and dancing scenes, dramatic and realistic scenes, scenes from fairy stories and tales, religious and biblical scenes, cine-photographic scenes, and scenes of arts and industries (Bousquet 1993, 1996). The criteria used to define these series are variable, including thematic content for certain of them, modes of production for others (the open-air scenes, for example), and stylistic register for yet others, and so on. The same observations apply to other catalogues. In the United States, Biograph's *Advance Partial List* of 1902 grouped films for sale under 14 headings: Comedy Views, Sports and Pastime Views, Military Views, Railroad Views, Scenic Views, Views of Notable Personages, Miscellaneous Views, Trick Pictures, Marine Views, Children's Pictures, Fire and Patrol Views, Pan-American Exposition Views, Vaudeville Views, and Parade Pictures (Neale 1995, p. 168). As far as Lumière's catalogue of 1907 is concerned, it expresses a desire to classify genres by views, by substituting a classification under headings for the alphabetic classification that society was using up until that date. However, his 11 headings, which are quite close to those of Pathé, do not show any greater evidence of taxonomic rigor. They include genre scenes, comic views, French military scenes, maritime scenes, dances, popular festivals, panoramas, journeys in France and in the French colonies, journeys to foreign lands, and official festivals.[4] All of these categories are shown to be still less precise when one considers the contents under each heading. Apart from the heading "Miscellaneous Views" in the Biograph catalogue, the name of which is sufficient to indicate its heterogeneity, the genre scenes in Lumière's catalogue of 1907 contain, among others, scenes of children, of fire-fighters, of bull-fighting, 13 views from *The Life and Passion of Christ*, historical views, and scenes of reconstruction. Direct representations and reconstructions rub shoulders in it just as they do under the heading "General views – Genre scenes" in Pathé's catalogue of 1900, which only includes nine headings. This series, which had disappeared from the catalogue by 1907 – a clear testimony to the changeableness of the productions and generic labels of early cinema – groups together films that are quite different, such as street scenes (*Sortie d'église en Bohême*) (*Exit from a Church in Bohemia*), circus numbers (*L'Homme-serpent*) (*The Serpent-Man*), and a "true scene in five tableaux," *Le Mariage de raison* (*The Marriage of Reason*) (Belloï 1998, p. 72). Among these relatively eccentric generic labels, there always seems to exist one label, in French production at least, that provides a certain unity, designating films that contain recurrent thematic and formal traits: the fairy story. As Frank Kessler demonstrates, in contrast to other series, this designation gives a precise indication of the type of diegesis and structure of the films involved, undoubtedly because of its close relationship with the staged fairy story that was very popular in the nineteenth century: a piece with grand spectacle that combines a fantastical or marvelous subject with scenes of dancing and special effects ending with a sumptuous grand finale. This genre is distinguished not so much by its repertory of characters (since films with fairies existed, such as *La Fée Carabosse* (*Carabosse the Fairy*) (1906) by Méliès, that are not classed as fairy stories) as by a series of morphological traits. Kessler highlights four of them, each of which complements the others: the presence of dance scenes, often not motivated by the narration; a concluding grand finale in the form of a tableau that exploits all the registers of the spectacular; an engaging quality, which the fairy story shares with trick-films, emphasized by a head-on mode of presentation; and the fairly systematic use of colorization. While Méliès is undeniably the specialist in this genre, Gaumont, as well as Pathé, also produced a significant number of fairy stories built around the same formula.

Finally, we should note that the dozen or so series or headings presented by the different catalogues ought not to mask the plethora of sub-categories, in which adjectives, according to an advertising logic, magnify and "anticipate the expected effect of the films, at the same time as promising them" (Jost 1998, p. 102).

This heterogeneity of generic terms is certainly far from being the exclusive preserve of early cinema (cf. chapter 1), but the very great changeability of appellations and their overall imprecision distinguishes them sharply from genres outside cinema. Another distinguishing characteristic of the generic regime during this era was that it combined several generic logics in a distinctive way: that of publishers, mindful of classifying their films in order to sell them to cinema managers, as we have just seen; those of exhibitors, who presented films to the audience in their programs – to which should be added those of articles in the specialized corporatist press. Exhibitors very often redefined the genres of films they had bought so as to integrate them into a program comprising several films characterized by variety. That is why promises of quality, of the spectacular, of exhilarating comedy, etc. were added to, or substituted for, generic terms. The logical system of the cinema managers, however, was not merely commercial, since the appellations they gave to films projected in the same program also function as a "program of emotions," which organizes the time sequence of the session and the emotional journey of the spectators. Indeed, as François Jost shows in analyzing the programs of the Gaumont-Palace in 1911–12, the program is composed in accordance with a recurrent three-part schedule that begins and ends with a short piece played by the orchestra (Jost 1998, pp. 108–109). The projections alternate genres and emotions according to an identical pattern that is sustained from one session to another. Thus, the program of the first part always begins with a serious direct reproduction (Panorama, Voyage) that is always followed by a drama, which in turn gives way to a scene accompanied by a recording, then an attraction that invites the viewer to marvel at the new possibilities of cinema. One should note, then, that the short length of the films is essential in the generic regime of early cinema, since it involves the composition of a program.

Finally, the press of the day contains discussions about genres that are distinct from the labels of publishers, billposting strategies, and the programs of cinema managers. Starting with the *Ciné Journal* and *L'Illustration* of 1908, as well as "Les Vues cinématographiques," a text from Méliès that appeared in 1907 in *L'Annuaire Général et International de la Photographie*, François Jost proposes to organize the map of genres in early French cinema according to four terms that had an important place in the realm of genres in the period. The first two, which determine the two poles of an axis along which films came to be ranged, consist of direct reproduction at one end, and invention at the opposite end, usually in the form of effects that were unattainable until then, made possible by the new cinematograph. Thus, open-air scenes, which comprise most of the views, but also theater scenes (because they are only considered as recorded souvenirs), are strongly situated on the side of direct reproduction, while fairy stories, special-effects films, or realist imitation – for example, Feuillade's series *La Vie telle qu'elle est* (*Life Such as It Is*) (1911–12) – are placed on the side of invention. The two other terms, life and theater (conceived here as the realm of the fictive, as opposed to reality), comprise another axis that intersects the first. Accordingly, realist imitation is located on the side of life, fairy stories on the side of theater, and reconstructed current events are a mixture of life and theater (Jost 1998, pp. 104–106).

Another approach to the understanding of genres, inspired by formalism, proposes a theory of the genres of early cinema based not on the observation of generic appellations and modes of film classification in vogue at the time, but on a defining criterion based on morphology, a spatiotemporal articulation of the different shots and levels that make up the *bandes* and the films. This method of theorizing genres, initiated by Tom Gunning (1984), is concerned more particularly with the whole early period, that is, the period before 1907. This period does not only involve narrative cinema, and the model proposed is both theoretical and historical, given that the four genres identified correspond to four successive moments in the development of early cinematography. Gunning distinguishes, then:

- The genre of single-shot narrative films – an uninterrupted structure of which *L'Arroseur arrosé* (*The Sprayer Sprayed*) (Lumière, 1895) is both the first of its kind, and also the most representative.
- The non-continuity genre. It is composed of narrative films with at least two shots, in which the lack of continuity between the shots is accentuated and justified by a discontinuity and rupture at the level of the story. This is the case, for example, with *Let Me Dream Again* (Smith, 1900), in which the first shot shows a man in the act of drinking and amusing himself in the company of a young and pretty woman. The second shot, articulated through an in-fade effect, shows the same man waking up in his bed, lying alongside his wife, obviously a good deal less young and attractive.

Films with special effects, such as *L'Escamotage d'une dame* (*The Vanishing Lady*) (Méliès, 1896), whatever the technique used to bring about the transformation, can also be included in this genre.

- The continuity genre, in which a continuity of action is achieved through cutting, with the discontinuity between the different shots being attenuated by a temporal overlapping of the action that repeats the same action from one part to the other, through juxtaposition. This is found in pursuit films, such as *Stop Thief!* (Williamson, 1901), that were very popular in the early years of the twentieth century, in which all the shots show a character pursued by others in the process of running away, lasting until the pursued and the pursuers disappear out of the field of the shot: in the last shot, the two groups join up again, the fugitive is captured . . . and that is the end of the film.

- The discontinuity genre in which the continuity of the action goes hand-in-hand with a discontinuity in the action, as a result of alternating montage. The pursuit film often metamorphoses into a film of rescue, in which the interweaving of two parallel actions creates a real suspense, as in *The Fatal Hour* (1908) and many of the films by Griffith made before Biograph.

Genres and generic regimes have, then, variable forms and statuses, and are organized according to the particular logic that inheres in each context. It is on this basis that the study of a genre, considered individually, can just as easily be constructed as the studies of genres from a particular period or a particular cinema. By adopting this perspective when studying genres, one avoids transforming them into universal archetypes, and replaces the question, often posed outside the context of classical Hollywood, "Do genres exist in early French and Italian cinema, contemporary cinemas, etc.?"[5] with an interrogation of the nature, role, and function of genres. In other words, instead of making the Hollywood studio system into the measure by which one evaluates the genericity of other cinemas, it is more appropriate to examine how in each cinematic, historic, and ideological context generic logical systems are put in place whose relations not only provide films, but also producers and those involved in the critical reception of films, with generic categories, the sense and particular meaning of which constitute the very concept of genre.

Notes

1 On the French colonial film of the 1930s, see Michèle Lagny, Marie-Claire Ropars, and Pierre Sorlin (Eds.) (1986) *Génériques des années 30*, Saint-Denis, Presses Universitaires de Vincennes; and Abdelkader Benali (1998) *Le Cinéma colonial au Magreb. L'imaginaire en trompe-l'oeil*, Paris, Cerf.

2 For a discussion of the question of genre in a French context and for an approach to French cinema genres, see Raphaëlle Moine (Ed.) (2005) *Le Cinéma français face aux genres*, Paris, AFRHC.

3 I prefer this neologism to the term "strangeness" (*étrangeté*) as a way of acknowledging that early cinema is not "strange" (*étrange*), but rather "foreign to us" (*étranger*). See André Gaudreault and Denis Simard (1995) "L'Extranéité du cinéma des premiers temps: bilan et perspectives de recherches." In Jean A. Gili, Michèle Lagny, Michel Marie, and Vincent Pinel (Eds.) *Les Vingt premières années du cinéma français*, Paris, Presses de la Sorbonne Nouvelle, pp. 15–28.

4 For an analysis of Lumière's "views," see, for example, Vincent Pinel (1994) *Louis Lumière, inventeur et cinéaste*, Paris, Nathan, pp. 110–111.

5 See chapter 4, pp. 122–126, for the question of genres in contemporary cinema.

Conclusion

Far from arranging themselves neatly on a general map, cinema genres constitute (to use a comparison suggested by Rick Altman) a kind of "Jurassic Park in which genres that are created in very different eras compete for possession of the landscape" (1995, p. 28). To extend the metaphor and return to some of the points underlined earlier in this book, one should recall that genres, like the creatures that populate the amusement park in Spielberg's film, are also artifacts, given that they are simultaneously collections of films, appellations produced and used at different moments, and discursive acts that influence the circulation of films, not only governing them, but also allowing them to be interpreted. One remembers that the dinosaurs created through biotechnology, programmed to be all of the same sex in order to avoid the possibilities of uncontrolled natural reproduction, changed their biological sex as a result of a logic of adaptation. In the same way, genres, because they have an ideological and social function, are subject to redefinition as well as semantic or syntactic shifts that respond to, and perpetuate, historical, social, cultural, and cinematic changes. Moreover, just as the DNA of a frog was combined with that of extinct monsters to give birth to a new kind of dinosaur, genres hybridize and mingle with one another. This process is the key to the phenomenon of genrification itself – a process that is invisible to its contemporaries, which explains the creation of new cycles that in turn become stabilized and form

205

new genres. This strategy of mixing and of innovation, in the first case scientific and technological, and in the second case artistic and cultural, is, moreover, guided by a comparable economic and commercial interest: to attract numerous visitors, and to seduce numerous viewers. Finally, as Altman's comparison suggests, the coexistence in Jurassic Park of species, whether animal or vegetable, that have appeared and developed in different eras and ecosystems, corresponds in our generic consideration to a juxtaposition of genres and generic appellations that belong to various different periods, being the products and constituents of different generic regimes. Thus, contemporary audiences, producers, and filmmakers are presented with several competing and mixed generic systems.

While it is clear from this that the question of genres cannot be answered on the basis of a logic of classification (it would be just as futile to try and impose laws in the territory of genres as to pretend to be able to organize and control the island of dinosaurs), any conception of genres has to take account of layering and successive stratifications, to propose models capable of explaining the play of complex interactions that form and shape cinema genres. Because of this, a genre cannot be considered a closed, static, and definitive collection; rather, it constitutes a point of equilibrium, a metastable state of a generic process. Any general definition of cinematic genres, then, can only be partially recursive. It is not always a matter of recognizing, to quote Tudor, that "genre is what we collectively believed it to be" (1995, p. 5), but of separating – in order to establish the relations between them – groups of films and categories that one calls cinematic genres, on one hand, and, on the other, a generic dynamical system that is maintained by economic, communicative, and ideological motivations, which this book hopes to have clarified in the course of its chapters. The theory of genres is, in fact, a theory of this generic process.

Cinema genres can therefore be considered as *cinematographic sites*, to use the analogy of anthropological sites, a site in which meaning is inscribed and symbolized. My intention here is not to substitute the notion of "site" for that of "genre" (as certain ritualist approaches have been able to do with myth), but to better identify how the activities of naming, recognition, and mediation work with respect to cinematic genres. The anthropological site is a space that is "a principle of meaning for those who inhabit it, and a principle of intelligibility for those who observe it," in which are put in place cultural points of reference for establishing identity and otherness (Augé 1992, p. 68). The notion of a site thus refers both to real spaces and to relationships that those who operate in these spaces maintain between themselves, just as the concept of genre refers both to concrete groups of films and to an awareness of genres. Anthropological sites have an identifying function because a certain number of individuals recognize themselves in them and define themselves in terms of them. These sites are relational, because one can read in them modes of relation with others, and also historical, given that in joining together identity and relationships, they are defined in terms of a minimal stability. They preserve traces of a former implantation (in the case of spaces *stricto sensu*) or of a tradition, and those who inhabit them recognize "reference points that are known without having to have been learned" (Augé 1992, p. 71). The sites are thus contexts of life as well as frames of reference, which also means that they exercise a constraint in fixing reference points, and that they can undergo a stereotypical reduction. The collective practices and uses of generic categories, then, construct cinematic and cultural sites, and generic denominations affect films at these sites, giving them an identity, establishing their relationship with other films, and situating them in history. Finally, symbolic spaces that cease to be inhabited or "experienced" become sites of memory, dear to historians, in which we find the image of that which we no longer are, and therefore of difference. Anthropological sites are not such by virtue of their own structure, but because those who operate in them invest them with social meaning, and thus turn them into places in which they are the actors. An airport, for example, a non-place for the passenger, is undoubtedly a site for the personnel who work in it, which will be inhabited in different ways by the different categories of professionals (pilots, hostesses and stewards, ground staff, security agents, and so on). Similarly, genres are only "living" for a community to the exact extent that its members find themselves in them, and see their relationships with others and the world mediated through them.

Select Bibliography

Abel, R. (2002) A Nation for Exports. American Westerns (1911–1912). In Barnier, M. & Moine, R. (Eds.) *France/Hollywood. Échanges cinématographiques et identités nationales*. Paris, L'Harmattan, pp. 147–172.

Albera, F. (Ed.) (1996) *Les Formalistes russes et le cinéma. Poétique du film*, Paris, Nathan.

Allan, R. & Gomery, D. (1985) *Film History: Theory and Practice*, New York, McGraw-Hill.

Alloway, L. (1971) *Violent America: The Movies 1946–1964*, New York, Moma.

Althusser, L. (1966) *Pour Marx*, Paris, Maspero.

Altman, R. (1981) Intratextual Rewriting: Textuality as Language Formation. In Steiner, W. (Ed.) *The Sign in Music and Literature*. Chicago, University of Chicago Press, pp. 39–51.

Altman, R. (1989) *The American Film Musical*, Bloomington, Indiana University Press.

Altman, R. (1995) Emballage réutilisable: les produits génériques et le processus de recyclage. *Iris*, 20, pp. 13–30.

Altman, R. (1999) *Film/Genre*, London, BFI.

Amengual, B. (1993) Bon chic, bon genre? *CinémAction*, 68, pp. 198–203.

Amossy, R. (1991) *Les Idées reçues. Sémiologie du stéréotype*, Paris, Nathan.

Anderson, B. (1991) *Imagined Communities*, London, Verso.

Aristotle (1987) *Poetics*, Indianapolis, Hackett.

Arroyo, J. (Ed.) (2000) *Action/Spectacle Cinema: A Sight and Sound Reader*, London, BFI.

Astruc, A. (2001 [1954]) Quand un homme. . . . In Baecque, A. d. (Ed.) *Politique des auteurs*. Paris, Éditions des Cahiers du cinéma, p. 43.

209

Select Bibliography

Augé, M. (1992) *Non-lieux. Introduction à une anthropologie de la surmodernité*, Paris, Seuil.

Augé, M. (1994) *Le Sens des autres. Actualité de l'anthropologie*, Paris, Fayard.

Aumont, J. (2002) *Les Théories des cinéastes*, Paris, Nathan.

Aumont, J. & Marie, M. (1988) *L'Analyse des films*, Paris, Nathan.

Aziza, C. (Ed.) (1998) Le péplum. L'Antiquité à l'écran. *CinémAction*, 89.

Baecque, A. D. (1991) *Les Cahiers du cinéma. Histoire d'une revue I et II*, Paris, Éditions des Cahiers du cinéma.

Baecque, A. D. (2001) *Politique des auteurs*, Paris, Éditions des Cahiers du cinéma.

Balandier, G. (1988) *Le Désordre*, Paris, Fayard.

Barthes, R. (1957) *Mythologies*, Paris, Seuil.

Basinger, J. (1986) *The World War II Combat Film: Anatomy of a Genre*, New York, Columbia University Press.

Basinger, J. (1993) *A Woman's View: How Hollywood Spoke to Women, 1930–1960*, London, Chatto and Windus.

Bazin, A. (1995) Évolution du western. *Qu'est-ce que le cinéma?* Paris, Cerf, pp. 229–239.

Belloï, L. (1998) Répétitions, variations, reconfigurations: à propos du concept de 'genre' dans le cinéma des premiers temps. In Quaresima, L., Raengo, A., & Vichi, L. (Eds.) *La Nascita dei generi cinematografici. Atti del V Convegno Internazionale di Studi sul Cinema*, Undine, Forum, pp. 69–86.

Benali, A. (1998) *Le Cinéma colonial au Maghreb. L'imaginaire en trompe-l'oeil*, Paris, Cerf.

Bidaud, A.-M. (1994) *Hollywood et le Rêve américain. Cinéma et idéologie aux États-Unis*, Paris, Masson.

Billard, P. (1995) *L'Âge classique du cinéma français. Du cinéma parlant à la Nouvelle Vague*, Paris, Flammarion.

Binh, N. T. & Pilard, P. (Eds.) (2000) *Typiquement british. Le cinéma britannique*, Paris, Centre-Pompidou.

Bondebjerg, I. (2000) Singing and dancing in Copenhagen. Hollywood et la construction du film musical danois. In Bertin-Maghit, J.-P. (Ed.) *Les Cinémas européens des années cinquante*. Paris, AFRCH, pp. 199–214.

Borde, R. & Chaumeton, É. (1988 [1955]) *Panorama du film noir américain (1941–1953)*, Paris, Flammarion.

Bordwell, D. (2000) *Planet Hong Kong: Popular Culture and the Art of Entertainment*, Cambridge, MA, Harvard University Press.

Bordwell, D., Staiger, J., & Thompson, K. (1985) *The Classical Hollywood Cinema: Film Style and Mode of Production to 1960*, New York, Columbia University Press.

Bourgeois, J. (1946) La Tragédie policière. *La Revue du cinema*, 2, pp. 70–72.

Bourget, J.-L. (1983) *Le Cinéma américain (1895–1980): de Griffith à Cimino*, Paris, Presses Universitaires de France.

Bourget, J.-L. (1985) *Le Mélodrame hollywoodien*, Paris, Stock.

Bourget, J.-L. (1998) *Hollywood. La norme et la marge*, Paris, Nathan.

Bousquet, H. (1993) *Catalogue Pathé des années 1896 à 1914: 1907–1908–1909*, Paris, Éditions Henri Bousquet.

Bousquet, H. (1996) *Catalogue Pathé des années 1896 à 1914: 1896–1906*, Paris, Éditions Henri Bousquet.

Bretèque, F. D. L. (1993) Un Essai de typologie: en relisant 'Les genres du cinéma'. *CinémAction*, 68, pp. 11–15.

Browne, N. (Ed.) (1998) *Refiguring American Film Genres: Theory and History*, Berkeley, University of California Press.

Brunetière, F. (1890) *L'Évolution des genres dans l'histoire de la littérature*, Paris, Hachette.

Brunsdon, C. (1993) Un sujet d'actualité pour les années 1970. *CinémAction*, 67, pp. 59–64.

Burch, N. (1990) *La Lucarne de l'infini. Naissance du langage cinématographique*, Paris, Nathan.

Burch, N. (Ed.) (1993) *Revoir Hollywood. La nouvelle critique angloaméricaine*, Paris, Nathan.

Burch, N. (2000) Double speak. *Réseaux*, 99, pp. 99–130.

Burch, N. & Sellier, G. (1996) *La Drôle de guerre des sexes du cinéma français, 1930–1956*, Paris, Nathan.

Buscombe, E. (1970) The Idea of Genre in the American Cinema. *Screen*, 2, pp. 33–45.

Carroll, N. (1981) Nightmare and the Horror Film: The Symbolic Biology of Fantastic Beings. *Film Quarterly*, 34, pp. 16–25.

Carroll, N. (1990) *The Philosophy of Horror, or Paradoxes of the Heart*, New York, Routledge.

Casetti, F. (1979) Les Genres cinématographiques. Quelques problèmes de méthode. *Ça cinéma*, pp. 37–40.

Casetti, F. (1998) Film Genres, Negotiation Processes and Communicative Pact. In Quaresima, L., Raengo, A., & Vichi, L. (Eds.) *La Nascita dei generi cinematografici*. Atti del V Convegno Internazionale di Studi sul Cinema, Undine, Forum, pp. 23–36.

Casetti, F. (1999) *Theories of Cinema 1945–1995*, Austin, University of Texas Press.

Cavell, S. (1993 [1981]) *À la recherche du bonheur. Hollywood et la comédie du remariage*, Paris, Éditions de l'Étoile/Cahiers du cinéma.

Cawelti, J. (1976) *Adventures, Mystery and Romance: Formula Stories as Art and Popular Culture*, Chicago, University of Chicago Press.

Chartier, J.-P. (1946) Les Américains aussi font des films "noirs." *La Revue du Cinéma*, 2, pp. 67–70.

Cook, P. (1978) Duplicity in *Mildred Pierce*. In Kaplan, E. A. (Ed.) *Women in Film Noir*. London, BFI, pp. 68–82.

Creton, L. (2001) *Économie du cinéma. Perspectives stratégiques*, Paris, Nathan.

Doane, M. A. (1984) The Woman's Film: Possession and Address. In Doane, M. A., Mellecamp, P., & Williams, L. (Eds.) *Re-vision: Essays in Feminist Film Criticism*. Frederick, MD, American Film Institute/ University Publications of America, pp. 67–82.

Doane, M. A. (1987) *The Desire to Desire: The Woman's Film of the 1940s*, Bloomington, Indiana University Press.

Drummond, L. (1996) *American Dreamtime: A Cultural Analysis of Popular Movies, and Their Implications for a Science of Humanity*, Laham, Rowman & Littlefield.

Dubuisson, D. (1993) *Mythologies du XXᵉ siècle (Dumézil, Lévi-Strauss, Éliade)*, Lille, Presses Universitaires de Lille.

Eco, U. (1984) Narrative Structures in Flemming. In *The Role of The Reader: Explorations in the Semiotics of Texts*. Bloomington, Indiana University Press, pp. 144–174.

Eisenschitz, B. (1999) *Le Cinéma allemand*, Paris, Nathan.

Elsaesser, T. (1995) Tales of Sound and Fury: Observations on the Family Melodrama. In Grant, B. K. (Ed.) *Film Genre Reader II*. Austin, University of Texas Press, pp. 350–380.

Erlich, V. (1955) *Russian Formalism: History, Doctrine*, The Hague, Mouton.

Esquenazi, J.-P. (1997) Le Renouvellement d'un jeu de langage. Genres et canaux. *Réseaux*, 81, pp. 105–118.

Esquenazi, J.-P. (2000) Le film, un fait social. *Réseaux*, 99, pp. 13–47.

Esquenazi, J.-P. (2001a) *Hitchcock et l'aventure de Vertigo. L'Invention à Hollywood*, Paris, CNRS Éditions.

Esquenazi, J.-P. (2001b) Les critiques et les films: le cas d'*Alphaville*. *Sociologie de l'art*, 13, pp. 97–118.

Feuer, J. (1995) The Self-Reflexive Musical and the Myth of Entertainment. In Grant, B. K. (Ed.) *Film Genre Reader II*. Austin, University of Texas Press, pp. 441–455.

Frank, N. (1946) Un nouveau genre 'policier', l'aventure criminelle. *L'Écran français*, 61, pp. 8–9, 14.

Gallagher, T. (1986) Shoot-Out at the Genre Corral: Problems in the 'Evolution' of the Western. In Grant, B. K. (Ed.) *Film Genre Reader*. Austin, University of Texas Press, pp. 202–216.

Gaudreault, A. & Gunning, T. (1989) Le Cinéma des premiers temps, un défi à l'histoire du cinéma. In Aumont, J., Gaudreault, A., & Marie, M. (Eds.) *Histoire du cinéma. Nouvelles approches*. Paris, Presses de la Sorbonne Nouvelle, pp. 49–63.

Gaudreault, A. & Simard, D. (1995) L'Extranéité du cinéma des premiers temps: bilan et perspectives de recherches. In Gili, J. A., Lagny, M., Marie, M., & Pinel, V. (Eds.) *Les Vingt premières années du cinéma français*. Paris, Presses de la Sorbonne Nouvelle, pp. 15–28.

Gauthier, G. (1995) *Le Documentaire. Un autre cinéma*, Paris, Nathan.

Genette, G. (1982) *Palimpsestes*, Paris, Seuil.

Genette, G. (1986) Introduction à l'architexte. In Genette, G., Jauss, H. R., Schaeffer, J.-M., Scholes, R., Stempel, W. D., & Viëtor, K. (Eds.) *Théorie des genres*. Paris, Seuil, pp. 97–106.

Genette, G., Jauss, H. R., Schaeffer, J. M., Scholes, R., Stempel, W. D., & Viëtor, K. (1986) *Théorie des genres*, Paris, Seuil.

Giacomini, F. (2000) Quand Naples défiait Hollywood. Le film musical italien. In Bertin-Maghit, J.-P. (Ed.) *Les Cinémas européens des années cinquante*. Paris, AFRHC, pp. 215–226.

Gili, J. (1983) *La Comédie italienne*, Paris, Henri Veyrier.

Gomery, D. (1986) *The Hollywood Studio System*, New York, St. Martin's Press.

Grant, B. K. (Ed.) (1986) *Film Genre Reader*, Austin, University of Texas Press.

Grant, B. K. (Ed.) (1995) *Film Genre Reader II*, Austin, University of Texas Press.

Gunning, T. (1984) Non-Continuity, Continuity, Discontinuity: A Theory of Genres in Early Film. *Iris*, 1, 101–112.

Gunning, T. (1990) The Cinema of Attractions: Early Film, Its Spectator and the Avant Garde. In Elsaesser, T. (Ed.) *Early Film: Space, Frame, Narrative*. London, BFI, pp. 56–62.

Gunning, T. (1995a) Those Drawn with a Very Fine Camel's Hair Brush: The Origins of Film Genres. *Iris*, 20, pp. 49–61.

Gunning, T. (1995b) Attractions, truquages et photogénie. L'explosion du présent dans les films à truc français produits entre 1896 et 1907. In Gili, J. A., Langy, M., Marie, M., & Pinel, V. (Eds.) *Les Vingt*

213

premières années du cinéma français. Paris, Presses de la Sorbonne Nouvelle, pp. 177–193.

Guynn, W. (1990) *A Cinema of Nonfiction*, Cranbury, NJ, Associated University Presses.

Harvey, S. (1993) La Place de la femme: absence de la famille dans le film noir. In Burch, N. (Ed.) *Revoir Hollywood. La nouvelle critique anglo-américaine*. Paris, Nathan, pp. 189–199.

Haskell, M. (1974) *From Reverence to Rape: The Treatment of Women in the Movies*, Chicago, University of Chicago Press.

Hegel, G. W. F. (1998) *Aesthetics: Lectures on Fine Art*, Oxford, Clarendon Press.

Henriet, J. M. G. (1989) *Géographies du western. Une nation en marche*, Paris, Nathan.

Hougron, A. (2000) *Science-fiction et société*, Paris, Presses Universitaires de France.

Ishaghpour, Y. (1982) *D'une image à l'autre*, Paris, Denoël.

Jauss, H. R. (1978) *Pour une esthétique de la réception*, Gallimard, Tel.

Jost, F. (1997) La Promesse des genres. *Réseaux*, 81, pp. 13–31.

Jost, F. (1998) Logiques des genres cinématographiques début de siècle. In Quaresima, L., Raengo, A., & Vichi, L. (Eds.) *La Nascita dei generi cinematografici*. Atti del V Convegno Internazionale di Studi sul Cinema, Undine, Forum, pp. 99–112.

Jullier, L. (1997) *L'Écran post-moderne. Un cinéma de l'allusion et du feu d'artifice*, Paris, L'Harmattan.

Kaminsky, S. (1974) *American Film Genres: Approaches to a Critical Theory of Popular Film*, Dayton, Pflaum.

Kaplan, E. A. (Ed.) (1978) *Women in Film Noir*, London, BFI.

Kitses, J. (1969) *Horizons West: Anthony Mann, Budd Boetticher, Sam Peckinpah: Studies of Authorship Within the Western*, London, Thames and Hudson.

Kral, P. (1984) *Le Burlesque ou morale de la tarte à la créme*, Paris, Stock.

Kral, P. (1986) *Les Burlesques ou parade des somnambules*, Paris, Stock.

Krutnick, F. (1991) *In a Lonely Street: Film Noir, Genre, Masculinity*, London, Routledge.

Kuhn, A. (1993) Hollywood et les nouveaux women's films. *CinémAction*, 67, pp. 53–58.

Lacasse, A. (Ed.) (1995) Sur la notion de genre au cinéma, *Iris*, 20.

Lagny, M., Ropars, M.-C., & Sorlin, P. (1986) *Génériques des années 30*, Saint-Denis, Presses Universitaires de Vincennes.

Langman, L. (1992) *A Guide to Silent Westerns*, Westport, CT, Greenwood Press.

Lenne, G. (1989) *Histoire du cinéma fantastique*, Paris, Seghers.

Lesuisse, A.-F. (2002) *Du film noir au noir. Traces figurales dans le cinéma hollywoodien*, Brussels, De Boeck Université.

Leutrat, J.-L. (1985) *L'Alliance brisée. Le Western des années 20*, Lyon, Presses Universitaire de Lyon-Institut Lumière.

Leutrat, J.-L. (1987) *Le Western. Archéologie d'un genre*, Lyon, Presses Universitaires de Lyon.

Leutrat, J.-L. (1995) *Vie des fantômes. Le Fantastique au cinéma*, Paris, Éditions de l'Etoile/Cahiers du cinéma.

Leutrat, J.-L. & Liandrat-Guigues, S. (1990) *Les Cartes de l'Ouest. Un genre cinématographique: le western*, Paris, A. Colin.

Lévi-Strauss, C. (1963) *Structural Anthropology*, New York, Basic Books.

Lévi-Strauss, C. (1966) *Les Mythologies II. Du miel aux cendres*, Paris, Plon.

Lipman, W. (1922) *Public Opinion*, New York, Penguin Books.

Lipsitz, G. (1993) Film noir et guerre froide. In Burch, N. (Ed.) *Revoir Hollywood. La nouvelle critique anglo-américaine*. Paris, Nathan, pp. 167–176.

McArthur, C. (1972) *Underworld USA*, New York, Viking Press.

McCarty, J. (1984) *Splatter Movies: Breaking the Last Taboo of the Screen*, New York, St. Martin's Press.

Maltby, R. (1995) *Hollywood Cinema: An Introduction*, Oxford, Blackwell.

Masson, A. (1981) *La Comédie musicale*, Paris, Stock.

Mauduy, J. & Henriet, G. (1989) *Géographies du western. Une nation en marche*, Paris, Nathan.

Metz, C. (1974) *Language and Cinema*, The Hague, Mouton.

Moine, R. (1999) Stéréotypes et clichés. In Vanoye, F. (Ed.) *Cinéma et littérature*. Nanterre, Publidix, pp. 159–170.

Moine, R. (2002) Les Remakes américains de films français. Une question d'identités. In Barnier, M. & Moine, R. (Eds.) *France/Hollywood. Échanges cinématographiques et identités nationales*. Paris, L'Harmattan, pp. 63–81.

Moine, R. (Ed.) (2005) *Le Cinéma français face aux genres*, Paris, AFRHC.

Morgan, J. & Andrew, D. (Eds.) (1996) European Precursors of Film Noir/Précurseurs européens du film noir, *Iris*, 21.

Morin, E. (1962) *L'Esprit du temps*, Paris, Grasset.

Musser, C. (1984) The Travel Genre in 1903–1904: Moving Toward Fictional Narratives. *Iris*, 20, pp. 47–59.

Nacache, J. (1995) *Le Film hollywoodien classique*, Paris, Nathan.

Naremore, J. (1996) American Film Noir: The History of an Idea. *Film Quarterly*, 49, pp. 12–28.

Naremore, J. (1998) *More than Night: Film Noir in Its Contexts*, Berkeley, University of California Press.

Neale, S. (1995) Questions of Genre. In Grant, B. K. (Ed.) *Film Genre Reader II*. Austin, University of Texas Press, pp. 159–183.

Neale, S. (1998) *Genre*, London, BFI.

Neale, S. (2000) *Genre and Hollywood*, London, Routledge.

Neale, S. (Ed.) (2002) *Genre and Contemporary Hollywood*, London, BFI.

Neisser, U. (1976) *Cognition and Reality: Principles and Implications of Cognitive Psychology*, San Francisco, W. H. Freeman.

Niney, F. (2000) *L'Épreuve de réel à l'écran. Esai sur le principe de réalité documentaire*, Brussels, De Boeck Université.

Odin, R. (1994) Sémio-pragmatique du cinéma et de l'audiovisuel. Modes et institutions. In Müller, J. E. (Ed.) *Towards a Pragmatics of the Audiovisual*. Münster, Nodus Publikationen, pp. 33–46.

Paul, W. (1994) *LaughingScreaming: Modern Hollywood Horror and Comedy*, New York, Columbia University Press.

Perron, B. (1995) Une machine à faire penser. *Iris*, 20, pp. 76–84.

Philippe, O. (1996) *Le Film policier français contemporain*, Paris, Cerf.

Pinel, V. (1994) *Louis Lumière, inventeur et cinéaste*, Paris, Nathan.

Pinel, V. (2000) *Écoles, genres et mouvements au cinéma*, Paris, Larousse-Bordas/HER, Comprendre/Reconnaître.

Piotrovski, A. (1996) Vers une théorie des ciné-genres. In Albéra, F. (Ed.) *Les Formalistes russes et le cinéma. Poétique du film*. Paris, Nathan, pp. 143–163.

Puiseux, H. (1988) *L'Apocalypse nucléaire et son cinéma*, Paris, Cerf.

Puiseux, H. (1997) *Les Figures de la guerre. Représentations et sensibilités, 1839–1996*, Paris, Gallimard.

Quaresima, L., Raengo, A., & Vichi, L. (1998) *La Nascita dei generi cinematografici*. Atti del V Convegno Internazionale di Studi sul Cinema, Undine, Forum.

Ramonet, I. (1980) Les Films-catastrophes américains. Des fictions pour la crise. In *Le Chewing-gum des yeux*. Paris, Éditions Alain Moreau.

Rey, H.-R. (1948) Démonstration par l'absurde: les *films noirs*. *L'Écran français*, 157, p. 13.

Richie, D. (2001) *A Hundred Years of Japanese Film. A Concise History, with a Selective Guide to Videos and DVDs*, Tokyo, Kodansha International.

Rieupeyrout, J.-L. (1953) *Le Western ou le cinéma américain par excellence*, Paris, Cerf.

Rieupeyrout, J.-L. (1987) *La Grande aventure du western. Du Far-west à Hollywood: 1894–1963*, Paris, Ramsay.

Rolot, C. & Ramirez, F. (1997) *Cinéma, le genre comique. Actes du colloque de Montpellier, 9 et 10 mai 1996*, Montpellier, Université Paul Valéry.

Rosow, E. (1978) *Born to Lose: The Gangster Film in America*, New York, Oxford University Press.

Rouyer, P. (1997) *Le Cinéma gore. Un esthétique du sang*, Paris, Cerf, 7è Art.

Sarris, A. (1978) The Sex Comedy Without Sex. *American Film*, 3, pp. 8–15.

Schaeffer, J.-M. (1986) Du texte au genre. In Genette, G., Jauss, H. R., Schaeffer, J.-M., Scholes, R., Stempel, W. D., & Viëtor, K. (Eds.) *Théorie des genres*. Paris, Seuil, pp. 179–205.

Schaeffer, J.-M. (1989) *Qu'est-ce qu'un genre littéraire?* Paris, Seuil.

Schatz, T. (1981) *Hollywood Genres: Formula, Filmmaking and the Studio System*, New York, McGraw Hill.

Schifano, L. (1995) *Le Cinéma italien, 1945–1995. Crise et création*, Paris, Nathan.

Searle, J. R. (1969) Expressions, meaning and speech acts. In *Speech Acts: An Essay in the Philosophy of Language*. Cambridge, Cambridge University Press, pp. 20–50.

Seguin, J.-C. (1994) *Histoire du cinéma espagnol*, Paris, Nathan.

Sellier, G. (1999) Henry Bernstein et le cinéma français des années 30. *CinémAction*, 93, pp. 82–88.

Serceau, M. (Ed.) (1987) La Comédie italienne. De Don Camillo à Berlusconi. *CinémAction*, 42.

Serceau, M. (Ed.) (1993) Panorama des genres au cinéma. *CinémAction*, 68.

Silver, A. & Ursini, J. (Eds.) (1999) *Film Noir Reader II*, New York, Limelight.

Simon, J.-P. (1979) *Le Filmique et le comique*, Paris, Albatross.

Socci, S. (1993) Le Mélodrame italien. *CinémAction*, 68, pp. 112–120.

Solomon, S. (1976) *Beyond Formula: American Film Genres*, New York, Harcourt Brace & Jovanovich.

Sorlin, P. (2000) Ce qu'était un film populaire dans l'Europe des années 50. In Bertin-Maghit, J.-P. (Ed.) *Les Cinémas européens des années cinquante*. Paris, AFRHC, pp. 19–46.

Stanley S. (1976) *Beyond Formula: American Film Genres*, New York, Harcourt Brace & Jovanovich.

Tasker, Y. (1993a) *Spectacular Bodies: Gender, Genre and the Action Cinema*, London, Routledge.

217

Tasker, Y. (1993b) Criminelles: *Thelma et Louise* et autres délinquantes. *CinémAction*, 67, pp. 92–95.

Tessier, M. (1990) *Images du cinéma japonais*, Paris, Henri Veyrier.

Tessier, M. (1997) *Le Cinéma japonais*, Paris, Nathan.

Todorov, T. (1965) *Théorie de la littérature. Textes des formalists russes*, Paris, Seuil.

Todorov, T. (1973) *The Fantastic: A Structural Approach to Literary Genre*, Cleveland, Case Western Reserve University Press.

Tudor, A. (1995) Genre. In Grant, B. K. (Ed.) *Film Genre Reader II*. Austin, University of Texas Press, pp. 3–10.

Vallet, A. (1963) *Genres du cinéma*, Paris, Ligel.

Vanoye, F. (2001) D'un rêve l'autre: Bergman, Lynch, Kubrick. In Lescot, D., Moine, R., & Triau, C. (Eds.) *Rêves: cinéma/théatre*. Nanterre, Publidix, pp. 21–30.

Vernet, M. (1980) Genre. In Collett, J., Marie, M., Percheron, D., Simon, J.-P., & Vernet, M. (Eds.) *Lectures du film*. Paris, Albatross, pp. 108–114.

Vincendeau, G. (1997) Hijacked. *Sight and Sound*, July, pp. 22–25.

Vincendeau, G. (2003) *Jean-Pierre Melville: An American in Paris*, London, BFI.

Vincendeau, G. & Gautier, C. (1993) *Jean Gabin, anatomie d'un mythe*, Paris, Nathan.

Vincendeau, G. & Reynaud, B. (Eds.) (1993) 20 ans d'études féministes sur le cinéma. *CinémAction*, 67.

Virmaux, A. & Virmaux, O. (Eds.) (1994) *Dictionnaire du cinéma mondial. Mouvements, écoles, courants, tendances et genres*, Paris, Éditions du Rocher.

Viviani, C. (1982) *Le Western*, Paris, Henri Veyrier.

Walker, J. (1993) Hollywood, Freud et la représentation des femmes. In Burch, N. (Ed.) *Revoir Hollywood. La nouvelle critique anglo-américaine*. Paris, Nathan, pp. 220–240.

Warshow, R. (1962a) Movie Chronicle: The Western. In *The Immediate Experience: Movies, Comics, Theatre and Other Aspects of Popular Culture*. New York, Atheneum, pp. 135–154.

Warshow, R. (1962b) The Gangster as Tragic Hero. In *The Immediate Experience: Movies, Comics, Theatre and Other Aspects of Popular Culture*. New York, Atheneum, pp. 127–133.

Whright, J. H. (1995) Genre Films and the Status Quo. In Grant, B. K. (Ed.) *Film Genre Reader II*. Austin, University of Texas Press, pp. 41–49.

Williams, L. (1993) *Mildred Pierce*, la Seconde Guerre Mondiale et la théorie féministe du cinéma. *CinémAction*, 67, pp. 113–120.

Williams, L. (1998) Melodrama Revised. In Browne, N. (Ed.) *Refiguring American Film Genres: Theory and History*. Berkeley, University of California Press, pp. 42–88.

Wittgenstein, L. (1953) *Philosophical Investigations*, Oxford, Blackwell.

Wood, R. (1986) *Hollywood from Vietnam to Reagan*, New York, Columbia University Press.

Wright, W. (1975) *Six Guns and Society: A Structural Study of the Western*, Berkeley, University of California Press.

Filmography

1492: Conquest of Paradise (Ridley Scott, USA, 1992)

1974, une partie de campagne (*A Summer Outing*) (Raymond Depardon, France, 1974)

2001: A Space Odyssey (Stanley Kubrick, UK, 1968)

Adventures of Robin Hood, The (William Keighley, Michael Curtiz, USA, 1938)

Affair to Remember, An (Leo McCarey, USA, 1957)

Airplane – Flying High (Jim Abrahams, David Zucker, Jerry Zucker, USA, 1980)

Alice Doesn't Live Here Anymore (Martin Scorsese, USA, 1974)

Alien (Ridley Scott, UK, 1979)

All Through the Night (Vincent Sherman, USA, 1942)

Alle går rundt og forelsker sig (*Everybody Falls in Love*) (Emanuel Gregers, Denmark, 1941)

Alphaville, A Strange Adventure of Lemmy Caution (Jean-Luc Godard, France, 1962)

America (David Wark Griffith, USA, 1924)

American in Paris, An (Vincente Minnelli, USA, 1951)

An Affair to Remember (Leo McCarey, 1957)

Ange de la nuit, L' (*Angel of the Night*) (André Berthomieu, France, 1942)

Anglaise et le Duc, L' (*The Lady and the Duke*) (Éric Rohmer, France, 2001)

Anthony Adverse (Mervyn LeRoy, USA, 1936)

AristoCats, The (Wolfgang Reitherman, USA, 1970)

Arroseur arrosé', L' (*The Sprayer Sprayed*) (Louis Lumière, 1895)

Aventures de Rabbi Jacob, Les (*The Adventures of Rabbi Jacob*) (Gérard Oury, France, 1973)

220

Band Wagon, The (Vincente Minnelli, USA, 1953)
Bandera, La (*Escape From Yesterday*) (Julien Duvivier, France, 1935)
Barbouzes, Les (*The Great Spy Chase*) (Georges Lautner, France, 1964)
Barkleys of Broadway, The (Charles Walters, USA, 1949)
Barry Lyndon (Stanley Kubrick, UK, 1975)
Beast with Five Fingers, The (Robert Florey, USA, 1946)
Bellissima (Luchino Visconti, Italy, 1951)
Ben-Hur (Fred Niblo, USA, 1925)
Ben-Hur (William Wyler, USA, 1959)
Bidasses en folie, Les (*Rookies Run Amok*) (Claude Zidi, France, 1971)
Big Trail, The (Raoul Walsh, USA, 1930)
Billy the Kid (King Vidor, USA, 1930)
Birds, The (Alfred Hitchcock, USA, 1963)
Birth of a Nation (David Wark Griffith, USA, 1915)
Blade Runner (Ridley Scott, USA, 1982)
Blonde Venus (Josef von Sternberg, USA, 1932)
Blood Feast (Herschell Gordon Lewis, USA, 1963)
Bossu, Le (*The Hunchback of Paris*) (André Hunebelle, France, 1960)
Broadway Melody, The (Henry Beaumont, USA, 1929)
Broken Arrow (Delmer Daves, USA, 1950)
Bronenosets Potyomkin (*The Battleship Potemkin*) (Sergei M. Eisenstein, USSR, 1925)
Brutti sporchi e cattivi (*Ugly, Dirty, and Bad*) (Ettore Scola, Italy, 1975)
Buffalo Bill and the Indians (Robert Altman, USA, 1976)
Butch Cassidy and the Sundance Kid (George Roy Hill, USA, 1969)
C'era una volta il West (*Once Upon a Time in the West*) (Sergio Leone, Italy, 1969)
Cabiria (Giovanni Pastrone, Italy, 1914)
Calino veut être cowboy (*Calino Wants to Be a Cowboy*) (Jean Durand, France, 1911)
Canyon Passage (Jacques Tourneur, USA, 1946)
Capitaine Fracasse, Le (*Captain Fracasse*) (Pierre Gaspard-Huit, France, 1961)
Capitan, Le (*Captain Blood*) (André Hunebelle, France, 1960)
Casta Diva (Carmine Gallone, Italy, 1955)
Cat People (Jacques Tourneur, USA, 1942)
Catene (*Chains*) (Raffaele Matarazzo, Italy, 1950)
Chagrin et la pitié, Le (*The Sorrow and the Pity*) (Marcel Ophuls, France, 1969)
Chèvre, La (*The Goat*) (Jacques Veber, France, 1981)

Filmography

Cheyenne Autumn (John Ford, USA, 1964)
Chienne, La (*The Bitch*) (Jean Renoir, France, 1931)
Chinatown (Roman Polanski, USA, 1974)
Chute de la maison Usher, La (*The Fall of the House of Usher*) (Jean Epstein, 1928)
Ciel est à vous, Le (*The Sky is Yours*) (Jean Grémillon, France, 1943)
Citadel, The (King Vidor, USA, 1938)
Classe tout risque (*The Big Risk*) (Claude Sautet, France, 1960)
Cleopatra (Joseph L. Mankiewicz, USA, 1963)
Close Encounters of the Third Kind (Steven Spielberg, USA, 1977)
Colosso di Rodi, Il (*The Colossus of Rhodes*) (Sergio Leone, Spain-Italy-France, 1960)
Come Drink with Me (King Hu, Hong Kong, 1965)
Compères, Les (*ComDads*) (Jacques Veber, France, 1983)
Comte de Monte-Cristo, Le (*The Count of Monte Cristo*) (Robert Vernay, France, 1954)
Count of Monte Cristo, The (Rowland V. Lee, USA, 1934)
Covered Wagon, The (James Cruze, USA, 1923)
Creature from the Black Lagoon (Jack Arnold, USA, 1954)
Curse of Frankenstein, The (Terence Fisher, UK, 1957)
Dance of the Vampires (Roman Polanski, USA, 1967)
Dancer in the Dark (Lars von Trier, Denmark, 2000)
Dead Men Don't Wear Plaid (Carl Reiner, USA, 1982)
Dégourdis de la 11ème, Les (*The Smart Guys of the Eleventh Company*) (Christian-Jaque, France, 1937)
Deuxième Souffle, Le (*Second Breath*) (Jean-Pierre Melville, France, 1966)
Dick Tracey (Alan James, Ray Taylor, USA, 1937)
Die Hard (John McTiernan, USA, 1988)
Distant Drums (Raoul Walsh, USA, 1951)
Doctor Jekyll and Mister Hyde (Victor Flemming, USA, 1941)
Dodge City (Michael Curtiz, USA, 1939)
Donne-moi tes yeux (*My Last Mistress*) (Sacha Guitry, France, 1943)
Double Indemnity (Billy Wilder, USA, 1944)
Dr. Erlich's Magic Bullet (William Dieterle, USA, 1940)
Dr. No (Terence Young, UK, 1962)
Dracula (Tod Browning, USA, 1931)
Dragonwyck (Joseph L. Mankiewicz, USA, 1946)
Drums along the Mohawk (John Ford, USA, 1939)
Du Rififi chez les hommes (*Rififi*) (Jules Dassin, France, 1954)
Duel in the Sun (King Vidor, USA, 1946)

Dumbo (Walt Disney/Ben Shapsteen, USA, 1941)
E.T. (Steven Spielberg, USA, 1982)
Earthquake (Mark Robson, USA, 1974)
East of Eden (Elia Kazan, USA, 1954)
Elle court, elle court la banlieue (*The Suburbs Are Everywhere*) (Gérard Pirès, France, 1973)
Entr'acte (René Clair, France, 1924)
Escamotage d'une dame, L' (*The Vanishing Lady*) (Georges Méliès, France, 1896)
Étroit Mousquetaire, L' (*The Three Must-Get-Theres*) (Max Linder, USA, 1922)
Exorcist, The (William Friedkin, USA, 1973)
Face/Off (John Woo, USA, 1997)
Faculty, The (Roberto Rodriguez, USA, 1998)
Fantasia (Walt Disney, USA, 1940)
Fantasia chez les Ploucs (*Fantasia among the Squares*) (Gérard Pirès, France, 1970)
Fantomas (André Hunebelle, France, 1964)
Fantomas contre Scotland Yard (*Phantoms Against Scotland Yard*) (André Hunebelle, France, 1966)
Fantomas se déchaîne (*Fantomas Strikes Back*) (André Hunebelle, France, 1965)
Fatal Hour, The (David Wark Griffith, USA, 1908)
Fathers' Day (Ivan Reitman, USA, 1997)
Fatiche di Ercole, Le (*Labours of Hercules*) (Pietro Francisci, Italy, 1957)
Fée Carabosse, La (*Carabosse the Fairy*) (Georges Méliès, France, 1906)
Fist of Fury (Luo Wei, Hong Kong, 1972)
Fistful of Dollars, A (Sergio Leone, Italy, 1964)
Floorwalker, The (Charlie Chaplin, USA, 1916)
For a Few Dollars More (Sergio Leone, Italy, 1965)
Frankenstein (James Whale, USA, 1931)
Frankenstein Junior (Mel Brooks, USA, 1974)
Friday the 13th (Sean S. Cunningham, USA, 1980)
From Russia with Love (Terence Young, UK, 1963)
Fugitifs, Les (*The Fugitives*) (France, Jacques Veber, 1986)
Gaietés de l'escadron, Les (*Fun in Barracks*) (Maurice Tourneur, France, 1932)
Galaxy Quest (Dean Parisot, USA, 1999)
Gaslight (George Cukor, USA, 1944)
General, The (Buster Keaton, Clyde Bruckman, USA, 1926)
Ghost of Zorro (Fred C. Brannon, USA, 1949)
Gigi (Vincente Minnelli, USA, 1958)

Girlfriends (Claudia Weill, USA, 1978)
Gladiator (Ridley Scott, USA, 2000)
G-Men, The (William Keighley, USA, 1935)
Godfather, The (Francis Ford Coppola, USA, 1972)
Godfather: Part II, The (Francis Ford Coppola, USA, 1974)
Gojira (*Godzilla*) (Inoshiro Honda, Japan, 1954)
Gold Diggers of 1933 (Mervyn LeRoy, USA, 1933)
Gold Diggers of 1935 (Busby Berkeley, USA, 1935)
Gold Diggers of 1937 (Lloyd Bacon, Busby Berkeley, USA, 1937)
Gold Rush, The (Charlie Chaplin, USA, 1925)
Good, the Bad and the Ugly, The (Sergio Leone, Italy, 1966)
Grand Jeu, Le (*The Big Game*) (Jacques Feyder, France, 1933)
Grande Silenzio, Il (*The Great Silence*) (Sergio Corbucci, Italy, 1968)
Grande Vadrouille, La (*Don't Look Now – We're Being Shot At*) (Gérard Oury, France, 1966)
Great Train Robbery, The (Edwin Stratton Porter, USA, 1903)
Gunfight at the OK Corral (John Sturges, USA, 1957)
Heimat (*Homeland – A German Chronicle*) (Edgar Reitz, West Germany, 1981–4)
High Noon (Fred Zinnemann, USA, 1952)
High, Wide and Handsome (Rouben Mamoulian, USA, 1937)
Holiday (George Cukor, USA, 1938)
Home from the Hill (Vincente Minnelli, USA, 1959)
Homme de Rio, L' (*That Man From Rio*) (Philippe de Broca, France, 1963)
Hôtel du Nord (Marcel Carné, France, 1938)
Hunchback of Notre Dame, The (William Dieterle, USA, 1939)
I Am a Fugitive from a Chain Gang (Mervyn LeRoy, USA, 1932)
Invasion of the Body Snatchers (Don Siegel, USA, 1956)
Invasion of the Body Snatchers (Philip Kaufman, USA, 1978)
Invisible Man, The (James Whale, USA, 1933)
Island of Dr. Moreau (Don Taylor, USA, 1976)
Island of Dr. Moreau (John Frankenheimer, USA, 1996)
Island of Lost Souls (Erle C. Kenton, USA, 1932)
It Happened One Night (Frank Capra, USA, 1934)
Jagdzenen aus Niederbayern (*Hunting Scenes from Bavaria*) (Peter Fleischman, West Germany, 1969)
Jaws (Steven Spielberg, USA, 1975)
Jazz Singer, The (Alan Crosland, USA, 1927)
Johnny Guitar (Nicholas Ray, USA, 1954)
Journey to the Center of the Earth (Henry Levin, USA, 1959)

Juge, Le (The Judge) (Philippe Lefebvre, France, 1984)
Julia (Fred Zinnermann, USA, 1977)
Jungle Girl (William Witney, John English, USA, 1941)
Jurassic Park (Steven Spielberg, USA, 1993)
Kind Hearts and Coronets (Robert Hamer, UK, 1949)
Kindergarten Cop (Ivan Reitman, USA, 1990)
King Kong (Merian Cooper, Ernest B. Schoedsack, USA, 1933)
King of the Rocket Men (Fred C. Brannon, USA, 1949)
Kingukongu no gyakushu (King Kong Escapes) (Inoshiro Honda, 1967)
Lady from Shanghai (Orson Welles, USA, 1946)
Ladykillers, The (Alexandra Mackendrick, UK, 1955)
Last of the Mohicans, The (Maurice Tourneur, Clarence Brown, USA, 1920)
Last of the Mohicans, The (George B. Seitz, USA, 1936)
Last of the Mohicans, The (Michael Mann, USA, 1991)
Last of the Redmen (George Sherman, USA, 1947)
Laura (Otto Preminger, USA, 1944)
Le Gorille vous salue bien (The Gorilla Greets You) (Bernard Borderie, France, 1958)
Le Jour se lève (Daybreak) (Marcel Carné, France, 1939)
Le Tigre aime la chair fraîche (The Tiger Likes Fresh Meat) (Claude Chabrol, France, 1964)
Le Tigre se parfume à la dynamite (An Orchid for the Tiger) (Claude Chabrol, France, 1965)
Les femmes s'en balancent (Dames Don't Care) (Bernard Borderie, France, 1954)
Leave Her to Heaven (John M. Stahl, USA, 1946)
Legioni di Cleopatra, Le (Legions of the Nile) (Vittorio Cottafavi, Italy, 1960)
Lemmy pour les dames (Ladies' Man) (Bernard Borderie, France, 1961)
Let Me Dream Again (George Albert Smith, UK, 1900)
Life of Emile Zola, The (William Dieterle, USA, 1937)
Liste noire (Black List) (Alain Bonnot, France, 1983)
Little Big Man (Arthur Penn, USA, 1969)
Little Caesar (Mervyn LeRoy, USA, 1931)
Lo chiavamano Trinita (My Name is Trinity) (E. B. Clucher/Enzo Barboni, Italy, 1970)
Logan's Run (Michael Anderson, USA, 1976)
Lone Ranger, The (William Witney, John English, USA, 1938)
Looking for Mr Goodbar (Richard Brooks, USA, 1977)
Lost Highway (David Lynch, USA, 1997)

225

Filmography

Lost Weekend, The (Billy Wilder, USA, 1945)
Love Affair (Leo McCarey, USA, 1939)
Love Parade, The (Ernst Lubitsch, USA, 1929)
Lumière d'été (*Light of Summer*) (Jean Grémillon, France, 1942)
Madame Curie (Mervin LeRoy, USA, 1943)
Magnificent Obsession (Douglas Sirk, USA, 1953)
Mais où est donc passée la 7ᵉ compagnie? (*Now Where Did the Seventh Company Get to?*) (Robert Lamoureux, France, 1973)
Malaspina (Armando Fizzarotti, Robert Amoroso, Italy, 1947)
Maltese Falcon, The (John Huston, USA, 1941)
Man from Laramie, The (Anthony Mann, USA, 1955)
Man in the White Suit, The (Alexander Mackendrick, UK, 1951)
Man Who Shot Liberty Valance, The (John Ford, USA, 1961)
Man Who Wasn't There, The (Joel and Ethan Coen, USA, 2001)
Marche de l'Empereur, La (*March of the Penguins*) (Luc Jacquet, France, 2005)
Marito per Anna Zaccheo, Un (*A Husband for Anna*) (Giuseppe De Santis, Italy, 1953)
Mars Attacks! (Tim Burton, USA, 1996)
Martin (George Romero, USA, 1977)
Masque de fer, Le (*The Iron Mask*) (Henri Decoin, France, 1962)
Massacre en dentelles (*Massacre in Lace*) (André Hunebelle, France, 1951)
Matrix, The (Andy and Larry Wachowski, USA, 1999)
Meet Me in St Louis (Vincente Minnelli, USA, 1944)
Méfiez-vous des blondes (*Beware of Blondes*) (André Hunebelle, France, 1950)
Mélo (*The Dreamy Mouth*) (Alain Resnais, France, 1986)
Mélo (Paul Czinner, France, 1932)
Microcosmos, le people et l'herbe (*Microcosmos*) (Claude Nuridsany, Marie Perennou, France, 1996)
Mildred Pierce (Michael Curtiz, USA, 1945)
Mission à Tanger (*Mission in Tangier*) (André Hunebelle, France, 1949)
Môme Vert-de-Gris, La (*Poison Ivy*) (Bernard Borderie, France, 1953)
Monocle noir, Le (*The Black Monocle*) (Georges Lautner, France, 1961)
Monty Python and the Holy Grail (Terry Gilliam, France, 1974)
Mostri, I (*The Monsters*) (Dino Risi, Italy, 1963)
Mullholland Drive (David Lynch, USA, 2001)
Mummy, The (Karl Freund, USA, 1932)
Murder My Sweet (Edward Dmytryk, USA, 1944)
My Darling Clementine (John Ford, USA, 1946)
Napoléon (*Napoleon*) (Abel Gance, France, 1927)

Nave delle donne maledette, La (*Ship of Lost Women*) (Raffaello Matarazzo, Italy, 1954)

Nevada Smith (Henry Hathaway, USA, 1966)

Nez de cuir (*Leathernose*) (Yves Allégret, France, 1951)

Night of the Living Dead, The (George Romero, USA, 1969)

Nightmare on Elm Street, A (Wes Craven, USA, 1985)

Northwest Passage (King Vidor, USA, 1940)

Nosferatu (Friedrich W. Murnau, Germany, 1922)

O.K. Nerone (*O.K. Nero*) (Mario Soldati, Italy, 1952)

Objective Burma! (Raoul Walsh, USA, 1945)

Ocean's Eleven (Steven Soderbergh, USA, 2001)

Œil de Vichy, L' (*The Eye of Vichy*) (Claude Chabrol, France, 1993)

Oklahoma! (Fred Zinnemann, USA, 1955)

On the Town (Gene Kelly, Stanley Donen, USA, 1949)

One-Eyed Jacks (Marlon Brando, USA, 1961)

Orphans of the Storm (David Wark Griffith, USA, 1921)

Others, The (Alejandro Amenabar, USA, 2001)

Pacte des Loups, Le (*Brotherhood of the Wolf*) (Christophe Gans, France, 2001)

Parapluies de Cherbourg, Les (*The Umbrellas of Cherbourg*) (Jacques Demy, France, 1964)

Party Girl (Nicholas Ray, USA, 1958)

Passport to Pimlico (Henry Cornelius, UK, 1949)

Peau d'âne (*Donkey Skin*) (Jacques Demy, France, 1970)

Phantom of the Opera, The (Arthur Lubin, USA, 1943)

Philadelphia Story, The (George Cukor, USA, 1940)

Pocahontas (Mike Gabriel, Eric Goldberg, USA, 1995)

Pocahontas II: Journey to the New World (Tom Ellery, Bradley Raymond, USA, 1998)

Poseidon Adventure, The (Ronald Neame, USA, 1972)

Princesse de Clèves, La (*Princess of Cleves*) (Jean Delannoy, France, 1961)

Professionals, The (Richard Brooks, USA, 1966)

Public Enemy, The (William Wellman, USA, 1931)

Pure Luck (Nadia Tass, USA, 1991)

Purple Rose of Cairo, The (Woody Allen, USA, 1985)

Quai des brumes, Le (*Port of Shadows*) (Marcel Carné, France, 1938)

Quatermass Experiment, The (Val Guest, UK, 1955)

Quo Vadis? (Enrico Guazzoni, Italy, 1912)

Raiders of the Lost Ark (Steven Spielberg, USA, 1981)

Rambo: First Blood (Ted Kotchev, USA, 1982)

Reazione a catena (*A Bay of Blood*) (Mario Bava, Italy, 1971)

Filmography

Rebecca (Alfred Hitchcock, USA, 1940)
Red River (Howard Hawks, USA, 1948)
Remember My Name (Alan Rudolph, USA, 1978)
Riding High (Frank Capra, USA, 1950)
Rigoletto (Carmine Gallone, Italy, 1947)
Rio Bravo (Howard Hawks, USA, 1959)
River of No Return (Otto Preminger, USA, 1954)
Rocky Horror Picture Show, The (Jim Sharman, UK, 1975)
Roman d'un Spahi, Le (*The Story of a Soldier*) (Michel Bernheim, France, 1936)
Romolo e Remo (*Duel of the Titans*) (Sergio Corbucci, Italy, 1961)
Rosemary's Baby (Roman Polanski, USA, 1968)
Run of the Arrow (Samuel Fuller, USA, 1957)
Rush Hour (Brett Ratner, USA, 1998)
Safety Last! (Fred Newmaver, Sam Taylor, USA, 1923)
Saving Private Ryan (Steven Spielberg, USA, 1998)
Scarface (Howard Hawks, USA, 1932)
Scarlet Street (Fritz Lang, USA, 1945)
Schindler's List (Steven Spielberg, USA, 1994)
Schwarzwaldmädel (*The Black Forest Girl*) (Hans Deppe, West Germany, 1950)
Scipione l'Africano (*Scipio the African*) (Carmine Gallone, Italy, 1937)
Scream (Wes Craven, USA, 1997)
Searchers, The (John Ford, USA, 1956)
Secret Beyond the Door (Fritz Lang, USA, 1948)
Senso (*Livia*) (Luchino Visconti, Italy, 1954)
Seven Brides for Seven Brothers (Stanley Donen, USA, 1954)
Shall We Dance? (Mark Sandrich, USA, 1937)
Shane (George Stevens, USA, 1953)
Sherlock Holmes and the Voice of Terror (John Rawlins, USA, 1942)
Shining, The (Stanley Kubrick, UK, 1980)
Si Versailles m'était conté (*Royal Affairs in Versailles*) (Sacha Guitry, France, 1953)
Signora senza camelie, La (*Camille Without Camelias*) (Michelangelo Antonioni, Italy, 1957)
Singin' in the Rain (Stanley Donen, Gene Kelly, USA, 1952)
Single White Female (Barbet Schroeder, USA, 1992)
Sixth Sense, The (M. N. Shyamalan, USA, 1999)
Soldier Blue (Ralf Nelson, USA, 1970)
Soliti ignoti, I (*Big Deal*) (Mario Monicelli, Italy, 1958)

Some Came Running (Vincente Minnelli, USA, 1958)
Some Like it Hot (Billy Wilder, USA, 1959)
Spartacus (Stanley Kubrick, USA, 1960)
Stachka (*The Strike*) (Sergei M. Eisenstein, USSR, 1925)
Stagecoach (John Ford, USA, 1939)
Star Wars (George Lucas, USA, 1977)
Steamboat Bill, Jr. (Charles F. Reisner, Buster Keaton, USA, 1928)
Stella Dallas (King Vidor, USA, 1937)
Stop Thief! (James Williamson, UK, 1901)
Story of Alexander Graham Bell, The (Irving Cummings, USA, 1939)
Story of Louis Pasteur, The (William Dieterle, USA, 1935)
Straight Shooting (John Ford, USA, 1917)
Suddenly Last Summer (Joseph L. Mankiewicz, USA, 1959)
Susana demonio y carne (*The Devil and the Flesh*) (Luis Buñuel, Mexico, 1951)
Suspicion (Alfred Hitchcock, USA, 1941)
Tanguy (Étienne Chatiliez, France, 2001)
Tarzan the Ape Man (W. S. Van Dyke, USA, 1932)
Taxi (Gérard Pirès, France, 1997)
Taxi Driver (Martin Scorsese, USA, 1976)
Ten Commandments, The (Cecil B. De Mille, USA, 1923)
Ten Commandments, The (Cecil B. De Mille, USA, 1956)
Terminator II: Judgment Day (James Cameron, USA, 1991)
Thelma and Louise (Ridley Scott, USA, 1991)
There's Something About Mary (Bobby and Peter Farrelly, USA, 1998)
They Made Me a Criminal (Busby Berkeley, USA, 1939)
Thin Red Line, The (Terrence Malick, USA, 1998)
Three Faces of Eve, The (Nunnally Johnson, USA, 1957)
Three Fugitives, The (Francis Veber, USA, 1989)
Three Men and a Baby (Leonard Nimoy, USA, 1988)
Three Women (Robert Altman, USA, 1977)
Tiger Boy (Cheh Chang, USA, 1960)
Tontons flingueurs, Les (*Crooks in Clover*) (Georges Lautner, France, 1963)
Top Hat (Mark Sandrich, USA, 1935)
Tormento (*Torment*) (Raffaele Matarazzo, Italy, 1951)
Tosca, La (Carmine Gallone, Italy, 1956)
Totale!, La (*The Jackpot!*) (Claude Zidi, France, 1991)
Touch of Zen, A (King Hu, Hong Kong, 1972)
Touchez pas au grisbi (*Grisbi*) (Jacques Becker, France, 1954)
Towering Inferno, The (John Guillerman, USA, 1974)

Traviata, La (Carmine Gallone, Italy, 1947)

Trois frères, Les (*The Three Brothers*) (Didier Bourdon, Bernard Campan, France, 1995)

Trois hommes et un couffin (*Three Men and a Cradle*) (Coline Serreau, France, 1985)

True Lies (James Cameron, USA, 1994)

Ugetsu Monogatari (*Tales of a Pale and Mysterious Moon After the Rain*) (Kenji Mizoguchi, Japan, 1953)

Unconquered (Cecil B. De Mille, USA, 1947)

Unmarried Woman, An (Paul Mazursky, USA, 1978)

Vénus aveugle (*Blind Venus*) (Abel Gance, 1940)

Vérité sur Bébé Donge, La (*The Truth About Bebe Donge*) (Henri Decoin, France, 1951)

Vertigo (Alfred Hitchcock, USA, 1958)

Viaggio in Italia (*Journey to Italy*) (Roberto Rossellini, Italy, 1953)

Virginia City (Michael Curtiz, USA, 1940)

Visiteurs, Les (*The Visitors*) (Jean-Marie Poiré, France, 1992)

Voile bleu, Le (*The Blue Veil*) (Jean Stelli, France, 1942)

Voyage dans la lune, Le (*Voyage to the Moon*) (Georges Méliès, France, 1902)

Whirlpool (Otto Preminger, USA, 1949)

Whiskey Galore! (Alexander Mackendrick, UK, 1949)

Wild and Woolly (John Emerson, USA, 1917)

Wild Bunch, The (Sam Peckinpath, USA, 1969)

Wizard of Oz, The (Victor Fleming, USA, 1939)

Wolf Man, The (George Waggner, USA, 1941)

Woman in the Window, The (Fritz Lang, USA, 1944)

Woodstock (Michael Wadleigh, USA, 1970)

Written on the Wind (Douglas Sirk, USA, 1955)

You Only Live Once (Fritz Lang, USA, 1937)

Zelig (Woody Allen, USA, 1983)

Ziegfeld Follies (Vincente Minnelli, USA, 1946)

Index

Index